SPEAKING OF JACK
A C.S. LEWIS DISCUSSION GUIDE

WILL VAUS

WINGED
LION
PRESS

Speaking of Jack: A C. S. Lewis Discussion Guide
Copyright © 2011 Will Vaus

Winged Lion Press
Hamden, CT

All rights reserved. Except in the case of quotations embodied in critical articles or reviews, no part of this book may be reproduced or transmitted in any form or by any means, electronic or mechanical, including photocopying, recording, or by any information storage or retrieval system, without written permission of the publisher.
For information, contact Winged Lion Press www.WingedLionPress.com

Winged Lion Press titles may be purchased for business or promotional use or special sales.

Cover photograph used by permission of
The Marion E. Wade Center, Wheaton College, Wheaton, IL

10-9-8-7-6-5-4-3-2-1

WINGED
LION
PRESS

ISBN-13 978-1-936294-12-1

DEDICATED TO
THE C. S. LEWIS SOCIETIES OF
COLUMBIA, SOUTH CAROLINA
PITTSBURGH, PENNSYLVANIA
&
HARRISONBURG, VIRGINIA

DEDICATED TO
THE C. S. LEWIS SOCIETIES OF
COLUMBIA, SOUTH CAROLINA
PITTSBURGH, PENNSYLVANIA
&
HARRISONBURG, VIRGINIA

Contents

Why Another Book About C. S. Lewis?	1
A Timeline of C. S. Lewis' Life	4
A Reading Schedule	15
Introductions & Discussion Questions to Lewis' Works	17
Boxen	17
Spirits in Bondage	21
Dymer	25
The Pilgrim's Regress	32
The Allegory of Love	43
Out of the Silent Planet	51
The Personal Heresy	58
The Problem of Pain	64
The Screwtape Letters	69
A Preface to Paradise Lost	77
Perelandra	81
The Abolition of Man	88
That Hideous Strength	94
The Great Divorce	99
Miracles	103
The Weight of Glory	109
The Lion, the Witch and the Wardrobe	115
Prince Caspian	121

Mere Christianity	126
The Voyage of the Dawn Treader	132
The Silver Chair	136
The Horse and His Boy	140
English Literature in the Sixteenth Century	145
The Magician's Nephew	152
Surprised by Joy	156
The Last Battle	163
Till We Have Faces	167
Reflections on the Psalms	171
The Four Loves	176
Studies in Words	181
The World's Last Night and Other Essays	186
A Grief Observed	192
An Experiment in Criticism	198
Letters to Malcolm: Chiefly on Prayer	202
The Discarded Image	209
Poems	214
Letters of C. S. Lewis	218
Christian Reflections	223
Letters to an American Lady	232
God in the Dock	238
Books About C. S. Lewis	243
Jack: A Life of C. S. Lewis by George Sayer	243
Lenten Lands by Douglas Gresham	248

Surprised by Joy: An Introductory Class on C. S. Lewis	252
Planning a C. S. Lewis Tour	263
A Select Bibliography	269
Resources for Further Study	276

Why Another Book About C. S. Lewis?

There are now more books in print about C. S. "Jack" Lewis than the forty-one books he wrote during his lifetime. What is it about this Oxford don, Cambridge professor, Christian apologist and fantasy writer who died in 1963 that makes him so popular? And why should there be yet another book about him and his work?

People have been analyzing for decades what makes Lewis so popular. The Narnia stories account for at least half of C. S. Lewis book sales. So one reason why Lewis is so well known is because he wrote what have become seven classic children's fairy tales. However, before Lewis ever walked through the wardrobe into Narnia he was already well known as a Christian apologist due to his numerous talks over BBC radio during the Second World War and his bestselling book, *The Screwtape Letters*. Thus Lewis' popularity can also be traced to the fact that his books appeal to a wide variety of audiences: those interested in a logical presentation of Christianity, as well as those desiring in a more imaginative approach to the faith. Perhaps Lewis is popular because he is so knowledgeable about the whole Western tradition, from the classics of Greek and Rome down to nineteenth century English literature, and he brings all of this tradition to bear, in an accessible way, through his books. On the other hand, maybe Lewis is so widely read simply because he is a great writer, one who delivers scintillating prose, intriguing storylines, and fascinating characters. Whatever the reason, Lewis is without doubt the bestselling author of Christian theology outside of the Bible, with over 100 million copies of his books in print: and that's apart from Narnia! The Narnia books altogether have sold another 100 million copies and continue to sell at a rate of one million per year.

But why write another book about Lewis? The answer: because so many people want to read Lewis' work and discuss it. C. S. Lewis Societies have been popping up around the globe since the first one started in New York in 1969. I have started and led three groups myself. And what you have in your hands is all the material I have passed on to those three groups: introductions to most of Lewis' books, and questions designed to stimulate discussion about Lewis' work and his life story. The best part about this book is that these materials have been "road- tested".

I became interested in being part of a C. S. Lewis Society, devoted to discussing Lewis' life and works, a number of years ago. Since there was no such Lewis Society in my geographical area at that time, I decided to start one. First I contacted other Lewis Societies to see how they had done it. After sorting through those materials I picked a place to meet–a Barnes & Noble bookstore in my area. I advertised our first and subsequent meetings in a local newspaper and on a nearby radio station. Barnes & Noble also advertised the meetings in their store calendar. We had over thirty people show up for the first meeting! We were overflowing the café area in the bookstore. It was a great size group for the delivery of a lecture, but it was not conducive to book discussion. So we multiplied into two groups which met on two different nights, once per month. I made up a reading list and we discussed a different book by Lewis each month, starting with his most popular works: *The Screwtape Letters*, *Mere Christianity*, and *The Lion, the Witch and The Wardrobe*.

I wrote introductions for each book we discussed, and I read those introductions at the beginning of each meeting. I also came up with helpful reading guides for some of the books—like a glossary to guide readers through the maze of abstract terminology in *The Pilgrim's Regress*, and listings of chapter topics for *The Screwtape Letters* and *Letters to Malcolm: Chiefly on Prayer*.

Some of the discussion questions in this book are designed to highlight certain important facts in various Lewis books. Other questions are more open-ended. In almost every case I have written more questions than can possibly be discussed in one meeting of a book discussion group. I led one group through a study of Lewis' works, reading one book per month in chronological order according to original publication date. Since that time the group has continued without my leadership. However, they continue to use the original discussion questions I wrote, in order to dig deeper into each book than they did in their first discussion. So, when you use the discussion questions, pick your favorites to discuss, and leave some questions for the next time your group reads the particular book in question.

In addition to the discussion questions there is: a timeline of Lewis' life, a reading schedule that will take you through most of Lewis' major works in a little under three years–one book per month, some suggestions for how to organize an introductory six-week class on Lewis' life and work, a guide to planning a C. S. Lewis Tour of Ireland and England, a bibliography, and a listing of resources for further study.

There are a few different ways you might use this book:

1. In an existing book discussion group.
2. To start a C. S. Lewis Society where you live.
3. To discuss Lewis' life and works in your high school or college classroom, Sunday School class or small group, or
4. You could use the questions to stimulate your own solo exploration of Lewis' books.

Whatever way you choose: may this book lead you "further up and further in".

A Timeline of C. S. Lewis' Life[1]

1894   Florence "Flora" Hamilton and Albert James Lewis married at St. Mark's Church, Dundela, Belfast, Northern Ireland on August 29.

1895   Warren "Warnie" Hamilton Lewis (C. S. Lewis' brother) born on June 16, at home in Dundela Villas (one of a pair of semidetached houses rented by the Lewis family from a relative, Thomas Keown, in Strandtown, a suburb of Belfast).

         Arthur Greeves (Lewis' Belfast neighbor and lifelong friend) is also born this year.

1898   Clive Staples Lewis born at home in Dundela Villas, Belfast, Northern Ireland, November 29.

1900   August 6-27 Flora, with the assistance of a nurse, takes her two sons on holiday to Ballycastle, County Antrim: a seaside resort north of Belfast.

1901   In June and July, Flora, along with nurse/housemaid Lizzie Endicott, takes her sons to the seaside resort of Castlerock.

1903   In May, Flora and her sons vacation at the Spar Hotel in the seaside resort town of Ballynahinch, County Down. During this holiday C. S. Lewis chooses the nickname of Jacksie for himself. The name is later shortened to Jacks, and finally to Jack.[2]

1904   From June to August, Flora and sons vacation once again

---

[1] For a complete yet succinct biography of C. S. Lewis suitable for readers 8th grade and up see Will Vaus, *The Professor of Narnia: The C. S. Lewis Story*, Washington, DC: Believe Books, 2008. This timeline is based, in part, on the timelines which appear in Gilbert, Douglas and Kilby, Clyde S., *C. S. Lewis: Images of His World*, Grand Rapids: Eerdmans, 1977, pp. 9-15 and Kilby, Clyde S. and Mead, Marjorie Lamp, *Brothers & Friends: The Diaries of Major Warren Hamilton Lewis*, New York: Harper & Row, 1982, pp. xi-xxiv.

[2] For the story behind Lewis' nickname see *The Professor of Narnia*, pp. 6-8.

at Castlerock. Also in the month of August construction begins on the new Lewis family home, to be named Little Lea, a short distance from Dundela Villas.

1905 On April 21, the Lewis family moves into Little Lea. On May 10, Warnie is enrolled by his mother at Wynyard School, Watford, Hertfordshire, England. In September Flora and her sons go on holiday to the seaside resort of Killough, County Down.

1906 In September, Flora and her sons vacation again at Castlerock.

1907 From August to September, Flora and sons go on holiday to Berneval in northern France.

1908 On February 15, Flora undergoes major cancer surgery.

On April 2, C. S. Lewis' grandfather, Richard Lewis, dies.

On May 20, Flora takes Jack to Larne Harbor, north of Belfast, for a holiday while Warnie is away at school.

On July 8, Warnie returns home early from Wynyard School because of his mother's illness.

Flora Lewis dies on August 23, Albert's forty-fifth birthday.

In September, Joseph Lewis, Albert's brother, dies. Also this month Albert sends Jack to Wynyard School along with Warnie.

1909 In May, Albert and his sons visit Dublin together. Then in September Warnie becomes a student at Malvern College, Great Malvern, Worcestershire, England.

1910 July 12 is Jack's last day as a student at Wynyard. The school is soon closed and the headmaster, Robert Capron, is later certified insane.

On August 19, Albert and sons visit Albert's brother, William, in Scotland.

In September Jack is enrolled as a student at Campbell College, Belfast, not far from Little Lea.

1911 In January, while Warnie continues as a student at Malvern College, Jack is enrolled as a student at Cherbourg Preparatory School, just up the hill. While Jack is a student here he becomes an atheist, partly under the influence of his matron, Miss Cowie. Warnie and Jack both become "confirmed smokers" during their time at school.

In August, Albert and his sons visit Dunbar, Scotland for a joint holiday with the family of Albert's brother, Richard Lewis.

1913 In May of this year, Warnie decides on a career in the Royal Army Service Corps (RASC).

In July, Warnie completes his education at Malvern College. In September, he begins private tutoring under William T. Kirkpatrick in Great Bookham, Surrey, England, in preparation for the entrance examination to the Royal Military Academy at Sandhurst.

On September 18, Jack enrolls at Malvern College.

1914 In January, Warnie wins a prize cadetship to Sandhurst and enters the Academy there in February.

On August 5, Warnie is recalled to Sandhurst during his holiday at Little Lea because of England's declaration of war on Germany.

On September 19, Jack begins private tutoring under W. T. Kirkpatrick, also an atheist, for whom he will develop a great affection. Kirkpatrick prepares Jack to take the entrance examination for Oxford University.

On September 30, Warnie is appointed as a second lieutenant in the RASC.

November 4, Warnie is sent to France where he will serve with the 4th Company 7th Divisional Train British Expeditionary Force.

1916 Jack receives a scholarship to University College, Oxford.

1917 April 28, Jack informally begins his studies at Oxford.

In May Jack is drafted into a cadet battalion and is housed at Keble College, Oxford while in training to take a commission. His roommate is fellow Irishman, E. F. C. "Paddy" Moore.

In September, Jack is appointed as a second lieutenant in the 3rd Battalion of the Somerset Light Infantry.

On November 29, his nineteenth birthday, Jack arrives in France where he will serve in the trenches of The Great War.

1918   On April 15, Jack is wounded by an English shell on Mount Bernenchon during the Battle of Arras near Lillers, France.

On April 24, Warnie visits Jack in the Liverpool Merchant's Mobile Hospital in Etaples, France.

May 25, Jack is transferred to Endsleigh Palace Hospital in London.

In July, Jack is transferred again, this time to Ashton Court Hospital in Bristol, England where he can be close to Paddy Moore's mother, Mrs. Janie King Moore,

In September, Paddy Moore is officially declared dead.

November 11, the Armistice is signed and The Great War is over.

1919   In January, Jack is demobilized from the army and returns to Oxford as a student. Here he eventually establishes a household with Janie King Moore and her daughter Maureen in fulfillment of a promise made to Paddy to care for his family in the event of his death.

In March, Jack has his first book published by William Heinemann; it is a collection of short poems entitled: *Spirits in Bondage, a Cycle of Lyrics.*

In August, Jack and Albert have a serious quarrel over Jack's school expenses.

On November 19, Warnie is reassigned by the army to service in England.

1920	Jack earns a First Class degree in Classical Honour Moderations at Oxford University.[3]
1921	On March 9, Warnie sails on the *Appam* to Sierra Leone, West Africa where he continues his army service.
	On March 22, W. T. Kirkpatrick dies.
	By the summer, Jack has moved out of his college housing and into a rented house in Warneford Road, Oxford with the Moores.
	In July, Albert visits Jack, briefly, in Oxford. Jack keeps his housing arrangement with the Moores a secret from his father.
1922	On April 7, Warnie arrives home from his service in Africa.
	Another First Class degree, this time in the Final Honour School, is won by Jack.[4]
	On August 1, Jack and the Moores move to Hillsboro, a home in the Western Road, Headington, a suburb of Oxford. On August 5, Warnie meets the Moores for the first time.
	In October, Warnie is assigned to an army position in Colchester, England.
1923	Another First Class degree, this time in English Literature, is gained by Jack. He is one of a small handful of people to earn a "Triple First" at Oxford in the twentieth century.
1924	Jack substitutes for E. F. Carritt as a philosophy tutor for one year at University College, Oxford.
1925	May 20, Jack is elected to a fellowship in English literature and language at Magdalen College, Oxford.
1926	Warnie is reassigned to duty in Woolwich, England.

---

3 Classical Honour Moderations is a classics course of study at Oxford with a final exam in Latin and Greek.

4 The Final Honour School, or second half of the classics course called "Greats" at Oxford, is completed when one passes an examination in ancient Greek and Roman history as well as ancient Greek and modern philosophy.

Jack publishes *Dymer*, an epic poem.

During the Christmas holidays, Albert, Warnie and Jack are all together for the last time.

1927 On April 11, Warnie sails for duty in China on the *Derbyshire*.

1928 On May 2, Albert retires as Belfast Corporation County Solicitor, a position he has held since 1889.

1929 Jack becomes a theist during Trinity Term at Oxford.

On July 25, Albert goes to a Belfast nursing home for x-rays. He is later diagnosed with cancer.

On August 13, Jack returns home to Little Lea to nurse his father in his final illness.

Albert Lewis dies on September 25.

1930 On February 24, Warnie sails from Shanghai, via the United States, returning home to help Jack settle their father's estate.

In April, Warnie and Jack are together at Little Lea for the last time.

On May 10, Warnie decides to edit and arrange the Lewis family papers, which becomes a lifelong project of great importance to future C. S. Lewis studies.

On May 15, Warnie is reassigned by the army to service in Bulford, England.

On May 25, Warnie decides to accept Jack's and Mrs. Moore's invitation to live with them once he retires from the army.

On July 7, the Lewis brothers and Mrs. Moore inspect an Oxfordshire home for sale known as The Kilns. They purchase the house later that month and move into this lovely house in Headington Quarry, a suburb of Oxford, during the month of October.

1931 In January, Jack and Warnie take their first walking tour together. This one is a 54 mile trek along the Wye Valley in Wales.

On May 9, Warnie returns to the Christian faith.

On September 19, Jack has a very important discussion about Christianity and myth with J. R. R. Tolkien and Hugo Dyson.

On September 28, Jack returns to the Christian faith while on a motorcycle ride with his brother to Whipsnade Zoo.

On October 1, Jack writes to Arthur Greeves, his Belfast friend, about his return to Christian faith. Then on October 5, Warnie returns to China for his second tour of duty there.

1932 On December 21, Warnie retires from the RASC and moves permanently into The Kilns.

1933 Jack and Warnie take another walking tour of the Wye Valley in January. They continue their practice of a January walking tour, in various locations, until the beginning of the Second World War.

Jack publishes *The Pilgrim's Regress*.

The informal literary gathering known as the Inklings begins to meet under Lewis' leadership. Members of the group eventually include: J. R. R. Tolkien, Warnie Lewis, Hugo Dyson, Robert Havard, Nevill Coghill, Charles Wrenn, David Cecil, Colin Hardie, Owen Barfield and Charles Williams, among others. The group will soon meet on Thursday nights in Lewis' rooms at Magdalen College, and on Tuesdays at the Eagle and Child pub in Oxford.

1936 Jack publishes *The Allegory of Love*. He also meets the author, Charles Williams, and begins a friendship with him.

1938 Jack publishes *Out of the Silent Planet*, the first in his science fiction trilogy.

1939 Jack begins a pen friendship with Sister Penelope, an Anglican nun living in a religious community in Wantage, England. She has written to Jack about *Out of the Silent Planet*.

In September, England declares war on Germany. On September 2, child evacuees arrive at The Kilns. On September 4, Warnie is recalled to active service and assigned to Catterick, Yorkshire. Jack begins volunteer service as a religious lecturer to the Royal Air Force.

In October, Warnie is reassigned to Le Havre, France.

1940 In May, Warnie is evacuated with his unit from Dunkirk to Wenvoe Camp, Cardiff, Wales. In August, he begins serving as a private soldier with the 6th Oxford City Home Guard Battalion.

Jack publishes *The Problem of Pain*. In October, he decides to begin seeing an Anglican priest for weekly spiritual direction. He chooses as his spiritual director Father Walter Adams, one of the priests of the Anglican Society of Saint John the Evangelist in Cowley, a suburb of Oxford.

1941 Jack gives BBC broadcast talks beginning in this year and continuing through 1944. Warnie begins serving as Jack's secretary due to the flood of mail he receives as a result of the BBC broadcasts. These talks will later be collected and published as *Mere Christianity* in 1952.

Jack also begins presidency of the Socratic Club, an Oxford Christian debate society, which position he will hold until 1954.

1942 Warnie begins writing his first book, *The Splendid Century: Some Aspects of French Life in the Reign of Louis XIV*, which will be published in 1953.

Jack publishes *The Screwtape Letters* with Geoffrey Bles, Ltd., after having them circulated in *The Guardian*, a Church of England newspaper.

1943 In February, Warnie and Jack travel to Durham in northern England where Jack delivers the Riddell Memorial Lectures, which will be published later in the year under the title, *The Abolition of Man*.

Jack publishes *Perelandra*, the second in his science fiction trilogy.

1945 Jack publishes *That Hideous Strength*, the third in his science fiction trilogy.

The war ends on May 9 and on May 15 Charles Williams dies.

1946 In June, Jack and Warnie travel to Scotland where Jack receives an honorary Doctorate of Divinity from St. Andrew's University.

1947 Jack publishes *Miracles*. His portrait appears on the cover of *Time Magazine*, September 8.

1948 Jack begins work on his autobiography.

1950 On January 10, Jack receives a letter from American writer Helen Joy Davidman Gresham.

On April 29, Mrs. Moore is admitted to Restholme, a nursing home in Oxford.

Jack publishes *The Lion, the Witch, and the Wardrobe*. The other six books in *The Chronicles of Narnia* will be published one per year through 1956.

1951 Mrs. Moore dies, January 12.

Jack writes to the Prime Minister of the United Kingdom declining the honor of being named Commander of the Order of the British Empire.

1952 Jack and Joy Gresham meet in September after having corresponded at length.

1953 Joy returns to the United States in January. After separating from her husband, William Lindsay Gresham she returns to England in December, this time with her two young sons, David and Douglas. They visit the Kilns for four days.

1954 Jack publishes *English Literature in the Sixteenth Century*.

He is elected Professor of Medieval and Renaissance English Literature at Magdalene College, Cambridge and delivers his inaugural lecture there on his birthday, November 29.

On December 3, Jack gives his last tutorial at Magdalen College, Oxford.

1955 Jack publishes his autobiography, *Surprised by Joy*.

He assumes chair in Cambridge.

During the summer, Joy and her two sons move from London to 10 Old High Street, Headington, just one mile from The Kilns. She publishes her commentary on the Ten Commandments entitled *Smoke on the Mountain*, with a foreword by Jack.

1956 Jack publishes *Till We Have Faces*. Jack and Joy marry in a civil ceremony at the Oxford registry office, April 23, so that Davidman may obtain British citizenship and avoid deportation to the United States.

By November, Joy is near death from a recurrence of cancer.

1957 Jack marries Joy in a death-bed ecclesiastical ceremony in the Churchill Hospital, March 21, 1957. The priest, Peter Bide, prays for Joy's healing at this time. By December, Joy is walking again.

1958 Jack publishes *Reflections on the Psalms*.

By June, Joy's cancer is arrested, and in July the couple honeymoon in Ireland.

1959 In October, x-rays reveal the return of Joy's cancer.

1960 Jack publishes *The Four Loves*.

Three months after a physically painful trip to Greece with Jack, Joy dies on July 13.

1961 Jack publishes *A Grief Observed* and *An Experiment in Criticism*.

1963 During the summer Jack meets correspondent Walter Hooper. In the absence of Warnie, who has gone to Ireland for an unknown period of time, Jack invites Hooper to serve as his secretary.

On June 15, Jack is admitted to the Acland Nursing Home following a heart attack.

In August, Jack returns to the Kilns.

In September, Warnie returns from Ireland and resumes his duties as Jack's secretary, Walter Hooper having returned to the United States to wind up his affairs there in preparation for a move to England.

Jack dies on November 22, 1963, the same day as President John F. Kennedy and writer Aldous Huxley.

1964 *Letters to Malcolm: Chiefly On Prayer* and *The Discarded Image* published posthumously.

1966 Arthur Greeves dies, August 29.

1973 Warren Lewis dies, April 9.

A Reading Schedule

Year	Month	Book	Year First Published
1	January	*Boxen*	1985
1	February	*Spirits in Bondage*	1919
1	March	*Dymer* (from *Narrative Poems*)	1926
1	April	*The Pilgrim's Regress*	1933
1	May	*The Allegory of Love*	1936
1	June	*Out of the Silent Planet*	1938
1	July	*The Personal Heresy*	1939
1	August	*The Problem of Pain*	1940
1	September	*The Screwtape Letters*	1942
1	October	*A Preface to Paradise Lost*	1942
1	November	*Perelandra*	1943
1	December	*The Abolition of Man*	1943
2	January	*That Hideous Strength*	1945
2	February	*The Great Divorce*	1946
2	March	*Miracles*	1947
2	April	*The Weight of Glory*	1949
2	May	*The Lion, The Witch and the Wardrobe*	1950
2	June	*Prince Caspian*	1951
2	July	*Mere Christianity*	1952
2	August	*The Voyage of the Dawn Treader*	1952
2	September	*The Silver Chair*	1953
2	October	*The Horse and His Boy*	1954
2	November	*English Literature in the Sixteenth Century*	1954
2	December	*The Magician's Nephew*	1955

3	January	*Surprised by Joy*	1955
3	February	*The Last Battle*	1956
3	March	*Till We Have Faces*	1956
3	April	*Reflections on the Psalms*	1958
3	May	*The Four Loves*	1960
3	June	*Studies in Words*	1960
3	July	*The World's Last Night*	1960
3	August	*A Grief Observed*	1961
3	September	*Letters to Malcolm: Chiefly on Prayer*	1964
3	October	*The Discarded Image*	1964
3	November	*Poems*	1964
3	December	*Letters of C. S. Lewis*	1966

Introductions & Discussion Questions

Boxen

Clive Staples Lewis was born in Belfast, Northern Ireland on November 29, 1898. He was the son of Albert Lewis, a police court solicitor, and Flora Hamilton Lewis, the daughter of a Church of Ireland (Anglican) clergyman and graduate of Queen's College, Belfast, with honors in mathematics. Both of Clive's parents loved books, especially some of those written by the great Victorian novelists. So it should come as no surprise that Clive himself developed an interest in books at a young age. However, Clive's literary tastes were rather different from his parents. From the time he was small, Clive developed a love of romantic poetry and fairy tales.

Clive had only one sibling, his brother Warren, or Warnie as he was called by family and friends. Warren was just three years older than Clive. Together Clive and Warren were cared for, not only by their parents, but by their beloved nurse, Lizzie Endicott. Lizzie was the one responsible for introducing Warren and Clive to some of the great legendary tales of Ireland.

These stories, among others, must have fired the imagination of the young Clive Staples Lewis. This was so much the case that he had to get the pictures in his mind out on to paper. He did this at first through drawing, then eventually through writing stories about the pictures popping into his mind.

Another source of inspiration for the creative young Clive was the world of "dressed animals" in the Beatrix Potter books. Clive worked hard at drawing his own dressed animals as well as human figures and making them look like they could really move.

A third source of inspiration, for Clive's drawings and stories, was the landscape of Northern Ireland all about him. There were castle ruins like those of Dunluce on the Antrim Coast. And there were the green Castlereagh Hills which Clive could see out the nursery window of his first home at Dundela Villas.

It was while Clive was living in his parents' first home that a momentous event took place. One day Clive decided to change his name. Various stories have been told about how this change of name came to be. I relate these in my book *The Professor of Narnia: The C. S. Lewis Story*. It is sufficient for our purposes here to say that one day Clive came home and said to his mother, pointing proudly to himself: "I is Jacksie." From that point on he refused to answer to any other name. The family shortened his nickname to Jacks, and eventually it became simply Jack. Thus the title of this book, *Speaking of Jack*, and thus I shall refer to C. S. Lewis throughout this discussion guide.

In 1905 the Lewis family moved from Dundela Villas to a larger home on the outskirts of the city of Belfast. This new home was dubbed "Little Lea". It was there, in "the Little End Room" on the third floor of that house that Jack continued drawing pictures and writing stories about his dressed animals. Jack's reading developed in him a love of knights in shining armor and so he included these in his stories as well. Out of these pictures, stories, and some stuffed animals, Jack created his own imaginary world which he called Animal Land.

While Jack was developing his tales of Animal Land his brother Warnie's interests were growing along other lines. Warnie was a lover of India. Thus for the two boys to be able to play effectively together Warnie's imaginary land of India and Jack's Animal Land had to be united. The end product came to be known as the federation of Boxen.

Even in writing these childhood stories Jack wanted to set the scene, so to speak, in The Middle Ages. How else can one have knights in armor? One can see how Jack's childhood make-believe eventually blossomed into a lifelong career, two careers really: that of a novelist, as well as that of a teacher of Medieval and Renaissance literature.

However, to keep his brother Warren content Jack's medieval Animal Land had to somehow be connected to Warnie's modern India with its trains and steamships. This led Jack to write up a little history of Animal Land from The Middle Ages down to modern times. And then he had to make a map to show how Animal Land was situated with reference to Warnie's India.

Sadly, writing stories and drawing pictures of Boxen was not to last forever. Before long, Warnie was sent off to boarding school in England. And Jack soon followed his brother there after the death of their mother in 1908 from cancer. During the couple of years while Warnie was in boarding school and Jack was still at home, they would write back and forth about their imaginary country. On one occasion Jack wrote to Warnie, "At present Boxen is *slightly* convulsed. The news has just reached her that King Bunny is a prisoner."[5]

Though Jack and Warnie one day stopped playing with stuffed animals and in fact buried all their toys in the garden at Little Lea after their father's death in 1929, we can be grateful that they saved some of the stories and pictures of Boxen. And we can be thankful too that these childhood stories written by C. S. Lewis and his brother have now been edited and published by Walter Hooper, Jack's secretary at the end of his life. For in these stories we catch some valuable glimpses of the man C. S. Lewis was to become; among other things we are allowed a window into the imaginary world of a boy who would one day write some of the most beloved fairy tales of all time.

---

5 Walter Hooper, editor, *The Collected Letters of C. S. Lewis*, Volume I, London: HarperCollins, 2000, p. 3.

Discussion Questions

1. C. S. Lewis wrote some of the stories in this collection as early as eight years old. What strikes you about these stories, considering that they were written by a child of that age?
2. These first stories were also written around the time that Jack lost his mother to cancer. How do you think young Jack might have used writing to cope with grief?
3. What else might the content of these stories and their subject matter tell us about Jack's life as a child and youth?
4. What hints, if any, do you get through Boxen of the later creation of Narnia? What is similar and dissimilar between the two worlds?
5. What do you think of Jack's artistic ability as a child as reflected in the drawings in this book?
6. What does the Encyclopedia Boxoniana reveal about Jack the literary critic and historian?
7. Obviously Jack and Warnie maintained a lifelong interest in these childhood stories. Why do you think that might have been the case?
8. What other insights or observations about Jack and Boxen do you have that you would like to share with the group?

Spirits in Bondage

According to Walter Hooper, C. S. Lewis began writing poetry in the Little End Room at Little Lea before he went away to boarding school at the age of ten.[6] Jack's earliest extant poem dates from 1912 when he was a student at Cherbourg preparatory school in Great Malvern, England. Inspired by Wagner's *Ring of the Nibelung*, Jack wrote 801 lines of a heroic poem. In 1913, another poem, *Carpe Diem*, won him a prize at his next boarding school, Malvern College, also in Great Malvern, England. Soon Jack aspired to be a great poet. During his years at Malvern College Jack also wrote a narrative poem entitled *Loki Bound* which was Norse in subject and Greek in form.

After his years in Malvern Jack was sent to a tutor by the name of William Kirkpatrick who lived in Great Bookham, Surrey. Kirkpatrick was responsible for preparing Jack to take the entrance examinations to Oxford University. During this time Jack continued to add to a collection of poems he entitled *Metrical Meditations of a Cod*. (According to Jack's brother, Warnie, "cod" was an expression of humorous and insincere self-deprecation used by inhabitants of Northern Ireland.) Between 1915 and 1917 Jack wrote fifty-two poems which he added to this collection, kept in a notebook. Fourteen of these poems eventually found their way into the book which became *Spirits in Bondage*. Jack first thought of getting these poems published while he was in the Officer Training Corps at Keble College, Oxford University in 1917.

---

6 Walter Hooper, editor, *Narrative Poems*, San Diego: Harcourt Brace & Company, 1979, p. vii.

Some of these lyrics, like *French Nocturne*, reflect Jack's experiences as a soldier during the First World War. Jack chose to write under the pseudonym of Clive Hamilton, the latter being his mother's maiden name. One reason why he chose anonymity was because while he served in the army he was concerned about what his fellow officers might think of him if they learned that he was writing poetry.

Jack was wounded during the war and some of his poems, like *Song*, were written during his convalescence. It was during his stay at Endsleigh Palace Hospital in London that he began to follow through on the idea of copying out all of his poems and having them typed up in preparation to send them to a publisher.

Macmillan was the first publisher to whom Jack sent his manuscript, initially titled *Spirits in Prison: a Cycle of Lyrical Poems*. The title was based upon 1 Peter 3:19 in the Authorized Version in which we read that Christ "went and preached unto the spirits in prison". By August 1918, Jack had received from Macmillan a polite rejection.

His next attempt was with the publisher William Heinemann. By September 1918 this try proved successful. Initially Heinemann wanted to remove a few of the poems submitted, saying that they were not on a level with the author's best work. Therefore Jack sent the publisher a couple of new poems as substitutes. Immediately upon hearing from Heinemann Jack wrote to his father, Albert, saying that this success gave him a pleasure which was perhaps childish, yet akin to greater things.

The main theme of these poems, as Jack noted in a letter to his Belfast friend Arthur Greeves, is that nature is evil and God, if he exists, is outside of and in opposition to the cosmos. Though baptized and confirmed in the Church of Ireland (Anglican) Jack had, for a number of reasons, become an atheist, perhaps as early as 1911, during his time at Cherbourg preparatory school in Great Malvern. He was later nurtured in his new-found atheism by his tutor, William Kirkpatrick. *Spirits in Bondage* is one of two published works of C. S. Lewis, the other being his epic poem *Dymer*, which in some ways reflects this atheistic period in his life.

Jack visited Heinemann's London office in October of 1918. At this time he met Mr. William Heinemann himself and signed his first book contract, guaranteeing him ten percent of the profits on the published price of twelve out of every thirteen copies sold.[7] Jack also learned at this meeting that John Galsworthy wanted to publish one of his poems, "Death in Battle", in a periodical entitled *Reveille*.

On March 20, 1919, William Heinemann published *Spirits in Bondage: a Cycle of Lyrics*. Jack's original title for the collection was replaced by this one due to the fact that Robert Hichens had already published a book in 1908 entitled *A Spirit in Prison*. Thus Jack's first book was published as *Spirits in Bondage*, a phrase borrowed from Milton's *Paradise Lost*.

Sadly, only about five hundred copies of Jack's first book were printed and it received only a few brief reviews of little consequence. *The Times Literary Supplement* found the lyrics to be "graceful and polished" but seldom rising above the "commonplace". The review in the *Bookman* was more encouraging, stating that Lewis' poems "confidently claim a place in the great tradition".

---

7   *The Collected Letters of C. S. Lewis*, Volume I, p. 410.

Discussion Questions

1. *Spirits in Bondage* is divided into three parts: *The Prison House, Hesitation,* and *The Escape.* What is "The Prison House" and who is imprisoned there? What is "the hesitation"? To where does the prisoner escape?

2. After *Spirits in Bondage* was published Jack told his father that in poems like *De Profundis* he wasn't cursing the God that his father or he believed in. Do you think Jack was telling the truth? What God is being cursed in this poem?

3. If you weren't told that these poems were written by C. S. Lewis what internal clues would reveal the identity of the author to you?

4. The poem, *Milton Read Again*, reveals Jack's love of *Paradise Lost.* Do you find it ironic that Lewis enjoyed Milton's poetry even during this atheistic period of his life?

5. Some Lewis scholars, like James Como, doubt that Lewis was ever an atheist. What do you think? What evidence do these poems provide either for or against that proposition?

6. How does this cycle of lyrics evoke Lewis' experience of World War I? If you have read any other poetry from this period how does Lewis' work compare?

7. Of what poets, if any, does Lewis remind you?

8. Which poem is your favorite? Why? Will you read it to the group?

Dymer[8]

C. S. Lewis began writing a prose version of *Dymer* during the Christmas holiday of 1916. He sent installments to his Belfast friend, Arthur Greeves, over the subsequent months while living with his tutor, William Kirkpatrick, in Great Bookham, Surrey. Despite Arthur's encouragement, Jack felt this first attempt at telling the story of Dymer was a failure. Thus he began writing a verse version of the same story in 1918 while recovering in a hospital in Eastbourne from his battle wounds suffered in the First World War. At that time he told Arthur that the main idea of the poem was that of development by self-destruction. According to Jack the story was based upon the assumption of good outside of and opposed to the cosmos.[9] This version was entitled "The Redemption of Ask". Thus Jack was thinking about redemption even in his atheistic years. In 1920 he made yet another attempt at the same story. This time it was called "The Red Maid" and took the form of a ballad.

In April 1922, while a student at Oxford University, Jack began a fourth attempt at telling the story of Dymer, this time in rhyme royal.[10] His diary from this period reveals that he worked on the poem regularly and shared it with his friends and fellow students at Oxford: Owen Barfield, Cecil Harwood, Leo Baker and Nevill Coghill.

---

8   Dymer is available as part of the collection entitled *Narrative Poems*, edited by Walter Hooper and published by Harcourt Brace & Company.
9   *Collected Letters*, Volume I, p. 419.
10 Walter Hooper, editor, *All My Road before Me: the Diary of C. S. Lewis 1922-1927*, San Diego: Harcourt Brace Jovanovich, 1992, p. 15.

All of these friends provided helpful advice which shaped the final outcome of Jack's work. Interestingly enough, Jack asked Coghill to keep the manuscript confidential; he still didn't want it spread abroad that he was writing poems. Jack kept a chronological account of the creation of *Dymer* from start to finish; this account, along with Jack's letters and diary entries, reveals more of his creative process in writing *Dymer* than what we have for any of his other books.[11]

A surviving original manuscript of *Dymer*, dating perhaps from 1924 or 1925, reveals that Jack toyed with the idea of making the story of Dymer a dream; this particular manuscript contains one additional stanza after Canto IX, 35 in which the dreamer awakes. The idea of the author awaking from a dream obviously appealed to Jack because, while he didn't, in the end, use this device in *Dymer*, he did use it in *The Pilgrim's Regress* and *The Great Divorce*.[12]

The final version of *Dymer* was presented first to William Heinemann for publication since Heinemann, as Jack's first publisher, had the right of first refusal on his second book. To Jack's great disappointment Heinemann rejected *Dymer* without a word of explanation, critique or encouragement. However, undaunted, Jack sent the manuscript to J. M. Dent, which company did finally publish the book in September 1926. Once again Jack published under the pseudonym of Clive Hamilton.

Dymer received some excellent reviews. *The New Leader* called it "a fine poem, indeed, marred only by an opening canto that is commonplace in comparison with the rest of the work." And *The Times Literary Supplement* said "Mr. Hamilton's poem is notable because it is in the epic tradition and yet is modern in idiom and reflects a profoundly personal intuition."

In the preface to the 1950 edition of *Dymer*, which was published under the name C. S. Lewis, Jack said that like many better books *Dymer* found some good reviews but almost no readers. He also described in this preface how he got the idea for this book and the main thrust of the narrative. He said that what came to him, apparently by pure inspiration, was the story of a man who, with a mysterious bride,

---

11   *Narrative Poems*, p. 176.
12   Ibid., p. x.

begets a monster. This monster, as soon as it has killed its father, becomes a god. This idea simply arrived in Jack's mind sometime during his seventeenth year.[13]

Jack provided some other helpful explanations in this same preface. He said that the Platonic and totalitarian state from which Dymer escapes was a natural invention for him since he disliked the state in Plato's *Republic*. Jack also lumped into this image his hatred of public school and the army.

He further explained that his hero was a man escaping from illusion. Jack and his friends, having read Freud, were much concerned about the issue of wishful thinking. As a result, by the time he wrote the final version of *Dymer* Jack had entered a state of angry revolt against the spell of what the Germans call *sehnsucht* and what he later called: longing, joy, or romanticism.

One more interesting point from Jack's 1950 preface is that the magician in Canto VI, 6-9 was modeled, at least in part, on William Butler Yeats. Jack had met Yeats during his student years in Oxford and was simultaneously impressed with and repelled by Yeats' belief in magic. Jack had come to believe that magic and spiritualism were part and parcel of the worst kind of fantasy. This view was due in part to his encounter with Yeats' work and Yeats the man. However, it was also due to his seeing a man descend into screaming mania just before his death, largely, Jack believed, due to the man's involvement in spiritualism. This man was none other than Dr. John Askins, the brother of Mrs. Moore who was, in turn, the mother of Jack's friend Paddy Moore killed in the First World War.

George Sayer, pupil, friend and biographer of C. S. Lewis, devotes an entire chapter in his book, *Jack: A Life of C. S. Lewis*, to the poem, *Dymer*. Sayer notes very intriguingly how Dymer's quest is the same as that of Anodos, the chief character in George MacDonald's myth, *Phantastes*, a book which profoundly influenced Jack. Anodos and Dymer both seek the feminine. And as Sayer notes, when Jack first read *Phantastes* the song of the sirens sounded, for the first time, like the voice of the two holy people Jack knew in childhood: his mother and his nurse.[14]

---

13 Ibid., p. 3.
14 George Sayer, *Jack*, Wheaton, Illinois: Crossway Books, 1994, p. 107.

Sayer notes that one critic, Marjorie Mack, interpreted *Dymer* as being essentially about Jack's search for his poetic muse. According to Mack, Lewis failed to find this muse in the palace of the romantic tradition set in nature. Only through disillusionment and suffering, only through the death of Jack as the romantic dreamer, can a new literary vision be reborn in God, the great and true romantic.[15]

Summary

Canto I: Dymer kills his teacher and flees the Perfect City naked.

Canto II: In a palace Dymer tries on new clothes, eats, drinks, and passes into a cool, dark place where the breathing body of a girl slides into his open arms.

Canto III: Dymer wakes in a forest to find the girl gone. He comes upon another palace where every entrance is blocked by an old woman.

Canto IV: Dymer encounters a dying man who tells him that he, Dymer, has been the cause of a rebellion in the Perfect City; the rebellion is led by a person named Bran.

Canto V: When he wakes up the next morning Dymer is filled with desolation at the thought of the havoc his life has wreaked.

Canto VI: Dymer continues his journey; coming to an old house he meets the Master Magician who tells him the shortcut back to happiness is to dream again, but deeper. Dymer falls for this and drinks from a magic cup.

Canto VII: We learn that the Magician is tormented by the same stimulant he has given Dymer to drink, but he keeps drinking it anyway. Dymer is disappointed by his dream of the girl and so, defying the Magician, he runs from his house; the Magician shoots and wounds Dymer.

Canto VIII: The bleeding Dymer is befriended by the woman he has longed for. As he looks back over his life he comes to the conclusion that he has never loved a real woman but only a spirit. The woman leaves him; Dymer continues on his journey until he comes to a gate leading to a graveyard.

---

15   Ibid., p. 213.

Canto IX: As Dymer lays dying his spirit ascends. In the heavens he meets an armed guard whose job is to protect him from the beasts of the upper air, and in particular, from a monster who threatens him. Dymer learns that the monster is his son, the product of his union with the immortal woman he met earlier. The monster ends up killing Dymer and as soon as he does so he becomes a god and the earth is reborn.

Discussion Questions

1. How does this poem express Lewis' theological/philosophical beliefs at the time of writing? How would you characterize his position at the time?
2. Do you think this poem evokes Lewis' experience of sehnsucht, joy, longing, desire, or romanticism? If so, how and where?
3. The nakedness of Dymer in the first canto seems to be an important image, as it is in much of Lewis' writing. Consider the nakedness of John in *The Pilgrim's Regress*, the Solid People in *The Great Divorce*, Eustace in *Voyage of the Dawn Treader*, and Shasta in *The Horse and His Boy*. What do you make of this image and its meaning in *Dymer*?
4. What is the significance of the fact that Dymer seeks the immortal feminine? Do you see any connection with Lewis' own life? What does the ancient matriarchal dreadfulness represent?
5. As the story moves along we find Dymer seeking objective truth in contrast to a subjective dream-world. Discuss the significance of this in Lewis' developing thought. You might wish to compare/contrast what Lewis says in this poem with what he writes later in *The Great Divorce* of heaven as the ultimate, objective reality.
6. This poem mentions the shadow-lands and the immortal forms. What role did the writings of Plato play in the development of Lewis' worldview?
7. What is the significance of the fact that the Master Magician wounds Dymer?
8. How do the ideas conveyed in this poem compare to the ideas conveyed in Lewis' *Pilgrim's Regress* written seven years later?
9. Compare/contrast Dymer's many deaths in Canto VIII with Eustace's sloughing off of the many layers of dragon skin in *The Voyage of the Dawn Treader*.

10. In Canto IX, 6 Lewis uses an image from biblical apocalyptic: "a moonset red as blood". What role do you think the Bible played in Lewis' developing thought and writing at this time?

11. What is the significance of the fact that the earth is reborn at the time of Dymer's death?

12. What is the significance of the monster killing Dymer and then turning into a god? Compare/contrast with the story of the man with the lizard on his shoulder in *The Great Divorce*.

13. Lewis claimed that Dymer was not a portrait of himself. What do you think? Why?

14. Do you have a favorite line or stanza in this poem? If so, would you read it aloud to the group?

15. How does this narrative poem compare to Lewis' lyric poetry? Which do you like better? Why?

16. One reviewer thought this story would be better told in prose. What do you think? Why?

The Pilgrim's Regress

*T*he *Pilgrim's Regress* was the first book C. S. Lewis had published after his return to the Christian faith. Jack wrote the book during a fortnight holiday in August 1932 with his childhood friend Arthur Greeves at the Greeves family home, Bernagh, across the street from the old Lewis family home, Little Lea, in Belfast. Jack had made an earlier prose attempt, in 1930, to describe his conversion to theism. This first attempt was never published, but a copy resides in the Bodleian Library, Oxford. A second account of his conversion, this time in verse, was attempted in early 1932. In this case the third attempt really was the charm. The fact that Jack wrote all of *The Pilgrim's Regress* in a fortnight holiday betrays something of his genius.

The manuscript was sent to J. M. Dent and Sons, the publisher of his narrative poem *Dymer*, in December 1932 and published in May 1933. Jack himself drew the sketch for the Mappa Mundi which appeared on the endpapers of the first and subsequent editions of *The Pilgrim's Regress*. This first edition only sold 650 out of 1000 copies printed.[16]

Some reviewers of *The Pilgrim's Regress* assumed wrongly that Jack was a Roman Catholic, perhaps because one of the chief characters in the book is Mother Kirk. This brought the book to the attention of Sheed & Ward, a Roman Catholic publishing house in London. Dent printed an additional 1500 copies for Sheed who re-issued the book in 1935.[17]

---

16 George Sayer, *Jack*, p. 230.
17 Ibid.

The blurb on the flyleaf of this second edition is really rather interesting. It says:

> The allegory obviously suggests *Pilgrim's Progress*, but the Giants and Demons are of a sort that Bunyan never knew, and Mr. Lewis' wit would probably seem to Bunyan sinful. Certainly his theology would.
>
> The hero, brought up in Puritania (Mr. Lewis himself was born in Ulster), cannot abide the religion he finds there. With many digressions he follows the Straight Path that runs past the City of Claptrap, between the tableland of the High Anglicans and the far-off marsh of the Theosophists. A fundamental problem throughout is to find the relation between the sexual instinct and the religious; on this the conclusion is neither that of Freud nor that of D. H. Lawrence.
>
> Many varieties of religious and aesthetic theorising come under the lash before the final chapters, in which the realm of controversy is altogether transcended.[18]

Jack's comment on this second edition is worth noting for it indicates how strong an Ulster Protestant he was at the time. He wrote to Arthur Greeves in December 1935 telling him of the publication of *Regress* by Sheed & Ward. He commented that he didn't like having a book of his, especially a religious one, brought out by a "Papist" publisher. The only reason he allowed it was because Sheed & Ward thought they could sell more copies than Dent could do. Jack noted that the blurb on the flyleaf was published without his authority; he felt it implied an attack on his own country of Northern Ireland and his own religion as a Protestant. Jack urged Arthur to explain to anyone who might be interested that he, Jack, was not consulted concerning the blurb and that the blurb itself was "a damnable lie told to try and make Dublin riff-raff buy the book."[19]

---

18 Flyleaf of my personal copy of the second edition of *The Pilgrim's Regress*

19 Walter Hooper, editor, *The Collected Letters of C. S. Lewis*, Volume II, New York: HarperCollins, 2004, p. 170.

Despite his displeasure with Sheed & Ward, Jack allowed them to re-issue the book again in 1944, this time with a preface. In the preface, which now appears as an afterword in some editions, Jack wrote that upon re-reading the book ten years after he wrote it, he felt its chief faults were needless obscurity, and an uncharitable temper.[20] He attempted to correct the needless obscurity of the book by supplying running headlines throughout. The temper he left as it was. The book is still obscure to the average reader who lacks a sufficient understanding of the philosophical movements of the 1920s in England. This obscurity can be somewhat clarified by reading Jack's spiritual autobiography, *Surprised by Joy*, alongside *The Pilgrim's Regress*. David C. Downing's book, *The Most Reluctant Convert: C. S. Lewis' Journey to Faith*,[21] also gives a helpful explanation of Jack's journey from popular realism to philosophical idealism, idealism to pantheism, pantheism to theism, and finally from theism to Christianity. For those in need of a handy translation and/or definitions of various terms in the *Regress* this introduction is followed by a glossary.

The overall purpose of *The Pilgrim's Regress* is summarized in the book's sub-title: *An Allegorical Apology for Christianity, Reason and Romanticism*, reason and romanticism being the two major things which led Jack to return to the Christian faith. As Jack notes in his preface, by romanticism he means experiences of intense longing, a mere wanting which is somehow a delight. Jack's romanticism is what the Germans call *sehnsucht* and Jack himself called joy in his own autobiography. He came to believe that if one would follow this romanticism, this longing, this joy, pursuing false objects until their falsity appeared and then abandoning them, then one would eventually come to the knowledge that the human soul was made to enjoy something which is never fully given in our earthly experience—that something which is a someone—namely God.

---

20 C. S. Lewis, *The Pilgrim's Regress*, Grand Rapids: Eerdmans, 1981, p. 200.
21 David C. Downing, *The Most Reluctant Convert: C. S. Lewis' Journey to Faith*, Downer's Grove, Illinois: InterVarsity Press, 2002.

Glossary[22]

Ahriman: Persian; Prince of Evil.

Angular: a caricature of T.S. Eliot who was an Anglo-Catholic. Lewis is satirizing Eliot's dry anti-Romantic approach to literature.

Archtype and Ectype: the original and the copy.

Behemoth & Leviathan: huge animals referred to in Job 3:8 and 40:15.

Benedict: Spinoza: contributed to 17th century rationalism.

Bernard: Bosanquet (1848-1923), British idealist.

Mr. Broad: the liberal church.

Claptrap: self-important, insincere and pretentious language. A trap is a two-wheeled carriage similar to Mr. Enlightenment's cart.

Classical: a caricature of Irving Babbitt, an American scholar who vigorously opposed Romanticism and died in 1933.

Clopinel: 13th century writer, Jean de Meun.

Dialectic of Desire: the pattern of pursuing the source of joy, being side-tracked, and then corrected.

"Dixit Insipiens" means "The fool hath said . . ." from the Vulgate, Psalm 53:1, "The fool hath said in his heart 'There is no God.'"

Druery: Lovemaking.

The Dwarfs: Fascists and Communists (Marxomanni). Mussolomini are Italian Fascists, Swastici are the Nazis (Hitler had just been elected Chancellor of Germany when Lewis wrote this), and the Gangomanni are gangsters.

Eschropolis: city of foul obscenity.

---

22 For much of the information in this glossary I am indebted to Kathryn Lindskoog, *Finding the Landlord: A Guidebook to C. S. Lewis' Pilgrim's Regress*, Chicago: Cornerstone Press, 1995.

"Esse Is Percipi" means "To be is to be perceived."

Evangelium eternum: the eternal gospel, pantheism.

Glugly: represents ugly and meaningless art. Lewis may have had the Dadaists of the 1920s in mind.

The Grand Canyon: the great chasm between God and man created by the sin of Adam, *Peccatum Adae*. It is also called the valley of Humiliation, a la Bunyan.

Mr. Halfways: represents the Romantic Poets. He is much like William Butler Yeats, whom Lewis had met and admired at one time. He also makes statements directly quoted from Keats.

Helot: a female serf in ancient Sparta.

Herbert: Spencer; coined the phrase "survival of the fittest."

Humanist: an atheist who lives to oppose optimism, romanticism, transcendentalism and humanitarianism. He is a thinly disguised George Santayana.

Ignorantia: ignorance brought about by overemphasizing scientific/technological knowledge and suppressing classical education.

Immanuel: Kant (1724-1804).

Io Paean: a traditional Greek shout of triumph and praise.

Jehovah-Jireh: God will provide. (Genesis 22:14)

Karl: Marx.

Landlord: God.

"Let Grill be Grill" refers to a character in Lewis' favorite allegory, Spenser's *Faerie Queene*. Gryll had been turned into a hog, and when a knight released him from the spell, Gryll abused the knight instead of thanking him.

Luxuria: one of the seven deadly sins; lust.

Mr. Mammon: wealth.

The Man: Christ.

Media Halfways: Media refers to the materials of artistic creation. Halfways indicates the insufficiency of the arts to finally satisfy John's longing.

Medium Aevum: The Middle Ages.

Mother Kirk: Kirk is Scottish for church. Mother Kirk represents Christianity.

Nella Sua Voluntade: In His Will. This refers to "In His will is our peace" from *Paradiso*, the third and last book of Dante's *Divine Comedy*.

Nomos: the Jewish Law, Vertue's father.

Northerners: According to Lewis the Northerners are "the men of rigid systems whether skeptical or dogmatic, Aristocrats, Stoics, Pharisees, Rigorists, signed and sealed members of highly organised 'Parties'."

Pagans: non-Jews.

Per-persecuted: extremely persecuted.

Phally: a nickname for Phallus. Probably represents D.H. Lawrence.

Pictures: Mythology.

Psittacosis: a parrot disease that men can catch.

"Quem Quaeritis in Sepulchro? Non Est Hic." is Luke 24:5-6 in the Vulgate: "Whom do you seek in the sepulcher? He is not here."

Romanticism: (as used in the title of *The Pilgrim's Regress*), an experience of intense longing or sweet Desire. Lewis said the mere wanting of this experience was to him, somehow, a delight; it was like a hunger which was better than any other fullness; it was like a poverty better than all other wealth.

Rudolph: Steiner (1861-1925), the first leader of the occult German Theosophic Association and later founder of the Anthroposophical Society, whose philosophy Lewis' friend Owen Barfield embraced.

The Rules: Morality.

Savage: a Nordic warrior much like Odin, god of war.

Mr. Sensible: common sense. He detests Reason, preferring common sense which seeks comfort instead of truth. He has a smattering of knowledge from many sources but does not fully understand any of the authors he has read, thus the many Latin, French and Greek quotes, which we will not translate here. Epicurus, who taught that the highest good is pleasure, was the founder of Mr. Sensible's house. In the end we find that Mr. Sensible is very insensible, and in fact–invisible.

Serpens nisi serpentem comederit: it is not a serpent if it doesn't eat serpents.

Shepherds: Jews.

A shaw: a small wood.

Sigismund: the son of Mr. Enlightenment; represents Sigmund Freud.

Slikisteinsauga: Sleekstone Eyes; a sleekstone is a rock used to polish something else. In Lewis' allegory this is an angelic guide.

Southerners: According to Lewis the Southerners are people whose minds are open to everything, especially any "Maenad or Mystagogue" who offers some sort of intoxication.

Superbia: pride, one of the seven deadly sins. Superbia is disgusted with all things physical and thus reduces her territory to sterile stone.

The Tableland: represents all high and dry states of mind including High Anglicanism.

Thrill: John's first thrill is delivery from fear of the Landlord; his second thrill is that of beautiful literature.

Vertue: human conscience.

Victoriana: Edith Sitwell, who wrote avant-garde poems but often dressed in medieval-style gowns.

Vieux jeu: French for "old hat".

Wisdom–Exoteric & Esoteric: readily understood wisdom and secret wisdom. Mr. Wisdom represents human wisdom apart from God and he teaches John basic Hegelianism. The Valley of Wisdom, in the end, turns out to be just one region in hell.

Worm: Snake.

Wormwood: a plant with a strong, bitter taste, used in Revelation 8:10-11 as a metaphor for calamity and sorrow; here used as the name for Mother Kirk's land-grabber.

Zeitgeistheim: home of the Spirit of the Age which is Freudian reductionism.

Discussion Questions

1. What do you think is the significance of the fact that John must regress rather than progress like Bunyan's Christian?
2. Lewis says that this book is an "allegorical apology for Christianity, Reason and Romanticism". How is this book a defense of each of these three entities?
3. What is the significance of the fact that John is born in the land of Puritania? How might this relate to Lewis' own life? How do Puritanism in Bunyan's allegory and Puritanism in Lewis' allegory compare and contrast?
4. How does John's experience of the primroses compare to Lewis' first experience of "joy"?
5. What is the meaning of the masks in Book I, chapter 3? Has your experience of religion ever been similar to John's? How?
6. What is the meaning of the Island? Is John's vision of the Island merely an aesthetic experience? Does reading John's story fill you with any desire to see the Island?
7. What is meant by the chapters entitled "Leah for Rachel"? Have you ever sought joy in a certain place only to find it wasn't there?
8. How does John's desire for the Island ultimately lead him to Mother Kirk? How did Lewis' experience of joy lead him to Christ? How about you– has desire played any role in leading you to God?
9. What role does Reason play in leading John to Mother Kirk? What role did Reason play in leading Lewis to Christianity? What role has Reason played in leading you closer to Christ?
10. What did you think of Mother Kirk's Story in Book V, Chapter 2? Do you find it more or less compelling than the corresponding biblical account of the fall? Why?
11. What is the significance of the Man's comment to John

that he and Vertue will both recover only if they keep together?

12. There is an element of fear in John that runs throughout the story, fear of the Landlord, fear of the black hole, fear of death, fear of Mother Kirk, fear of prayer. Why is John afraid and how is this fear ultimately transformed?

13. In the chapter entitled "Caught" John expresses one of his deepest wishes. What is that wish? How does this correspond to Lewis' own wishes before his conversion? Have you ever had this wish?

14. The essence of *The Pilgrim's Regress* is perhaps best summed up in John's words to the hermit that he set out to find an Island and he found a Landlord instead. How are the Island and the Landlord related? How did you feel when John finally crossed the Canyon and saw the Island and realized it was the other side of the Eastern Mountains?

15. The hermit tells John that there are two ways to the Landlord that were united in the Landlord's Son. What are these two ways? Who travels these two different routes? What do you think of Lewis' theology on this point?

16. In the second chapter entitled "Archtype and Ectype" John says he is afraid the things the Landlord wants for him may be completely unlike his own desires. Have you ever had this fear? How does the hermit answer John's fear?

17. What is the significance of the fact that John must dive into the pool to get across the Canyon? What does the dive into the pool symbolize?

18. Why does the world look different to John as he regresses? What is Lewis' meaning here?

19. John's angelic guide during his regress makes the statement that if anyone really wants to damage the Landlord's character, rather than say the Landlord is cruel he should say that the Landlord is an inveterate gambler. What do you think the angel means by this statement? How does this fit in to Lewis' theology? What do you think?

20. What do you think of Lewis' concept of hell as a tourniquet?

The Allegory of Love

In a letter to his friend Owen Barfield written on Whitsunday 1928 C. S. Lewis mentioned that during his most recent vacation from his newly assumed position as a Fellow and Tutor of English Literature at Magdalen College, Oxford, he had spent most of his time in the Bodleian Library doing research for a book. The subject was the *Romance of the Rose* and its school,[23] a topic which had been suggested to him by his former tutor, F. P. Wilson, in about 1925.[24] By July of 1928 Jack reported to his father Albert that he had actually begun writing the first chapter of this book which would become *The Allegory of Love*.[25]

Jack explained to his father that the book was to be about medieval love poetry and the medieval idea of love: a love which was at the same time both super-sensual *and* honorable since directed from a man toward a married woman, as in the case of Dante and Beatrice or Lancelot and Guinevere. In the first chapter of *The Allegory of Love* Jack enumerated the characteristics of courtly love as it appeared suddenly at the end of the 11th century in Languedoc: humility, courtesy, adultery and the religion of love. This service of love was closely modeled on that service which a feudal vassal in those days owed to his Lord.[26]

---

23   *Collected Letters*, Volume I, p. 764.
24   *Jack*, p. 242.
25   *Collected Letters*, Volume I, p. 766.
26   C. S. Lewis, *The Allegory of Love*, New York: Oxford University Press, 1967, p. 2.

By November of 1928 Jack finished writing the first chapter of this new book. However, he was concerned at the possibility of making an elementary blunder since no one else in Oxford at the time seemed to know anything about his subject. He was worried that some French scholar might easily point out his errors. At the same time one of the most successful aspects of the book was Jack's translation of certain writings in Old French into Middle English; he hoped thereby to convey the flavor of the period better than if he translated into modern English. Jack's translations passed muster with no less an expert than C. T. Onions, one of the chief lexicographers on the staff of the Oxford English Dictionary.[27]

Jack's painstaking scholarly work on this subject was slow-going. By May of 1929 he was able to report to his father that he had completed most of chapter two.[28] But by July he was still working on the same chapter.[29] Of course Jack had to fit his work on *The Allegory of Love* into odd moments between tutorials, being able to work at length only during the long vacations each summer.[30] One can picture Jack almost alone in the Bodleian during the long, hot summers, year after year, toiling away on this project. He wrote to his father in the summer of 1929 saying he would be glad to get out of the windless hollow of the Bodleian and see the ocean again.[31]

Sadly, Jack's Belfast holiday that summer was to be his last with his father, for the latter died of cardiac arrest on September 25 after a brief battle with cancer.[32] Jack's father Albert would never get to read the final fruit of his son's scholarly labors which he had enjoyed in its seminal period.

By the end of 1929 Jack was soliciting comments and criticism from one of his Oxford colleagues regarding the second chapter of *The Allegory of Love*.[33] While Jack was busily at work on this scholarly project and continuing his other duties as a Fellow and Tutor at

---

27 *Collected Letters*, Volume I, pp. 779-780.
28 Ibid., p. 796.
29 Ibid., p. 799.
30 Ibid., p. 957.
31 Ibid., p. 800.
32 Ibid., p. 822.
33 Ibid., p. 855.

Magdalen College, other developments were afoot in his spiritual life. During Trinity Term 1929 he became a theist and by September 1931 he had returned to full-bodied Christian faith. Thus his work on *The Allegory of Love* was slightly interrupted by the writing of an allegorical account of his conversion entitled *The Pilgrim's Regress* published in 1933.

Being made an English Examiner for Oxford University also devoured much of his time during the summers of 1932 and '33.[34] Nonetheless Jack completed the manuscript of *The Allegory of Love* by September 1935 and submitted it to The Clarendon Press of Oxford University for publication, which press accepted the book almost immediately.[35] By December Jack was working on correcting the galley proofs,[36] which laborious effort continued through February 1936 in amongst his other work.[37]

However, the galley proofs of *The Allegory of Love* provided Jack with more than just work: they eventually connected him with a man who would become one of his most important friends. In the spring of 1936 Jack read *The Place of the Lion* by Charles Williams. He called it one of the major literary events of his life, comparable to his first discovery of George Macdonald, G. K. Chesterton or William Morris. And on March 11 he wrote to Williams, a proofreader at The Oxford University Press office in London, thanking him for the book.[38] At the same time Williams, having read the proofs of *The Allegory of Love*,[39] wrote to Jack telling him of his admiration for the book. Thus was born a friendship which eventually, along with Jack's friendship with J. R. R. Tolkien, formed the nucleus of the literary gathering known as The Inklings.

The Allegory of Love was published by the Clarendon Press on May 21, 1936.[40] It was highly praised by reviewers at the time like

---

34 *Collected Letters*, Volume II, p. 127.
35 Ibid., p. 168-169.
36 Ibid., p. 174.
37 Ibid., p. 181.
38 Ibid., pp. 181-184.
39 Ibid., p. 186. Williams eventually wrote the blurb for the cover of the first edition of *The Allegory of Love*.
40 Ibid., p. 191.

Professor Ifor Evans writing for *The London Observer*: "Out of the multitude of volumes on literary history there arises once or twice in a generation a truly great work. Such I believe is this study by Mr. C. S. Lewis."[41] The reviewer for *Modern Language Notes* enthused, "The tremendous amount of information, the brilliance of the ideas, the felicitous phrasing and always delightful style, all combine to make *The Allegory of Love* a really outstanding contribution to medieval studies." And *The Times Literary Supplement* called it: "Scholarly, fascinating, and original".

According to George Sayer the publication of *The Allegory of Love* even led to an upsurge in the sales of otherwise obscure medieval works, at least among Oxford booksellers.[42] Jack's treatment of the poet, Spenser, was considered especially insightful. Whether they agree with Jack's conclusions or not, all later writers on Spenser have inevitably made use of *The Allegory of Love*. Again according to Sayer, *The Allegory of Love* is still the number one book on its subject. And while Jack has been criticized for an overemphasis on morality at the expense of literary criticism his approach is still helpful in dealing with essentially moralistic authors.[43]

---

41 *Jack*, p. 243.
42 Ibid., p. 244.
43 Ibid., p. 245.

A C. S. Lewis Discussion Guide

Discussion Questions

1. In chapter one, paragraph one, of *The Allegory of Love* Lewis states that humanity does not pass through phases like a train passing through stations. Since humanity is something alive it is always moving while at the same time it never leaves anything behind. Whatever humanity has been it will in some ways always be. Do you think this is true? Why or why not? Is it important to you to learn about the history of humanity? If so, how do you go about doing this?

2. In chapter one, paragraph four, Lewis states that the idea of romantic love, as it arose suddenly at the end of the 11th century, was a novelty. Our difficulty, Lewis maintains, is to imagine a world without it. How much, would you guess, is our contemporary fiction, and even nonfiction, preoccupied with the topic of romantic love? Did it ever occur to you before that this is a novelty within the history of humanity? What do you think of Lewis' contention?

3. In chapter one, paragraph thirteen, Lewis paraphrases the thought of Albertus Magnus who states that fallen humanity's real problem is not the strength of pleasure but the weakness of reason. Humanity before the fall could have enjoyed any amount of pleasure without losing sight of the First Good, namely God. Do you think Lewis himself agreed with Magnus? What is your view?

4. In chapter one, paragraph fifteen, Lewis states that the impression left on the medieval mind by its official teachers was that all love—at least the kind of love the courtly poets wrote about —was more or less wicked. This division between church and court on the issue of love was, Lewis maintains, the most striking feature of medieval sentiment. On which side in this debate does your sentiment lie: church or court? Why?

5. In chapter one, section three, paragraph four, Lewis says that where marriages are arranged by parents rather than based upon the choice of the individuals who marry any

theory which sees romantic love as a noble experience must be a theory of adultery. What does Lewis mean by this? Can you imagine living in a time where all marriages were arranged by parents, and where marriage based upon "falling in love" was a novelty?

6. At the beginning of chapter two Lewis says that the equivalence between the immaterial and the material may be used by the mind in two ways. A poet can start with an immaterial fact, such as the passions, and then invent a visible image or character to express those passions. This is allegory. But there is another way of using the equivalence between the immaterial and the material which Lewis calls sacramentalism or symbolism. If the passions, being immaterial, can be expressed by the material invention of the poet then, Lewis says, it is possible that our material world in its turn is the copy of an invisible world. How important are allegory and symbolism or sacramentalism in the work of C. S. Lewis? What examples can you provide?

7. In chapter two, section three, paragraph two, Lewis maintains that monotheism should be regarded as the maturity of polytheism, that the former is a natural development from the latter. Do you agree with Lewis? Why or why not?

8. In chapter two, section three, paragraph three, Lewis summarizes the view of Aristotle that a really good person is not a tempted person. The truly temperate person abstains from certain pleasures because he or she likes abstaining. The ease and pleasure of his or her good acts are symptoms of virtue. The biblical phrase 'Fight the good fight' would sound very odd in the midst of Aristotle's *Ethics*. Do you agree with Aristotle or do you have a different view? Explain.

9. In chapter two, section three, paragraph nine, Lewis asserts that there is no writer who admits us into the heart of the Middle Ages better than Augustine. In what ways does Lewis say Augustine helps us understand what was then new about the medieval mind?

10. In chapter three, section two, paragraph one, Lewis states that a poet's biography has little relevance for literary criticism. This was a strongly held belief of Lewis which he spelled out in his book *The Personal Heresy*. Do you agree? Why or why not?

11. In chapter three, section two, paragraph eight, Lewis talks about how in the *Romance of the Rose* Venus symbolizes sexual appetite, the mere natural fact, in contrast to the god of Love who symbolizes the refined sentiment of romantic love. Does this remind you of something Lewis says elsewhere? Where? What does this reveal about how Lewis' reading of great literature influenced his philosophy of life?

12. In chapter three, section five, paragraph ten, Lewis comments on the photographic memory of Jean de Meun. Who else is this true of? How did this power of memory affect his writing?

13. At the beginning of chapter four Lewis mentions the three most "germinal" books of the Middle Ages? What were these? How did each of these influence Lewis?

14. According to Lewis, at the beginning of chapter seven, where is accomplished the final defeat of courtly love by the romantic conception of marriage?

15. At the end of chapter seven, section one, Lewis refers to Johnson's ideal happiness which he would choose if he were regardless of futurity, as well as his own ideal. What was Lewis' ideal happiness? And what is your ideal happiness which you would choose regardless of futurity?

16. In chapter seven, section three, paragraph two, Lewis tells us that Spenser has been represented as one who preached Protestantism while his imagination was essentially Catholic. In what sense, do you think, the same could be said of Lewis?

17. In the very next paragraph Lewis says that not all allegory is Catholic, but that Catholicism is allegorical. Do you think Lewis' contention that all allegories are in danger of being mistaken for Catholic apologetic is true? Why or why not?

18. In that same paragraph Lewis maintains that when Catholicism goes bad it becomes merely a religion of amulets and holy places and priest-craft. When Protestantism goes bad it becomes a vague mist of ethical platitudes. Catholicism, Lewis says, is sometimes accused of being much too like all the other religions while Protestantism is accused of being unlike a religion at all. Plato, Lewis asserts, is *the* philosopher for Protestants while Aristotle is the one for Catholics. Do you think Lewis' analysis is accurate? Why or why not?

19. In chapter seven, section three, paragraph nine, Lewis states that an allegory is not a puzzle. The worst thing a person can do when reading an allegory is to keep his or her eyes peeled for clues, as some readers do when reading a murder mystery. How does Lewis' caution apply to reading his own works?

20. In the penultimate paragraph of chapter seven Lewis says of Spenser that to read his works leads to growth in mental health. Do you think the same can be said of reading Lewis? Why or why not?

Out of the Silent Planet

C. S. Lewis wrote his first science-fiction novel, *Out of the Silent Planet*, in 1937[44] and it was first published in 1938. Also in 1938, Lewis wrote to one of his students, Roger Lancelyn Green, about his motivation to write the book. He said that what spurred him to write was Olaf Stapledon's *Last and First Men*, published in 1931, along with an essay in J. B. S. Haldane's book *Possible Worlds*, published in 1927. Both of these books seemed to take the idea of space travel seriously and shared what Lewis considered to be the immoral outlook pilloried in his own character—Weston. Lewis said that he liked the whole inter-planetary idea as a mythology and wanted to conquer for his own Christian point of view a genre which had hitherto been used by people like H. G. Wells to promote atheism.[45]

According to George Sayer, Jack was fascinated with the space-travel thriller since boyhood. And thus it was natural that after becoming a Christian he should have a deep desire to develop his own space-travel novel from a Christian perspective. Concerned that such books were rare, Jack made a proposal to his friend J. R. R. Tolkien that Tolkien should write a time-travel story and he should write a space-travel tale.[46] Sayer tells us that Tolkien and Lewis took the bargain seriously. However, Tolkien's story, *The Lost Road*, was not published at that time. Lewis' book was at first rejected by J. M. Dent

---

44 Sayer, p. 254.
45 Roger Lancelyn Green & Walter Hooper, *C. S. Lewis: A Biography*, Glasgow: Collins, 1974, p. 163.
46 Sayer, p. 254.

and Sons, but subsequently was accepted by The Bodley Head. Even then Lewis' book did not sell well until after he became famous for his *Broadcast Talks* and *The Screwtape Letters*.[47]

On July 9, 1939 Jack answered some questions for Sister Penelope, one of his correspondents, about the book. His letter gives us further insight into some of his motives for writing and the reception which the book received. He noted that he intended the danger of "Westonism" to be real and that what set him about writing the book was the discovery that one of his students took the idea of interplanetary colonization seriously. Jack was afraid that many people held out hope for a scientific solution to the problem of death and that this hope was a real rival to Christianity. He told Sister Penelope that she would be both grieved and amused to learn that only two reviewers of *Out of the Silent Planet* realized that his idea of the fall of the Bent One was anything but a private invention of his own. But this fact gave Jack hope that theology could be smuggled into people's minds under the cover of fiction without their knowing it.[48]

By 1945, when Jack addressed a group of Anglican priests and youth leaders, he had further developed this idea of "smuggling in theology under the cover of romance." At that time he asserted that the world didn't need more books about Christianity, but more books written by Christians on other topics with their Christianity latent.[49] This is precisely what he set out to accomplish himself using the science fiction genre.

The effect of Jack's *baptized* science fiction on his readers is told in a letter which Dorothy Sayers wrote to Lewis on December 21, 1953 about a young friend of hers:

> He told me how, in his undergraduate days, he read "Out of the Silent Planet" with great enjoyment, accepting it quite simply as a space-travel story until quite suddenly near the end (not, I think, until Ransom had got to Meldilorn) some phrase clicked in his mind and he exclaimed: "Why, this is a story about Christianity. Maleldil is Christ,

---

47   Ibid., p. 256.
48   *Collected Letters*, Volume II, p. 262.
49   C. S. Lewis, *God in the Dock*, Grand Rapids: Eerdmans, 1970, p. 93.

and the Eldila are the angels!" He said it was a most wonderful experience, as though two entirely different worlds had suddenly come into focus together, like a stereoscope, and it's a thing he can never forget.[50]

In his book, *A Severe Mercy*, Sheldon Vanauken tells the story of his introduction to C. S. Lewis through reading *Out of the Silent Planet*:

> It was fortunate that I chose to read that C. S. Lewis science-fiction trilogy first, for, apart from being beautiful and enthralling, it made me conscious of an alliance with him: what he hated (*That Hideous Strength*) I hated and feared. Much more important, perhaps, the trilogy showed me that the Christian God might, after all, be quite big enough for the whole galaxy. Nothing was proved except that, quite reasonably, He might be big enough; but, in fact, an insuperable difficulty–that of Christianity's being only a local religion–was overcome.[51]

Vanauken later became a Christian then, subsequently, fell away from "the Obedience," as he called it, for a period of time. In his "Afterward on the Genesis of A Severe Mercy," Vanauken described how *Out of the Silent Planet* led him back into the Obedience:

> Then one October night I was comfortably reading a detective story in bed. Suddenly in mid-page I was seized by an urgent desire to reread the first Lewis book I'd ever read, "Out of the Silent Planet". I fetched it and read the first page, which had nothing significant upon it. Nevertheless, by the time I reached the bottom of that page, I was back in the Obedience. I prayed. God was first.[52]

One of the most captivating aspects of *Out of the Silent Planet* is the incredible beauty therein described. Writing in 1937, Jack was certainly ahead of his time, especially when it came to describing the glory of "the heavens". Clyde Kilby, in *The Christian World of C. S.*

---

50 Green & Hooper, p. 165.
51 Sheldon Vanauken, *A Severe Mercy: Davy's Edition*, New York: Harper & Row, 1980, p. 84.
52 Ibid., p. 235.

Lewis, notes how Scott Carpenter, the second American to circle the earth in space, said, "The colors glowed vigorously alive with light."[53]

However, even those who love Jack's writing are not without criticism for *Out of the Silent Planet*. Clyde Kilby felt that *Out of the Silent Planet* was not dominated by a single idea as was the later *Perelandra*.[54] And George Sayer felt that this otherwise magnificent piece of science fiction suffered from the weak characterization of Ransom. According to Sayer the reason for this was that Ransom was, to some extent, a self-portrait of Lewis who was, at that time, shy of writing about his own spiritual or private life.[55] Though Ransom is not a fully developed character in *Out of the Silent Planet*, we catch glimpses of his inner nature: his fear, his tendency to self-absorption when left alone, his struggle to be courageous. And if Ransom is not fully developed in this novel, by the end of Jack's cosmic trilogy, one cannot help but be satisfied with the literary depth of his character. On the whole, *Out of the Silent Planet* is well worth the read for its fascinating plot and haunting beauty, as well as for its spiritual implications.

---

53   Clyde S. Kilby, *The Christian World of C. S. Lewis*, Grand Rapids: Eerdmans, 1964, note on p. 85.
54   Ibid., p. 90.
55   Sayer, p. 257.

A C. S. Lewis Discussion Guide

Discussion Questions

1. It would appear that Lewis put a good bit of himself, as well as a good bit of J. R. R. Tolkien, into the character of Ransom. Ransom is thirty-five to forty years of age (the age Lewis was when he wrote *Out of the Silent Planet*). Ransom dresses with a particular kind of shabbiness (like Lewis). He is a philologist (like Tolkien). He is a fellow of a college in England (like Lewis and Tolkien). Ransom enjoys walking tours, whiskey and tobacco (like Lewis). He is an anti-vivisectionist (like Lewis). Ransom served in the War (like Lewis and Tolkien) and he is a Christian (like Lewis and Tolkien). Do you think Lewis' writing technique in this regard detracts from or enhances the development of Ransom as a character? Why? Is Ransom an interesting character to you? Why or why not?

2. What do you think of Weston's philosophy of life, that anything which is done to individual people now is justified if it serves to perpetuate the human race? Do you see any traces of this philosophy in our contemporary society?

3. What do you think of Ransom's reflection in the middle of chapter five regarding vacuity of space versus the realization that the heavens are the blazing womb of the worlds?

4. *Out of the Silent Planet*, among other things, is full of descriptions of the sheer beauty of Malacandra. How did some of these descriptions affect you as you read the book? Would you read one of these descriptions for the group?

5. How well do you think Lewis achieves the feat of creating a whole new world that is at once believable as well as intriguing and delightful? What is one of your favorite aspects of Malacandrian life?

6. One of the key concepts in this book is that Thulcandra, Earth, is "the silent planet". What do the Malacandrians mean by this? What do you make of this whole idea?

7. The Hrossa call Weston and Devine *bent* men. Do you think this is a helpful description? Why? Do you think this is an accurate description of all human beings? Why or why not? Ransom often displays a sense of shame in regard to his people and his planet. Why is this? Would you feel the same way if you were in Ransom's shoes?

8. What do the Eldila and Oyarsa in particular add to your understanding or imagination when it comes to your view of angels? Do you believe in the reality of angels? Why or why not?

9. Another underlying theme in *Out of the Silent Planet* is that of *pleasure*. What do you think of the hross' statement in chapter twelve that pleasure is fully developed only when it is remembered? Elsewhere Lewis has said that the one prayer that God never answers is "Encore!" Do you think the Hrossa ever say, "Encore!"? Do human beings do this? Why do you think there is such a difference between the Hrossa and human beings as species?

10. In chapter twelve Hyoi says to Ransom that he doesn't think the forest would be bright, nor would the water be warm, nor would love be sweet, if there wasn't danger in the lakes. Does this statement suggest to you one reason why God may have allowed evil to exist in the world? What do you think about this?

11. Lewis' constant theme of longing, desire, joy, sehnsucht, is quite present in this book. At the end of chapter sixteen Lewis as narrator says that Ransom thought much of the old forests on Malacandra; he contemplated what it would be like to grow up always seeing at a brief distance a land of color which could never be reached, but which had once been inhabited. Does reading this or any other passage in this story fill you with a sense of longing? If so, for what? What do you think the old forests of Malacandra correspond to in our world?

12. When Ransom meets Oyarsa the latter tells Ransom that Ransom has been afraid of him and running from him even though he, Oyarsa, has been calling to him. What spiritual reality do you think this corresponds to in our world? Has this ever been true of you?

13. What do you think were the "wonders" which Ransom showed to Oyarsa at the beginning of chapter twenty-one?

The Personal Heresy[56]

In 1930 C. S. Lewis wrote an essay entitled "The Personal Heresy in Criticism" which he sent in November of that year to T. S. Eliot hoping that Eliot would publish the essay in his periodical *The Criterion*. Lewis' essay was a response to Cambridge Professor E. M. W. Tillyard's contention in his book *Milton* that poetry is about the poet's state of mind. In May of 1931 Eliot wrote a demurring letter to Lewis and Lewis wrote back still hoping that Eliot would publish the essay at a later date.[57] However, publication in *The Criterion* never came to be. Instead, Lewis' essay was published in *Essays and Studies by Members of the English Association*, XIX (1934).[58]

---

56 I have chosen to omit from this discussion guide one book by C. S. Lewis which was published the same year as *The Personal Heresy*. *Rehabilitations and Other Essays* was published by Oxford University Press on 23 March 1939 and contained the following essays: "Shelley, Dryden, and Mr. Eliot", "William Morris", "The Idea of an 'English School'", "Our English Syllabus", "High and Low Brows", "The Alliterative Metre", "Bluspels and Flalansferes: A Semantic Nightmare", "Variation in Shakespeare and Others", and "Christianity and Literature". Sadly, *Rehabilitations* has long been out of print and is difficult to obtain at a reasonable price, though it is available in a number of college and university libraries worldwide. The essays on "High and Low Brows" and "Christianity and Literature" have been reprinted in the C. S. Lewis *Essay Collection* published in Great Britain in 2000.

57 Walter Hooper, editor, *The Collected Letters of C. S. Lewis*, Volume III, New York: HarperCollins, 2007, pp. 1521-1522.

58 *Collected Letters*, Volume II, p. 157, note 14.

Tillyard responded to Lewis' essay with "The Personal Heresy in Criticism: A Rejoinder" also published in *Essays and Studies*, Volume XX in 1935.[59] The debate between Tillyard and Lewis continued in print with Lewis' "Open Letter to Dr Tillyard" published the following year, again in *Essays and Studies*.

The two men met in public debate in Magdalen College, Oxford on February 7, 1939. Lewis told his friend Owen Barfield that he expected to be defeated in the controversy.[60] However, one of Lewis' students, John Lawlor, remembered the outcome differently. In his book, *C. S. Lewis: Memories and Reflections*, Lawlor wrote:

> There was a memorable occasion when in the Hall at Magdalen Dr. Tillyard met him [Lewis] to round off in debate the controversy begun with the publication of Lewis's indictment of "The Personal Heresy". I am afraid there was no debate. Lewis made rings round Tillyard; in, out, up, down, around, back again—like some piratical Plymouth bark against a high-built galleon of Spain. Never was there a more skilful demonstration of "the Great Knock's" skills. As to the issues of the debate, that perhaps, is another story. There is no doubt that immense dialectical skill can batter an opponent into silence. But, as Adam Fox once reminded us, in the words of Daniel Waterland, "It is one thing to understand the doctrine, and quite another to be masters of the controversy." Lewis's ambition was of course to know the doctrine and to be master of the controversy.[61]

All six of Lewis and Tillyard's essays were published in April 1939 by Oxford University Press as *The Personal Heresy: A Controversy*.

George Sayer, also a student of Lewis during this time period, noted that Lewis' reaction to the increasing role of biography in literary criticism "was the fruit of thirteen years of teaching, during which Jack often found that his pupils wrote essays about the lives or personalities of their authors instead of about their works. In fact,

---

59   Ibid., p. 1074.
60   *Collected Letters*, Volume II, p. 248.
61   John Lawlor, *C. S. Lewis: Memories and Reflections*, Dallas: Spence Publishing Company, 1998, p. 4.

his dislike of biographical criticism was lifelong."[62] Sayer, a teacher for many years at Lewis' alma mater, Malvern College, also noted that although *The Personal Heresy* "never sold well, the idea it presents has had an important influence on the teaching of English literature. Henceforward, boys and girls who had hardly heard of C. S. Lewis were liable to be severely reprimanded if they served up biography in the guise of literary criticism."[63]

---

62   Sayer, p. 261.
63   Ibid., p. 262.

A C. S. LEWIS DISCUSSION GUIDE

Discussion Questions

1. At the risk of committing the very heresy this book is about: What does the fact that C. S. Lewis published this book in conversation with another literary critic suggest about Lewis' openness to real debate involving possible alteration of his own views? Does this perhaps give us a different view of Lewis than that portrayed in the movie *Shadowlands* with Anthony Hopkins?

2. What do you think of Lewis' contention in his first essay that when we read poetry correctly we do not have before us any representation which claims to be the poet, in fact, we have no representation of *man, a character, or a personality at all*?

3. How does Lewis' argument in this book relate to his more general argument for objective values expressed especially in *The Abolition of Man*?

4. In his first essay Lewis suggests that the poet is more like a friend to the reader rather than a lover. The poet invites us to look at what he or she is looking at, rather than to look at him or her. Where else does Lewis express a similar idea in his later works?

5. To use another analogy, Lewis says we must make of the poet, not a spectacle, but a pair of spectacles. Following Professor Alexander's book, *Space, Time and Deity*, Lewis says we must *enjoy* the poet not *contemplate* him or her. Alexander's book was very influential in helping Lewis understand his own experience of joy. How did understanding this concept influence Lewis' return to Christian faith?

6. Do you think Lewis' argument against "the personal heresy" is more applicable to reading older poetry, or does it also apply to reading more modern poetry? Why?

7. Along with his hatred of "the personal heresy" Lewis despises imagery used in poetry which only the poet and his or her select friends can understand. This was one of

the main things Lewis disliked about the poetry of T. S. Eliot. Do you agree with Lewis? Why or why not?

8. What does Lewis maintain in his first essay is the driving force behind the personal heresy? Do you agree? Why or why not? (See paragraph 24.)

9. At the end of his first essay Lewis says that if the world is meaningless then we are meaningless. If we mean something, then we do not have meaning in ourselves alone. If we embrace either of these alternatives then we are free of the personal heresy. What does Lewis mean by this? What do you think?

10. Tillyard does not agree with Lewis that the personal heresy is a sign of modernity. What do you think?

11. Tillyard re-defines what he means by "personality" in his first essay. He says, "Now if it is heretical to hold that part of the value of poetry consists in gaining contact with the normal personality of the poet, then I am a heretic." What do you think? Are you a heretic?

12. In his second essay Lewis says that when reading Shakespeare he wants all of Shakespeare's invented characters but not Shakespeare. Why does Lewis say this? Do you agree or disagree? Explain your answer.

13. Lewis says that we owe to a poet and to poetry two different things. What are these? What do you think of Lewis' argument at this point?

14. How does Lewis modify his position in the course of this controversy?

15. Do we heed Lewis' warning against the personal heresy when we read his own work? If so, is it easy or hard to do this? Does Lewis' own writing style tempt us or repel us from committing the personal heresy when reading his books?

16. In chapter V Lewis distinguishes between two different kinds of poetry. What are the two kinds and what examples does he give of each? Which kind do you enjoy more? Why?

17. In chapter V Lewis states his greatest concern regarding the personal heresy, the fact that it leads to what he calls "poetolatry". What does Lewis mean by this? Do you share his concern? Why or why not?
18. Lewis was dead-set against the idea (expressed by T. S. Eliot) that only practicing poets could correctly evaluate poetry. Who do you agree with? Eliot or Lewis? Why?
19. How much do you think Lewis and Tillyard came to agreement by the end of their controversy?
20. If the arguments presented in this book were offered in a live debate who do you think would win, Tillyard or Lewis? Why?

The Problem of Pain

In June of 1997 I had the privilege of meeting Arthur R. Lewis, an Anglican priest and former missionary to Africa. Arthur Lewis, no relation to C. S. Lewis, went up to Oxford as an undergraduate in 1939. He attended the lectures of J. R. R. Tolkien and C. S. Lewis on English literature. According to Arthur Lewis, Jack's lectures on "Prolegomena to Renaissance Literature" and *Paradise Lost* were the best lectures given in Oxford at the time. Jack had the wonderful habit of inviting his students to simply listen to the lecture without taking notes. Then, if there was something specific Jack wanted his students to write down, he would stop, dictate something for his students to write, and then invite them just to listen once again to the lecture without taking notes.

Arthur Lewis became part of an informal study group which Jack organized in order to read to the group chapters from *The Problem of Pain* as he was writing the book. According to Arthur Lewis, Jack "picked the students' brains" on the subject; he wanted to be sure he was writing something which would be intelligible and meaningful to undergraduates. It was quite clear to Arthur Lewis that Jack did not keep himself in "safe" positions in his early years as an Oxford don, as depicted in the later movie, *Shadowlands*, with Anthony Hopkins and Debra Winger. Arthur Lewis' perspective on *The Problem of Pain* was that it was a book dealing with the intellectual problem of pain and not a book to offer to someone presently going through any bit of suffering. However, after reading *A Grief Observed*, Jack's chronicle of the period of grief which followed his wife's death, Arthur Lewis felt that Jack lived out what he had been teaching all along.

Jack wrote *The Problem of Pain* because he was invited to do so by Ashley Sampson, a senior editor with the publishing firm of Geoffrey Bles. Sampson had been favorably impressed by reading *The Pilgrim's Regress* and so invited Jack to contribute a volume on pain and suffering to his Christian Challenge Series. The idea of the book was appealing to Jack since one of his reasons for having been an atheist was this very problem of the existence of pain in the world.

Jack began writing the book in the autumn of 1939 just after England's declaration of war with Germany. He read installments to The Inklings, that group of literary friends which Jack gathered around himself and which included people like J. R. R. Tolkien and Charles Williams. One of The Inklings, Jack's doctor, R. E. Havard, wrote the appendix to the book. Thus *The Problem of Pain* is dedicated to The Inklings. Jack wrote to his brother Warnie on November 11, 1939 recounting a Thursday night meeting of the Inklings. The group dined at the Eastgate Hotel, across the High Street from Magdalen College. Afterwards they retired to Jack's rooms in college. That evening saw one of Jack's friends, Hugo Dyson, "a roaring cataract of nonsense". The rest of the evening's activities included a reading from Tolkien of his "new Hobbit book",[64] a nativity play from Charles Williams and a chapter out of the book on the problem of pain from Jack.

Williams once humorously said to Jack with tongue firmly in cheek: "The weight of the divine displeasure has been reserved for the 'comforters' of Job, the self-appointed advocates on God's side, the people who try to show that all is well, the sort of people who write books on the problem of pain".

The Problem of Pain was published in October 1940 and was a bestseller from the start. It was reprinted twice in 1940, four times in 1941, three times in 1942 and 1943. To this day it is one of C. S. Lewis' most popular books. At the time of publication the book received a number of positive reviews like this one in *The Guardian* (22 November 1940), p. 560:

> This is a strong book: strong in its background of sound scholarship never obtruded on the reader, but evident

---

64 "The new Hobbit" would become *The Lord of the Rings* trilogy.

to the discerning eye, strong in its frank admission of mysteries and unpalatable facts, strong above all in its uncompromising affirmation of the Christian revelation.

A C. S. Lewis Discussion Guide

Discussion Questions

1. What is "the problem of pain" which Lewis seeks to resolve? Even though God is omnipotent what is impossible for him to do? Why is it important to understand this?

2. How does Lewis define "total depravity"? Do you think his definition is correct? Do you think Lewis is right to reject the doctrine of total depravity? Why or why not?

3. According to Lewis, how does God's goodness relate to our own? Why is this important?

4. Lewis says that God has paid us "the intolerable compliment" of loving us, in the deepest, most tragic, most inexorable sense. What does Lewis mean by this? Do you agree with him? If this love be true, how does it help overcome the problem of pain?

5. Why does Lewis see a proper understanding of the fall as essential to resolving the problem of pain? Do you agree with him? In his chapter on the Fall of Man Lewis refers to the biblical account of the fall as a "myth." What does Lewis mean by "myth"?

6. Lewis also seems to allow for what has been called "theistic evolution". Do you agree with Lewis' view of the biblical account as myth? Do you agree with theistic evolution? Why or why not?

7. What do you think Lewis means when he says that pain is God's megaphone to rouse a deaf world? Do you agree with Lewis? Why or why not?

8. Lewis says, "I am not arguing that pain is not painful. Pain hurts. That is what the word means." What then is Lewis arguing for in this book?

9. In his second chapter on human pain Lewis says that the security we crave would teach us to rest in this world, whereas a few happy moments of pleasure do not so teach us. Lewis asserts that God will refresh us on our life's journey with some pleasant inns, but he will not encourage us to mistake them for home. Do you agree? Does this in any way help you deal with the problem of pain? How?

10. In chapter 8 Lewis deals with the problem of hell. He says that the problem of hell is not simply that of a God who condemns some people to final ruin. The problem of hell is knottier. How so? What do you think?

11. Lewis raises and seeks to answer five objections to hell. How does he answer these objections? Do these answers help you to see hell as morally justified?

12. In his chapter on animal pain Lewis distinguishes between sentience in animals and consciousness in humans, suggesting that animals do not experience pain as humans do. What do you think of Lewis' argument?

13. In his chapter on heaven Lewis reminds us that both Scripture and tradition put the joys of heaven into balance against the sufferings of earth, therefore no book on the problem of pain which does not treat of heaven can be a Christian one. Do you agree? Does Lewis, in this chapter, make heaven more believable to you? More desirable? Why or why not?

14. How do Lewis' thoughts on pain in this book compare to his thoughts in *A Grief Observed*? Which book has helped you more to deal with the problem of pain? Why?

The Screwtape Letters

In a letter to his brother Warnie, dated 20 July 1940, C. S. Lewis recorded the circumstances of the conception of *The Screwtape Letters*. That morning Jack went to church for the first time in many weeks due to an illness. Before the service was over he was struck by an idea for a book which he thought might be both useful and entertaining. At first he thought of calling it: "As one Devil to Another". From the first Jack conceived of the book consisting of letters from an elderly devil to a young devil who has just started work on his first "patient." His idea was to give all the psychology of temptation from the demonic point of view.[65]

Jack and Warnie attended Holy Trinity Church in Headington Quarry, just outside of Oxford. Ordinarily, the Lewis brothers attended the eight o'clock Communion service because Jack disliked almost all church music, and there was no music at the early service.[66] On this occasion, as Jack noted in his letter to Warnie, he went to the later service because he was ill and had slept late.

Jack wrote *The Screwtape Letters* quickly, completing one letter in just a few hours each week. In February 1941 after all thirty-one letters had been written, he sent them to *The Guardian*, a Church of England weekly newspaper. The letters were published weekly from May to November 1941. Jack was paid sixty-two pounds for all of the letters.[67] In the midst of the appearance of these letters in *The*

---

65 *Collected Letters*, Volume II, pp. 426-427.
66 Sayer, p. 272.
67 Ibid., p. 273. Jack instructed the editor of *The Guardian* to send the

Guardian Jack was asked by an Oxford undergraduate how many letters there were to be in the end. His reported reply was: "Thirty-one: Something diabolical for each day of the month!"[68]

The letters were an immediate success. One of the readers, Ashley Sampson, took the letters to the publisher, Geoffrey Bles, and suggested publishing them as a book.[69] Bles did so and soon had a bestseller on his hands.

Jack wrote all of his books in longhand and usually had his brother Warnie type the final drafts. He then customarily burned the original manuscripts because he didn't have room to store them. However, in the case of *The Screwtape Letters*, after Jack sent the only typewritten manuscript of the book to Geoffrey Bles, he sent the original handwritten manuscript to a friend, Sister Penelope, an Anglican nun of the Community of Saint Mary the Virgin at Wantage.[70] Jack wrote to Sister Penelope on 9 October 1941 asking her to keep the manuscript safe until the book was printed, just in case the one sent to the publisher should get "blitzed" during the German air raids on London. Jack told Sister Penelope that once the book was published she could basically use the manuscript for scrap paper.[71]

---

money to a charity which assisted the widows of Church of England clergymen. According to George Sayer, Jack had resolved even before the publication of *The Pilgrim's Regress* to give the money he received from writing religious books to charity. Jack didn't realize he would owe tax on this money until the revenue service of the United Kingdom informed him of the back taxes he owed. Jack's friend and solicitor, Owen Barfield, therefore helped Jack to form a charitable trust into which his income from religious writing was thereafter placed. Some people who knew Jack have estimated that he gave approximately two-thirds of his income away to charity.

68 This anecdote was related to me in personal conversation with the Rev. Canon John Fenton during the 2000 Oxford Summer School in Religious Studies at Wadham College.
69 Sayer, p. 273.
70 Ibid.
71 *Collected Letters*, Volume II, p. 493.

What I find most interesting about Jack's letter to Sister Penelope is his characteristic humility. He didn't attach any particular value to the original manuscript of what was to become one of the best-selling religious books of the twentieth century. The first 2,000 copies sold out before publication and it was reprinted eight times by the end of 1942. As of 1988 the book had sold at least two million copies worldwide.[72] And since the advent of the Walden Media film versions of *The Chronicles of Narnia*, *Screwtape* has frequently been in the *Publisher's Weekly* top-ten list of religious paperback bestsellers.

Screwtape was first published in February 1942, but even before then responses started flowing in. The correspondence being too much for Jack to handle alone, he enlisted Warnie's help.[73] Warnie helped answer his brother's mail for most of Jack's life from that time forward. Today the letters which were written by Warnie may be identified by their being type-written, whereas Jack always wrote out his responses by hand. Handwritten letters, signed by Jack, fetch thousands of dollars from collectors, even though some of the letters are merely written on scraps of paper. However, many, if not most of Jack's letters are now archived in the Bodleian Library in Oxford and the Wade Center of Wheaton College, Wheaton, Illinois, with each institution sharing copies of the original letters with the other.

Jack noted in his preface to the 1961 edition of *Screwtape* that though he had never written anything more easily, he never wrote with less enjoyment than while working on this book.[74] The reason Jack felt this way was because, as biographer and friend George Sayer noted: "He thought it was bad for his character to imagine himself a devil, thinking about how to tempt and pervert those around him."[75]

One can indeed imagine that some of the situations described in *Screwtape* are almost autobiographical. For example, there is the mention of the "patient's" relationship with his mother at the end of chapter three. From 1919 to 1951 Jack lived with and cared for Mrs. Janie King Moore, the mother of his friend Paddy Moore who was

---

72 Sayer, p. 274.
73 Ibid.
74 C.S. Lewis, *The Screwtape Letters*, New York: Macmillan, 1977, p. xiii.
75 Sayer, p. 274.

killed in the First World War. When Jack became a theist in 1929 and started attending church services, Mrs. Moore was rather miffed. She remained an atheist throughout her life and always seemed to resent Jack's conversion to theism, and later to Christianity. Does one see another portrait of Mrs. Moore in chapter seventeen of *Screwtape* where Jack describes the "gluttony of delicacy"? We know from Lewis' biographers, and from the pen of his brother Warnie, that Mrs. Moore could be rather demanding. Whether the "patient's" mother is a faint portrait of Janie King Moore we cannot be certain, but surely in the later chapters of *Screwtape*, when Jack comes to describe the "patient's" activities on home patrol during the War, we know for certain that Jack was writing from direct personal experience. Jack served on home patrol in Oxford during the dark days of World War II.

Jack's great achievement in *The Screwtape Letters* is that he gives us a unique portrait of the devils, unlike anything else before it in literature, and he gives us a fresh look at some of the temptations that people face in life. He tells us in his preface to the 1961 edition about the previous literary portraits of the devils he likes and the ones he doesn't like. He likes Dante but not Milton because Dante's devils in their rage, spite, and obscenity, must be more like the real thing than any of Milton's demons.[76] Jack seemed to think that Milton's devils were too beautiful and thus they did not convey to him the appropriate "dust, grit, thirst, and itch" of hell.[77] Likewise, Goethe has done great harm, according to Jack. Mephistopheles, in his humor, civilization, sensibility and adaptability has strengthened the illusion that evil is freeing.[78]

Jack, in a sense, paints over many of these old portraits of the devils. His demons are the ultimate bureaucrats and hell is the final police state. Nothing could be more calculated to translate the reality of the supernatural world into terms and images more accessible to the modern mind.

Likewise, Jack gives us a new look at the temptations faced by human beings. All the old categories of sin are there in *Screwtape*:

---

76   *The Screwtape Letters*, p. ix.
77   Ibid., p. xiv.
78   Ibid., p. ix.

anger, pride, sloth, gluttony, sexual immorality, selfishness, cowardice. But Jack rings the changes on these and many other topics. When it comes to humility, Screwtape urges Wormwood to conceal from his patient the true goal of humility. The patient should be taught to think of humility, not as a sort of self-forgetfulness, but rather as a low opinion of his own gifts and character.[79] As I have already mentioned, in the area of gluttony, Screwtape would have Wormwood tempt not only to "gluttony of Excess" in some patients but also to "gluttony of Delicacy" in others.[80] When it comes to unselfishness, Screwtape reminds Wormwood that men and women have different views of what it means to be unselfish; Wormwood is encouraged to exploit these differing views to his own ends. Screwtape concludes that a small bit of actual selfishness on the patient's part is often of less value in the long run for the purpose of securing his soul than the first beginnings of a fussy self-conscious unselfishness.[81]

This fresh look at the devils combined with the fact that Jack shows us human temptation from a different angle, the inverted world of Screwtape, makes for fun reading and good spiritual nourishment. Of course, one has to turn the book upside down in order to obtain the spiritual refreshment, but the extra effort is worth it.

---

79   Ibid., p. 63.
80   Ibid., p. 76.
81   Ibid., pp. 123-124.

Topical Index to the Letters

1. Preventing Conversion
2. The Church
3. The Family
4. Prayer
5. The War
6. War & Fear
7. Extremes
8. The Law of Undulation
9. Temptation in Trough Periods
10. Acquaintances
11. Laughter
12. The Safest Road to Hell
13. Repentance
14. Humility
15. Time
16. Attending the Parish Church
17. Gluttony
18. Sexual Temptation, Marriage & Family
19. God's Love and Being *In* Love
20. Sexual Temptation, Continued
21. Ownership
22. Losing in Love
23. Theology, Politics & The Historical Jesus
24. The Christian Inner Ring
25. Change
26. Unselfishness
27. Prayer, Free Will & Old Books
28. Life & Death
29. Cowardice & Courage
30. Reality
31. The Ultimate Failure & Victory

A C. S. Lewis Discussion Guide

Discussion Questions

1. In his 1961 preface to *Screwtape* Jack wrote that his purpose in writing these letters was not to speculate about the life of the demons but to shed light on human life from a new angle. Do you think Jack fulfilled his purpose? Why or why not? Is it possible to get something out of this book whether or not one believes in the existence of devils?

2. Jack said of writing *Screwtape* that though he never wrote anything more easily, he never wrote with less enjoyment. He explained that the mindset into which he had to project himself excluded every trace of beauty, freshness, and geniality. What do you make of Jack's concept of evil being the absence of good? Do you agree with this? Why or why not?

3. Describe your reaction to Jack's portrayal of Screwtape as a type of bureaucrat and hell as a type of police state. Do these images make belief in the supernatural more accessible to you than, say, the image of the devil in red tights with horns, tail and pitchfork?

4. In his first letter Screwtape says that human beings find it nearly impossible to believe in the unfamiliar while the familiar is right in front of them. Have you found this to be true in your own experience regarding belief in God? Why or why not?

5. What do you think of Screwtape's statement in letter #2 that one of the devils' greatest allies is the church? Do you think this is true or false and in what way?

6. One of the running themes in *The Screwtape Letters* is God's love for human beings. In Letter #8 Screwtape says that the Enemy really does want to fill the universe with a lot of copies of himself; according to Screwtape, God does this, not through absorption of human beings into himself, but by giving human beings the free choice to conform their small wills to his own larger will, or not. The devils want to suck human beings into themselves whereas God wants to give out. Do you think Screwtape

makes God attractive in a back-handed sort of way? Is Jack's portrayal of "the Enemy" attractive to you? Why or why not?

7. In Letter #12 Screwtape says that on arrival in hell one of his patients realized that he had spent his life doing neither what he ought to have done nor what he enjoyed doing. This suggests that the Christian life is meant to be enjoyable, what do you think?

8. In Letter #16 Screwtape tells Wormwood that if a person can't be cured of churchgoing then the next best thing is to send that person searching for a church that 'suits' him or her. What does Jack suggest, back-handedly through Screwtape, is the danger of what is commonly called "church-shopping"? Have you experienced this in your own life? How can Christians guard against this danger?

9. In Letter #28 Screwtape says about human beings that the devils have taught them to regard death as the ultimate evil, and survival as the greatest good. If death is not the prime evil and survival the main good, then what do you suppose the chief evil and the supreme good really are? How do you think one can inculcate more of an eternal perspective on life?

10. In Letter #30 Screwtape reminds Wormwood that he will soon find that the justice of hell is purely realistic, and concerned only with results. Throughout *The Screwtape Letters* Jack suggests that hell is a purely works-oriented society, that one's "salvation" or "success" in hell is dependent solely upon one's own efforts. What does this suggest that human salvation is dependent upon, from a heavenly perspective? Do you agree with the latter perspective? Why or why not?

A Preface to Paradise Lost

C. S. Lewis read *Paradise Lost* for the first time when he was nine years old. By the time he was sixteen years old, and a student of W. T. Kirkpatrick in Surrey, John Milton had become one of his favorite authors. Jack even composed a poem, *Milton Read Again (in Surrey)*, later published in *Spirits in Bondage*. The poem begins:

> Three golden months while summer on us stole
> I have read your joyful tale another time,
> Breathing more freely in that larger clime
> And learning wiselier to deserve the whole.[82]

What is somewhat striking is that Jack was an atheist when he wrote those lines. However, eventually he came to realize that all of his favorite authors had Christianity in common, and he too became a follower of Christ.

Jack's interest in Milton only grew stronger once he became a lecturer in the English School at Oxford. As a Fellow of Magdalen College, Jack taught a course on "The Text of Milton's Comus" to B.Litt. students in the Trinity Term of 1930. And in the Hilary Term of 1937 he gave a series of lectures in the English School on "Milton and the Epic Tradition".

In 1939 Jack's great friend, Charles Williams, came to live in Oxford. Jack arranged for Williams to lecture on Milton. Williams' second lecture on February 5, 1940, in the Divinity School, stirred Jack to the core of his being. Williams lectured nominally on *Comus*

---

82   *Spirits in Bondage*, p. 32.

but really on the virtue of chastity. Jack felt that here at last was a university being used for learning. He thought that, perhaps, no greater lecture had occurred in that lovely hall with its delicate fan vaulting for hundreds of years. Williams later contributed an Introduction to the 1940 edition of *The English Poems of John Milton* published by Oxford University Press. This too made a deep impression on Jack.

Jack probably would have written *A Preface to Paradise Lost* without the influence of Williams, but Williams' example spurred him on. What really pulled the trigger and caused Jack to produce this fourth work of literary criticism was an invitation from the University College of North Wales to deliver the Ballard Mathews Lectures during their session of 1941-42. While Jack wanted to respond positively to the invitation he was, at first, reluctant. This was due to the fact that he had just committed to a lectureship in theology to members of the Royal Air Force. In the end there was no conflict between the two commitments. By the close of October 1941 Jack had written his *Preface* and selected the highlights to deliver in three lectures in Wales on December 1-3, 1941. Jack's *Preface* was published by the Oxford University Press the following year.

One review was typical of the response to this *Preface to Paradise Lost*: "The book is one of very great moment indeed, and is, in fact, much more than an essay on Milton; it is above all the kind of criticism, of which it is an almost perfect instance that is immensely valuable and important. What is this kind? It includes, but is not exhausted by, a serious effort to rethink a writer's thoughts with him, to understand and for the moment to share his presuppositions (by a suspension of disbelief, if need be), to get out of one's own skin by history and to get into his. This is already to be released in some degree from contemporaneity and the domination of fashion and party-cries. It is also to begin to understand, whether one approves of it or not, what has been the cultural achievement of Christianity in Europe."[83]

---

83   V. G. Turner SJ, *The Tablet*, 181, 9 January 1943, p. 20.

A C. S. Lewis Discussion Guide

Discussion Questions

1. C. S. Lewis begins his *Preface* by asserting that the first requirement for accurately judging any piece of workmanship, whether it be a corkscrew or a cathedral, is that one must know *what* one is judging. Therefore, says Lewis, the first thing the reader needs to know about *Paradise Lost* is what Milton meant it to be. What does Jack suggest Milton meant *Paradise Lost* to be?
2. What are the similarities and differences between Jack's writing style in his scholarly books and his writing style in his more popular works?
3. In chapter II Jack takes issue, once again, with T. S. Eliot. In particular Jack had difficulty accepting Eliot's assertion that the best contemporary practicing poets are the only proper jury for judging *Paradise Lost*. Why does Jack take exception to Eliot's view? Do you think Jack wins the argument with Eliot?
4. What does Jack mean by primary and secondary epic? What examples does he give of both?
5. In chapter IX Jack asserts that if we are to enjoy our full humanity, then we need to have within ourselves and sometimes actualize in ourselves all the modes of feeling and thinking through which humanity has passed. This means that one must, in a sense, become "an Achaean chief while reading Homer, a medieval knight while reading Malory, and an eighteenth century Londoner while reading Johnson." How does this apply to reading *Paradise Lost*? What do you think of this approach to literature? How can this same approach to the reading of ancient literature help us in our spiritual life?
6. In chapter X Jack quotes Addison, "The great moral which reigns in Milton is the most universal and most useful that can be imagined, that Obedience to the will of God makes men happy and that Disobedience makes them miserable." Then Jack concludes that if we as readers can't be interested in that subject we can't really be interested in

Paradise Lost. What does this statement suggest about the reason why Jack wants readers to be interested in *Paradise Lost*? And what do you make of Jack's explanation of Milton's theology in this same chapter?

7. In chapter XI Jack writes about the idea of hierarchy, that it is not simply attached to Milton's poem where doctrine demands it. The concept of hierarchy is part of the inner life of Milton's entire work. How do you respond to this hierarchical idea? How do you think Jack responded?

8. Why do you think Jack spends multiple chapters exploring and explaining Milton's theology?

9. In chapter XIII Jack explains why Satan is the best drawn of Milton's characters. It is because Satan is the easiest character to draw. Why does Jack maintain this is the case? Do you agree?

10. In chapter XIV Jack writes that the only escape from hell is the way of humiliation, repentance, and restitution. This way is closed to Milton's devils because they will not repent. The door out of hell is securely locked by the devils themselves, on the inside. Does this statement remind you of something Jack says elsewhere?

11. In chapter XVIII Jack queries: What would have happened if instead of going along with Eve, Adam had scolded or even chastised her and then interceded with God on her behalf? We are not told the answer because Milton does not know the answer. Jack maintains that this ignorance is significant; we know the results of our evil actions, but we don't know what would have happened if we had obeyed God. Though Milton did not write about "the fall averted" Jack did in two of his stories. What stories did Jack write in order to make the "rejected goods" of original obedience visible? Do you think Jack was successful in these attempts to write about what Milton stepped back from exploring?

Perelandra[84]

C. S. Lewis once said that the starting point for his second novel, *Perelandra*, was a mental picture of floating islands. Once Jack had this picture in mind he had to work at creating a fictional world in which those floating islands could exist. So first there was a mental picture, but then the important question had to be answered: what would happen in this world? That's when Jack began dreaming of creating a story about a perfect world where a great fall is averted. After all, Jack once said, once you've got your people to an exciting new world, something must happen.[85]

So while *Perelandra* began from a picture in Jack's mind, it also began from an idea he wanted to illustrate: the basic idea of Paradise Retained. The idea of writing a novel about this subject may have developed out of Jack's reading of Milton's *Paradise Lost* from the age of nine. Jack wondered: What would have happened if Adam and Eve had obeyed God's command not to eat of the tree of knowledge of good and evil? Unfortunately Milton could not tell him the answer because Milton didn't know. Jack must have been enthralled with trying to answer that question and he must have spent many years trying to imagine the kind of perfect world that would result from

---

84 In between *A Preface to Paradise Lost* and *Perelandra* Jack had published *Broadcast Talks* and *Christian Behaviour*, the first two installments of his BBC Radio addresses. These two books, along with *Beyond Personality* published in 1944, were eventually gathered together in one collection published in 1952. Therefore I will deal with all three of these books under the heading of *Mere Christianity*.

85 C. S. Lewis, *On Stories*, San Diego: Harcourt Brace & Company, 1982, p. 144.

obedience. [86] What Jack set about to do was to make the "rejected goods" of obedience visible in a story. *Perelandra*, like *The Chronicles of Narnia* written many years later, is based upon a supposal. What if there is intelligent life on other planets? And what if that intelligent life on one planet is un-fallen? Will it remain so? What is essential to retaining Paradise? These are the questions Jack seeks to answer through this novel.

The literary influences upon *Perelandra* are several. The picture of the floating islands probably was influenced by Olaf Stapledon's *Last and First Men*. "In early days on Venus men had gathered foodstuffs from the great and floating islands of vegetable matter . . ."[87] Picturing Tor and Tinidril as having green bodies was, perhaps, an idea Jack got from reading Burton's *Anatomy of Melancholy* written in 1621. We can also detect in *Perelandra* the influences of Wagner and Dante. On October 29, 1944 Jack wrote to a correspondent, Charles Brady, telling him that he just missed detecting the Norse influence upon *Perelandra*. Jack noted how important Wagner was to the climax of the story which is very operatic.[88] Jack also told Mr. Brady that Tinidril, in her second appearance, owed something to Matilda at the

---

86 C. S. Lewis, *A Preface to Paradise Lost*, London: Oxford University Press, November 1942, p. 123.
87 Olaf Stapledon, *Last and First Men*, Chapter 13, Section I.
88 In fact, *Perelandra* was turned into an opera with music by Donald Swann and libretto by David Marsh. The opera was written in collaboration with Lewis between 1960 and Lewis' death in 1963. The opera was performed in concert in Oxford, Cambridge, and at the Mermaid Theatre, London in 1964, and in a student stage production in Haverford and New York City in 1969. It was well received. The review in *The Wall Street Journal* noted: "Swann's score is always effective theater music, tellingly keyed to the shifting dramatic tensions, and rising at moments to scalp-prickling power and threat. At other times it has a lambent lyricism". And the reviewer for *The New Yorker* commented: "soaring choruses and very singable arias follow one another with seemingly endless fecundity". The sale of the film rights to *Perelandra* shortly after Lewis' death prevented any dramatic presentations of the work for many years. However, more recently the legal situation changed allowing another performance of the opera to take place in Oxford in the summer of 2009.

end of Dante's *Purgatorio*.[89]

Jack once referred to his friend, Charles Williams', literary style as "clotted glory". The same could be said of Jack's style in some of his books, especially *That Hideous Strength,* which owes a lot to the influence of Williams. But what Jack does with the polyglot of influences in *Perelandra* is uniquely his own work. Who else has imagined with near perfection what temptation and a fall averted might look like on another planet?

Jack began writing *Perelandra* sometime in 1941. The first written reference to Jack's writing of this novel is contained in a letter to his friend, Sister Penelope, on November 9, 1941. He told the sister that he had just got Ransom to Venus and through his first conversation with Tinidril, the "Eve" of that world. Only when he had begun the actual writing of the story did Jack realize how difficult it was going to be. He wanted to create in Tinidril a character that was in some ways like a Pagan goddess and in other ways like the Virgin Mary. He figured that if he could get even a small portion of what he imagined Tinidril to be into writing it would be worth it. [90]

On May 11, 1942 Jack wrote again to Sister Penelope. This time he told her that "The Venus book" was finished, except for some rewriting which needed to be done on the first two chapters. He promised to send Sister Penelope the manuscript as soon as it was typed so she could show it to the Reverend Mother in order to gain her consent for the dedication.[91] Thus Jack dedicated the book to The Community of St. Mary the Virgin at Wantage, England. However, the dedication simply reads "To some ladies at Wantage". This dedication proved difficult for a later Portuguese translator of the book and thus was rendered: "To some wanton ladies".

Perelandra received a number of good reviews after it was published in April 1943. However, more than one reviewer thought that the matter of *Perelandra* would have been better handled in verse; how ironic for Jack who had longed to be a great poet and who actually began writing *Perelandra* in verse. Despite this critique Leonard Bacon

---

89   *The Collected Letters of C. S. Lewis*, Volume II, p. 630.
90   Ibid., p. 496.
91   Ibid., p. 520.

perhaps most succinctly summed up Jack's achievement: "*Perelandra* is the result of the poetic imagination in full blast... The reader is taken into an Eden with the dew on it, where not unnaturally the only rational inhabitants are a thoroughly interesting Eve and perhaps the only endurable Adam in literature."[92] Perhaps more importantly, *Perelandra* was a favorite of Jack's among his own books along with *Till We Have Faces*.

---

92 *Saturday Review of Literature*, 29 (25 May 1946), pp. 13-14.

A C. S. Lewis Discussion Guide

Discussion Questions

1. What do you think of Jack putting himself as a character into *Perelandra*? Do you think he put more of himself into his own character or the character of Ransom?
2. Do you think Jack's portrayal of supernatural beings, the eldils, is believable? Why or why not?
3. One of Jack's minor themes in *Perelandra* is summed up in the question: Are all things which appear as mythology on earth actually scattered throughout other worlds as realities? What do you think of this idea?
4. What is your response to Jack's descriptions of the flora and fauna of Perelandra? How do these descriptions make you feel?
5. Jack writes about Ransom in chapter four that while looking at a fine cluster of bubbles which hung above his head he thought how easy it would be to plunge into them once again and feel their magical refreshment. However, Ransom restrains himself. He wonders if the itch to have certain pleasures over and over again is the root of all evil. What do you think?
6. What do you think of Jack's characterization of Tinidril as a cross between a goddess and a Madonna? Is it successful?
7. What do you think of Jack's development of the character of Weston from *Out of the Silent Planet*? Is Jack's description of "demon possession" believable? What do you think of the final end of Weston, the Un-man? Was this the best way to end the struggle between good and evil? The only way?
8. What do you think of Weston/The Un-man's temptation of Tinidril? How does it compare to the serpent's temptation of Eve in the Garden?
9. What is the significance of the Fixed Island in *Perelandra* and why has Maleldil forbidden Tor and Tinidril to stay

on it over night? (See chapter seventeen.) To what do the fixed islands in *Perelandra* correspond in *Genesis*?

10. Based upon your reading of *Perelandra* how do you think Jack viewed the account of human temptation in *Genesis*? Do you think he viewed the Genesis account as history, myth, or both?

11. In chapter nine Tinidril says to Weston, "But if I try to make the story about living on the Fixed Island I do not know how to make it about Maleldil."[93] In what way might this statement summarize Jack's approach to storytelling?

12. What do you think of Tinidril's statement: "To walk out of His will is to walk into nowhere."?[94]

13. What is the significance of the name "Ransom"? What is the meaning of the wound in Ransom's heel? How is Ransom like Christ? How is he unlike Christ?

14. At the end of chapter 11 Jack as narrator reflects on Ransom's situation as Ransom contemplates the necessity of killing the Un-man. Jack says that, in a sense, the power of choice had been set aside and an inflexible destiny substituted for it. On the other hand, Ransom was being delivered from the rhetoric of his passions and emerging into unassailable freedom. Ransom could no longer see any meaning to the many arguments he had heard on the subject of predestination and freedom. What do you make of this?

15. What do you think of Ransom's hatred for the Un-man toward the end of the book and Jack's statement that Ransom had at last discovered what hatred was made for?

16. In chapter fourteen what does Ransom's starvation for light prove? What does human hunger for something more than the natural realm prove?

17. In chapter sixteen Jack says that older writers did not refer to mountains as masculine because they projected

---

93 C. S. Lewis, *Perelandra*, New York: Macmillan, 1965, p. 112.
94 Ibid., p. 116.

male characteristics into them. Actually the process works the other way around. Gender is a bedrock reality, more fundamental than sex. Sex, Jack says, is the mere adaptation to organic life of a basic polarity which divides all created beings. What do you think about this?

18. Jack, as narrator, says that the universe is like a spider's web connecting every human mind or a vast whispering gallery where no news travels unchanged, but at the same time no secret can ultimately be kept. What do you think Jack means by this? What do you think of this idea?

19. What was your reaction to the final scene on the mountaintop in Perelandra? Does this story fill you with awe, longing, something else?

20. What has been the overall impact on you from reading *Perelandra*?

The Abolition of Man

As noted in the timeline earlier in this book, C. S. Lewis gained a first class degree in philosophy at Oxford during his undergraduate days and subsequently served as a tutor in philosophy for one year at University College before accepting a post as Fellow of English Language and Literature at Magdalen College, Oxford. Jack's enthusiasm for philosophy did not wane until the late 1940's. Thus his interest in philosophy began when he was not a Christian and continued after his conversion.

During the 1920's, when Jack anticipated a life devoted to philosophy, he adhered to a sort of Stoical Monism as he described it in his autobiography, *Surprised by Joy*. During his year as a philosophy tutor he began a series of lectures on *The Good, its position among the values*. Later that same year he read a paper on *The Hegemony of Moral Values* to the Oxford Philosophical Society.[95]

At this time Jack distinguished very sharply his own concept of this philosophical "God" from "the God of popular religion" as he called it. There was no possibility in Jack's mind of entering into a personal relationship with such a God. All of that soon changed when, in the Trinity Term of 1929, Jack became a theist, later describing himself as "the most dejected and reluctant convert in all England".[96] It was another two years before Jack came to believe in Jesus Christ as the Son of God, a conversion which took place on a motorcycle journey to Whipsnade Zoo.

---

95 Jack mentions a "dissertation" on this same subject in his diary entry for 6 July, 1922. See *All My Road Before Me*, p. 64.
96 C. S. Lewis, *Surprised by Joy*, New York: Harcourt Brace Jovanovich, 1955, pp. 228-229.

Given this background it should come as no surprise that Jack would eventually write a philosophical book about objective values and morality called *The Abolition of Man*. The book came about as follows. Sometime in 1942 Jack was made aware by some of his students of the existence of school textbooks which taught the subjectivity of all literary and moral values. Around the same time he received from the publisher a book entitled *The Control of Language* written by two schoolmasters: Alec King and Martin Ketley.[97] The worldview behind King and Ketley's book seemed to Jack to spell the destruction of human stability and the dehumanization and de-rationalization of humanity.[98]

In the midst of his horror over this textbook Jack received an invitation from The University of Durham to deliver the three Riddell Memorial Lectures for 1943. Thus he jumped at the chance to use this lecture opportunity to speak on the subject of education with special reference to the teaching of English in the upper forms of schools.[99] In preparation Jack immersed himself in the thirteen-volume Encyclopedia of Religion and Ethics edited by James Hastings. This became Jack's main source of examples for the Tao, as he called it, included in the Appendix to *The Abolition of Man*.

In his first BBC broadcast talk Jack had already referred to the agreement in moral teaching between the ancient Egyptians, Babylonians, Hindus, Chinese, Greeks and Romans. In the Appendix to *The Abolition of Man* he demonstrated this agreement. In an essay entitled *On Ethics*, most likely written just prior to *The Abolition of Man*, Jack asserted: "In triumphant monotony the same indispensable platitudes will meet us in culture after culture."[100]

The Riddell Memorial lectures were delivered by Jack on three successive evenings in Newcastle-Upon-Tyne close by to the Cathedral and University town of Durham, February 24-26, 1943.[101] Warnie

---

97 Not wishing to attack King and Ketley directly Jack refers to them as Gaius and Titius and to their text as "The Green Book". See C. S. Lewis, *The Abolition of Man*, New York: Macmillan, 1978, p. 13.
98 Sayer, pp. 300-301.
99 Thus the sub-title was formed for *The Abolition of Man*.
100 Walter Hooper, editor, *Christian Reflections*, London: Geoffrey Bles, 1967, p. 55.
101 See Walter Hooper, *C. S. Lewis: Companion & Guide*, New York:

accompanied Jack on this jaunt from Oxford north to Durham and Newcastle. Though he mentioned nothing in his diary of Jack's lectures, he did give a delightful description of part of their journey:

> Arrived at Durham at 9.51 in the still early morning sunlight of a lovely day and set out on foot, down so steep a decline that we saw our own train trundling off many hundreds of feet over our heads....[Durham's] exquisite beauty came upon us with an impact I shall long remember. Crossing a high stone bridge over the Wear, which here runs in a wide steep timbered bed, we walked along under the wall which encloses castle, cathedral, university and Bishops Palace. Each and all lovely, but especially the Cathedral which is one of the most splendid Norman buildings I have ever had the good fortune to see, built of an almost honey coloured stone, with twin towers at the west end, and a great central tower.[102]

Jack's lectures were published by Oxford University Press under the title, *The Abolition of Man*, in January 1944. A new edition with some alterations was published by Geoffrey Bles in London on 12 August 1946 and by Macmillan in New York on 8 April 1947.[103]

George Sayer comments:

> The lectures are too closely argued to make for easy listening, and it seems that few members of his audience understood them. Nor were they well received when they were published as a pamphlet . . . None of the reviewers of the first edition seem to have realized its importance. They must have been put off by the title . . . Now, however, it is generally seen as his most important pamphlet and the best existing defense of objective values and the natural law, which he referred to as the Tao.[104]

Jack probably prized the opinions of his friends more than those of reviewers. One sign of this is the fact that he saved a letter from

---

HarperCollins, 1996, p. 331.
102 *Brothers and Friends*, p. 179.
103 *C. S. Lewis Companion & Guide*, p. 804.   Hooper's *Companion & Guide* mistakenly notes the original publication date as 1943. As I have a copy of the Oxford University Press publication in my library I know that the original publication date was 1944, not 1943.
104 Sayer, p. 301.

Owen Barfield written on 22 January 1944 in which Barfield said of *The Abolition of Man:*

> It is a real triumph. There may be a piece of contemporary writing in which precision of thought, liveliness of expression and depth of meaning unite with the same felicity, but I have not come across it.[105]

---

105 *Companion & Guide*, p. 341.

Discussion Questions

1. What does C. S. Lewis mean by the phrase *men without chests*? (See the end of chapter one.)
2. What do you think of St. Augustine's definition of virtue as "the ordinate condition of the affections in which every object is accorded that kind and degree of love which is appropriate to it"? (See chapter one, paragraph ten.)
3. Jack believed that one could become a better person through reading, especially through reading the classics. What do you think of this idea? Why do people read today, if they read at all?
4. Jack says that the purpose of education for those operating within the Tao is to train appropriate responses to literature into students. On the other hand, educators trying to operate outside the Tao must either decide to remove all sentiments in their students or encourage certain sentiments for their own idiosyncratic reasons. Jack gives an illustration of the process of removing all sentiments in one of his books. Do you remember which book? If so, remind the group of the illustration.
5. Which method of education is being followed most today? Based upon what Jack says in *The Abolition of Man*, what do you think Lewis was trying to accomplish by writing *The Chronicles of Narnia*?
6. Do you think there is a connection between the loss of a sense of objective values in our society and such events as the shooting at Columbine High School? If so, what is the connection? Do you think Jack would see a connection?
7. What is the problem with telling people to obey their instincts? (See chapter two, paragraph nine.)
8. What do you think of Jack's contention that there never has been, and never will be, a radically new judgment of value? Do you think he proves this point in the Appendix to *The Abolition of Man*?
9. What application do you think Jack's words about

contraceptives have to the issue of genetic engineering in our day? (See chapter three, paragraph two.)

10. What do you think of Jack's statement that if people in one period of time attain by eugenics and scientific education the power to make their descendants what they please then all people who live thereafter will be the patients of that power?

11. What does Jack mean when he says that humanity's final conquest may prove to be the abolition of humanity? Do you think this is happening in our time? How was it attempted in Jack's time? (See chapter three, paragraph fourteen.) How is humanity abolished?

12. Do you think Natural Law can be abolished? Why or why not?

13. How is science destroyed by rejecting the Tao? (See chapter three, paragraph sixteen.)

14. What do you think of Jack's conclusion that it's no use trying to see through first principles? What relevance do Jack's comments have to the whole movement of Deconstructionism in literature?

15. How would you summarize *The Abolition of Man*?

That Hideous Strength

C. S. Lewis probably began writing *That Hideous Strength* soon after he finished *Perelandra*. However, some of the ingredients in the recipe of this book go further back in the mix of Jack's imagination. Some time before World War I, he had read about an attempt by a German scientist to keep all the functions of a human head alive after it had been severed from its body. Jack ruminated on this idea for some time and, in fact, planned to write a horror play based upon this concept with his friend and fellow Oxford student, A.K. Hamilton Jenkin.

It wasn't until 1942 that Lewis began work in earnest on the book that was destined to become *That Hideous Strength*. He first mentions it in a letter to fellow author, E. R. Eddison, written on 30 December 1942. He sought from Eddison advice on the nuptial practices of bears! He wrote to Eddison again on 29 April 1943 to say that he had finished three hundred sheets of the book. He probably finished writing the manuscript a few months later since the preface to the American edition is dated Christmas Eve 1943.

The quote on the title page is from Sir David Lindsay whose *Voyage to Arcturus* spurred Jack to write his Cosmic Trilogy in the first place. Lindsay's line of verse, and Jack's title, *That Hideous Strength*, both refer to the Tower of Babel in Genesis 11:4-9.

That Hideous Strength reveals the influence of Jack's friend Charles Williams more than any other book that Jack wrote. Like Williams' novels, *That Hideous Strength* mixes the realistic and the supernatural. Jack especially liked this aspect of Williams' novels. In fact, as mentioned earlier, he and Williams first became friends when Jack wrote to congratulate Williams on his novel, *The Place of the Lion*, and Williams, at the same time, wrote to tell Jack how much he appreciated *The Allegory of Love*. During World War II Williams moved from London to Oxford along with the Oxford University Press and became a regular participant in The Inklings.

Jack's perverted N. I. C. E. scientists, who rely upon black magic, are reminiscent of some of the evil characters in Williams' *War in Heaven* and *Many Dimensions*. And the introduction of Merlin and the whole Arthurian matter in *That Hideous Strength* is definitely due to Williams' influence. At the time Jack was writing *That Hideous Strength* he was already working on a study of Williams' Arthurian poetry which would eventually be published under the title: *Arthurian Torso*.[106]

As Jack notes in his preface, *That Hideous Strength* makes, through fiction, the same serious point he sought to make, through nonfiction, in *The Abolition of Man*. In fact, one might say that the former book is an illustration of the latter. In addition to being an illustration of *The Abolition of Man*, *That Hideous Strength* contains many of Jack's own likes and dislikes. THS mirrors his hatred of "the inner ring" and "the progressive element", both of which he saw a bit at Oxford. According to George Sayer, Feverstone, Busby and Curry are thinly disguised characterizations of some of Jack's colleagues who purportedly rigged meetings and held traditional values in contempt. On the positive side, Belbury is contrasted with St. Anne's, a place of healing that welcomes all people.

That Hideous Strength was not well liked by initial reviewers of the book in the 1940's, though it was not exactly "universally damned" as Jack claimed. However, the reading public has, apparently, not agreed with the critics. *That Hideous Strength* has, for some time, been the most popular of Jack's four novels, and, for what it's worth, one of my personal favorites in the Lewisian corpus.

---

106 C. S. Lewis, *Arthurian Torso*, London: Oxford University Press, 1948.

Discussion Questions

1. What is *the* major theme of *That Hideous* Strength which is represented in the title of the book? What is the opposite of that hideous strength? (See the end of chapter 14, "Real Life is Meeting" for a clue.)

2. That *Hideous Strength* opens with the words from the Anglican wedding service about the purpose of marriage. What do you think Jack's message is about marriage in this book?

3. Jack tells us that Mark and Jane Studdock did not plan to have children for a long time. Based upon this book, what do you think Jack's view of contraception was? What do you think of his view? (See the beginning of chapter 1 and chapter 13, section 3.)

4. One of the sub-themes of this book is that of *The Inner Ring*. What does Jack mean by *The Inner Ring* and what temptations does this pose?

5. What do you think was Jack's view of modern science? What does Jack suggest are the dangers of modern science? (See chapter 9, section 5.)

6. Arthurian legend, reworked by Jack for his own purposes, plays a strong hand in THS. What do you think of this element in the book? Did you enjoy it? Why or why not?

7. Why do you think Jack uses Merlin as a character in the book? (See chapter 13, section 5.)

8. How well drawn are the three main communities in this book: Bracton College, Belbury and the N. I. C. E., and St. Anne's on the Hill? How did the book make you feel as you read about each of these communities? Which did you most enjoy reading about, or wish you could visit? Why?

9. What is the main purpose of the N. I. C. E.? What do you think of its purpose? (For a clue, see chapter 2, section 1.)

10. Another sub-theme of THS is retributive punishment vs. psychological rehabilitation (the humanitarian theory of punishment). What, do you gather, is Jack's view on this subject? What point is Jack subtly trying to make in THS? (See chapter 15, section 5.)

11. Why do you suppose there is "vagueness" in all the communications that take place between Mark and the leaders of the N.I.C.E.?

12. Some critics of Jack's work have said that he was not very successful in his creation of the character of Jane Studdock, that she turns out to be merely a cardboard character. Others have said that Jack betrays an anti-feminist streak in his characterization of Jane Studdock. What do you think?

13. What view of modern journalism does Jack portray in THS? Do you agree with his view? Why or why not?

14. What do you think of Jack's characterizations of various Christians as represented in Straik, at one end of the spectrum, and in the Dimbles, Dennistons and Ivy Maggs at the other end of the spectrum? What point do you think Jack is trying to make by these contrasting characters?

15. How do you think Jack viewed the gradual destruction of Edgestow and Cure Hardy by the N. I. C. E. and the construction of "model villages"? Do you see any corollaries in Jack's own life and times?

16. Another sub-theme of THS concerns the evil of vivisection. What do you think of the way in which good triumphs over evil in the banquet at Belbury?

17. One of the major themes of THS is the theme of hierarchy and equality. Both St. Anne's and Belbury have a *Head*. What point do you think Jack is trying to make about hierarchy and equality? Do you agree with him? Why or why not?

18. What do you think of Jack's portrayal of the gradual "conversions" of Mark and Jane Studdock? Are his

portrayals realistic? What glimmers of Jack's own conversion do you see in the book?

19. Another major theme of THS is that of gender roles. What do you think THS portrays as the proper roles of men and women in relation to one another? What does THS suggest about the larger issues of masculinity and femininity in general? (See chapter 14, section 5.)

20. How does Jack portray the demonic in THS? How does this portrayal compare with *The Screwtape Letters*?

21. Another major theme of THS is that of Logres vs. Britain. How are these two entities portrayed in the book? What do you think of Jack's thesis on this point? (See chapter 17, section 4.)

22. How does MacPhee stand in relation to all the other people at St. Anne's? What is his role? Do you recognize in MacPhee a portrait of anyone from Jack's own life?

23. What contrasting belief systems concerning Right and Wrong (Normal and Abnormal) are represented by St. Anne's and Belbury? How does Belbury's view lead to *the abolition of man*? Do you think Jack is successful, as a writer of fiction, in making *good* attractive?

24. Why do you think the Church, as an institution, does not appear in THS? What do you think of Jack's commentary on the modern day Church in THS? (See the end of chapter 13.)

25. What do you think of the descent of the gods towards the end of THS? Do you think Jack does a good job of tying together all the themes from the previous two books in the trilogy? What do you think of the ending of THS? Is it appropriate? Does it tie everything together?

The Great Divorce

C. S. Lewis first came across the idea which would form the nucleus of *The Great Divorce* around August or September of 1931, shortly before his return to Christian faith. Jack was reading the works of Jeremy Taylor, a 17th century Anglican divine. In one of Taylor's sermons Jack came across the idea of the Refrigerium—the idea that perishing souls in hell may sometimes have remission and refreshment. In the same sermon Taylor mentions Prudentius Aurelius Clemens, a fourth century Latin poet and hymn-writer, as a source for the idea of the Refrigerium. In his *Hymn for the Lighting of the Lamp* Prudentius writes: "Often below the Styx holidays from their punishments are kept, even by the guilty spirits . . . Hell grows feeble with mitigated torments and the shadowy nation, free from fires, exults in the leisure of its prison; the rivers cease to burn with their usual sulphur."

This idea remained in Jack's mind for some time. In April 1933 Warren Lewis recorded in his diary that his brother had "a new idea for a religious work, based upon the opinion of some of the Fathers, that while punishment for the damned is eternal, it is intermittent: he proposes to do sort of an infernal day excursion to Paradise. I shall be very interested to see how he handles it."[107]

Eleven years later, in April 1944, J. R. R. Tolkien wrote to his son Christopher about one of the meetings of the Inklings. Tolkien wrote about a meeting on April 13 in which "the best entertainment proved to be the chapter of Major Lewis' projected book – on a subject that does not interest me: the court of Louis XIV; but it was most wittily written [as well as learned]. I did not think so well of the

---

107 *Brothers & Friends*, pp. 102-103.

concluding chapter of C. S. L.'s new moral allegory or 'vision', based on the medieval fancy of the *Refrigerium*, by which lost souls have an occasional holiday in Paradise."[108]

These vignettes were originally titled: *Who Goes Home?* or *The Grand Divorce* and were published in twenty-three consecutive installments in *The Guardian*, a Church of England weekly newspaper, from November 1944 to April 1945. "Who goes home?" was the cry shouted by the policeman on duty in the House of Commons after the conclusion of a session and prior to the closure of its doors at the end of a day. Tolkien humorously suggested to the Inklings that the title of Jack's book should have been "Hugo's Home" after their mutual friend and fellow Inkling, Hugo Dyson. These vignettes were subsequently published in book form as *The Great Divorce* by the London publisher Geoffrey Bles in November 1945.

In his preface to *The Great Divorce* Jack urges the reader to remember that this story is a fantasy, it is a dream. The conditions of life beyond the grave are merely an imaginative supposal. Jack did not want to arouse factual curiosity about the details of the after-world. Certainly Jack himself believed in hell, purgatory and heaven. But the subject of *The Great Divorce* is really human choice in this life. Jack's point is that the choices we make in this life are leading us to either one ultimate destination or another, either heaven or hell. The message of the book is summed up in these words:

> There are only two kinds of people in the end: those who say to God, "Thy will be done," and those to whom God says, in the end, "*Thy* will be done." All that are in Hell, choose it. Without that self-choice there could be no Hell. No soul that seriously and constantly desires joy will ever miss it. Those who seek find. To those who knock it is opened.[109]

---

108 Humphrey Carpenter, editor, *The Letters of J. R. R. Tolkien*, Boston: Houghton Mifflin, 1980, p. 71.
109 C. S. Lewis, *The Great Divorce*, London: Geoffrey Bles, 1945, pp. 66-67.

A C. S. Lewis Discussion Guide

Discussion Questions

1. In his preface to *The Great Divorce* Jack says that we are not living in a world like a circle where all roads lead to a common center but in a world much more like a tree, where every so often every road forks and one must make a decision about which way to go. What do you think of Jack's statement as it applies to religion? Do you think it true or false? Why?

2. How do you react to Jack's concept of hell as a place where each of the inhabitants is gradually moving further away from each other? Does this depiction of hell make it more real to you? Why or why not?

3. Upon his arrival on the outskirts of heaven Jack's character in the story says he felt like he had gotten "out" in a way that made our solar system feel like an indoor affair. Is Jack's description of heaven one to which the 21st century mind is receptive? Is his depiction of heaven attractive to you? Does it make you want to go there? Why or why not?

4. In one of the first vignettes on the outskirts of heaven one of the ghosts from the grey city says that he is not asking for anyone's "bleeding charity". The response of one of the solid persons is to encourage him to ask for the "Bleeding Charity" at once. What do you think Jack intends to convey by the solid person's response? Why is it "Bleeding Charity"?

5. What do you make of the clerical ghost who doesn't believe in a literal heaven and hell? Does *The Great Divorce* make it easier for you to believe in heaven and hell?

6. What is your favorite line from this book? How about your favorite vignette? Do you see yourself in any of the characters? In which ones–if you dare to say?

7. Jack says that the book is intended to teach a moral. What moral do you think it teaches?

8. Why do you think Jack includes George MacDonald as a character in this dream? What do we learn about

MacDonald's theology and Jack's theology from this book?

9. What do you think of MacDonald's statement about heaven and hell working retroactively?

10. Perhaps *the* major theme of *The Great Divorce* is that of choice with regard to salvation. Based on this book, what would you say is Jack's view of free will and predestination?

11. One of the Spirits says that every artist, apart from the working of grace, is drawn away from love of the thing he or she writes or paints or makes music about to love of the art in and of itself, until in hell we find people who are no longer interested in God at all but only in what they can say about God. Can you identify with this at all or have you ever known anyone like this?

12. What do you think of MacDonald's statement: that there is only one good and that is God? He says that everything is good when it looks to God for life and evil when it turns away from God. According to MacDonald, the higher a creature is in the natural order of things, the more demonic it will be when it falls. Demons are made out of bad angels, not bad mice or bad men. Lust is lower than the false religion of mother-love or patriotism or art, but then lust is less likely to be made into a religion. What do you make of this?

13. One of the sub-themes of *The Great Divorce* is the concept of Time. In several places throughout the book we are reminded that "this moment contains all moments." What do you think Jack is saying about time as it relates to human free choice and predestination?

14. What do you think of Jack's point that hell will not be allowed to veto heaven? Does this make the reality of hell more acceptable to you?

Miracles

On May 13, 1943, Dorothy Sayers wrote a letter to C. S. Lewis complaining that there were not any up-to-date books about miracles. She also stated that she felt Lewis himself was the man to remedy the situation.[110] Apparently Jack agreed with her because he began writing his book *Miracles* a few weeks later. George Sayer tells us that Jack found this book difficult to write because, when he began it, his own ideas about miracles were not quite clear. He was still working on the book during the long vacation of 1945 just after the death of his friend Charles Williams. Sayer also tells us that, though there is no sign of Williams' influence in the book, Jack once said to him that he felt Williams was nearby, helping him to finish it.[111]

Miracles was published by Geoffrey Bles in 1947. Its publication coincided almost exactly with Bishop E. W. Barnes's *Rise of Christianity* in which he tried to explain away the miraculous.[112]

Jack's central argument in the book is that Naturalism contains a great self-contradiction. He quotes Professor Haldane in support of his view: "If my mental processes are determined wholly by the motions of atoms in my brain, I have no reason to suppose that my beliefs are true...and hence I have no reason for supposing my brain to be composed of atoms."[113] If the Naturalists are right and Nature is all there is then this begs the question, "Where does reason come from?" Jack posits that Reason can only come from outside of Nature.

---

110 Green & Hooper, *C. S. Lewis: A Biography*, p. 226.
111 Sayer, *Jack*, p. 306.
112 Green & Hooper, p. 227.
113 C. S. Lewis, *Miracles*, London: Geoffrey Bles, 1947, pp. 28-29.

If Nature is all there is then there is no purpose behind the existence of the universe. If there is no purpose then there is no Reason. If there is no Reason then all arguments for or against Naturalism are nonsensical and thus invalid.

Jack's argument for the self-contradiction inherent in Naturalism received criticism from Elizabeth Anscombe, later professor of philosophy at Cambridge. The criticism came in the form of a debate during a Socratic Club meeting in Oxford on February 2, 1948.[114] The particular statement in the first edition of *Miracles* to which Miss Anscombe objected was Jack's statement that "we may in fact state as a rule that no thought is valid if it can be fully explained as the result of irrational causes."[115] Anscombe insisted that a distinction should be made between irrational causes (such as passion, self-interest, obstinacy, and prejudice) and non-rational causes (such things as brain tumors, tuberculosis, and mental fatigue). She asked Jack to clarify what he meant by the word "valid". Anscombe also distinguished between the ground of a conclusion (the reasons a man would give if asked to explain why he thinks such and such) and the cause of a conclusion (brain tumors, prejudices, or whatever makes him think as he does). Jack admitted in the course of debate that his use of the word *valid* was unfortunate.[116]

After the debate Jack was apparently dejected. He told George Sayer that he felt his argument for the existence of God had been demolished.[117] But Jack did some further thinking on the whole issue of Naturalism and the end result was that he re-wrote chapter three of *Miracles* for the 1960 Fontana paperback version.[118]

Some Lewis scholars maintain that, after the debate with Anscombe, Lewis made a deliberate decision to no longer write any strictly theological or apologetic works.[119] Sayer maintains that Jack

---

114 Sayer, p. 307.
115 *Miracles*, p. 27.
116 Walter Hooper, Oxford's Bonny Fighter, in *C. S. Lewis at the Breakfast Table*, ed. James Como, Harcourt Brace, 1992, pp. 162-163.
117 Sayer, p. 307.
118 *C. S. Lewis at the Breakfast Table*, p. 164.
119 See A. N. Wilson, *C. S. Lewis: A Biography*, New York: Fawcett Columbine, 1990, pp. 214-215.

told him, with regard to *Miracles*, "I can never write another book of that sort."[120] But obviously, after Jack thought the matter through, he did not thoroughly give up on apologetics because he did re-write that chapter in *Miracles* and that only a few years before his death. Though Lewis was humbled by the encounter with Anscombe he did not in any way lose faith and he continued to stand by his early defenses of the Christian faith up to the time of his death.[121]

While *Miracles* contains many of Jack's own homespun illustrations it is, at the same time, obviously written for a more scholarly audience than *Mere Christianity*. The book is very closely reasoned and therefore presents some challenges for the average reader. Jack addresses Naturalists and Pantheists in the first part of the book, desiring to remove as many obstacles as possible to a thoroughgoing acceptance of Christian Supernaturalism. The chapters on *The Grand Miracle* and the *Miracles of the Old and New Creation* probably offer the most nourishing food for thought for those who have grown up in the church.

This reader believes that this Lewis book will clearly prepare the mind of any intelligent reader to accept the possibility of miracles. But human reason will only take a seeker for truth just so far. Then there is the leap of faith to be made into the loving arms of the Miracle-worker.

---

120 Sayer, p. 308.
121 See the last official interview with C. S. Lewis, reprinted in *God in the Dock*, pp. 261-262.

Discussion Questions

1. What do you think of Jack's statement in the first chapter that people who assume miracles can't happen are wasting their time examining texts because the outcome is already determined for them? How is it that Naturalism automatically rules out the possibility of miracles? How does Supernaturalism allow for the possibility of miracles without insisting upon it?

2. What is the cardinal difficulty of Naturalism according to C. S. Lewis? Do you agree with Jack's view? Why or why not?

3. What do you think of Jack's statement at the end of chapter 4 regarding Genesis 1 being told in the manner of a popular poet or folk tale?

4. How are Naturalists inconsistent when it comes to morality? Do you agree with Jack that Supernaturalism provides the only firm ground for morality?

5. How does Jack refute the idea that people in "olden times" believed in miracles because they didn't understand the laws of nature? (See chapter 7.) Have you ever held to this reason for disbelief in miracles? Does Jack's argument change your thinking? Why or why not?

6. Why does Jack say that the size of the universe is irrelevant to the question of miracles? (See chapter 7 again.) Do you agree? Why or why not?

7. Why does Jack say that it is inaccurate to define a miracle as something that breaks the laws of Nature? What illustrations does he give of this principle? (See chapter 8.) What do you think?

8. What do you think Jack means by saying that only Supernaturalists really *see* Nature? If you are a Christian, did you have a different response to the natural world after you became a Christian? If so, tell us about it.

9. Why is it that there can be no true Christianity without miracles? Are you now or have you ever tried to be a

Christian without believing in miracles? If so, tell us about your experience.

10. Why is it that we can never get rid of anthropomorphic images when talking about God or spiritual realities? Do you think it is important to hold on to the images used in Scripture to describe God? Why or why not?

11. How do you feel about Jack's statement at the end of chapter 11 that there comes a time when people who've been dabbling in religion suddenly draw back?

12. What does Jack mean when he says that theology offers a working arrangement which leaves the scientist free to continue his experiments and the believer free to continue his or her prayers? What do you think?

13. How is the difficulty of the Supernatural descending into the Natural overcome in every person? (See chapter 14.)

14. Does Jack make the Grand Miracle of the Incarnation seem more fitting to you? Why or why not?

15. How are the Christian miracles different from "mythological miracles"? (See beginning of chapter 15.)

16. According to Jack, what is the difference between miracles of the Old Creation and miracles of the New Creation? Which biblical miracles fall into each category? Does Jack's categorization of miracles help you in thinking about them? How?

17. Does Jack's statement that in all his miracles Jesus does suddenly and locally something that God has done or will do in general make the miracles of the Gospels more credible to you? Why or why not?

18. How does Jack defend the idea of the bodily resurrection of Christ and of the general resurrection of the body? How are Christ's resurrection and ascension inextricably tied together? Does Jack make these doctrines more credible to you? Why or why not?

19. How do you feel upon reading Jack's final paragraph in chapter 16? Does it fill you with any desire to participate in the resurrected life? What other story in Jack's writings does this remind you of?

20. Why does Jack suggest that we might not want to witness a miracle ourselves? How do you feel about this?

The Weight of Glory[122]

The Weight of Glory and Other Addresses was first published in 1949 by Macmillan in the United States and under the title *Transposition and other Addresses* by Geoffrey Bles in Great Britain. Originally this book contained only the following five addresses:

1. Transposition
2. The Weight of Glory
3. Membership
4. Learning in War-Time
5. The Inner Ring

"Transposition" was a sermon preached by C. S. Lewis on Whitsunday (Pentecost) 1944, in the chapel of Mansfield College, Oxford. As Walter Hooper notes, it was reported in *The Daily Telegraph* that "in the middle of the sermon Mr. Lewis, under stress of emotion, stopped, saying 'I'm sorry,' and left the pulpit. Dr. Micklem, the Principal, and the chaplain went to his assistance. After a hymn was sung, Mr. Lewis returned and finished his sermon . . . on a deeply moving note."[123] Anyone familiar with C. S. Lewis knows that such a display of emotion was unusual for him. Was it occasioned by

---

122 In between *Miracles* and *The Weight of Glory* C. S. Lewis had published *Arthurian Torso*, which contains his commentary on the poetry of Charles Williams. Since *Arthurian Torso* is primarily a work by and about Williams I have left it out of this discussion guide. Though *Arthurian Torso* has long been out of print, the last time I checked it was available online.

123 Walter Hooper, ed., *The Weight of Glory and Other Addresses*, New York: Macmillan, 1980, p. xxii.

the subject with which he was dealing, or by some personal trying circumstance in his own life? We shall probably never know the answer.[124]

"The Weight of Glory" became one of Jack's most famous sermons. It was originally preached in the University Church of St. Mary the Virgin, Oxford on June 8, 1941. The sermon was first published in *Theology* (November 1941) and by the SPCK in 1942.

"Membership" was an address given to the Fellowship of St. Alban and St. Sergius in 1945. This Fellowship came into being in 1928. It was organized by members of the Eastern Orthodox and Western Christian Churches for the purpose of prayer and work toward Christian unity. Jack was no doubt invited to give this address by his friend, Nicholas Zernov, who was instrumental in founding this Fellowship which still exists in Oxford.[125] The fact that Jack spoke to this group on the topic of "Membership" displayed his heart-felt desire for Christian unity. This address was first printed in the Fellowship's publication *Sobornost*.

"Learning in War-Time" was Jack's first sermon preached in St. Mary the Virgin, the University Church in Oxford. It was then published as a pamphlet by the Student Christian Movement under the title, *The Christian in Danger*. Subsequently, the publisher Ashley Sampson, who had also invited Jack to contribute *The Problem of Pain* to the Christian Challenge series of books he was bringing out, now asked Jack if he could include his sermon in an anthology he was editing entitled: *Famous English Sermons*. Jack wrote to his brother Warnie saying that he couldn't make up his mind whether he should be grateful for the honor or fearful of looking a fool if his sermon should appear alongside the work of such historical figures as Bede, Latimer and Donne. When Jack later included this sermon in *Transposition and*

---

124 "Transposition", preached on Pentecost, naturally dealt at least tangentially, with the topic of "speaking in tongues" and the gift of the Holy Spirit. For a summary of Lewis' beliefs on this topic see Will Vaus, *Mere Theology: A Guide to the Thought of C. S. Lewis*, Downers Grove, Illinois: InterVarsity Press, 2004, pp. 91-96.
125 For more information see www.sobornost.org.

Other Addresses he changed the title to "Learning in War-Time".[126]

In 1980 a revised and expanded edition of *The Weight of Glory and Other Addresses* appeared, edited by Walter Hooper. The new edition contains these additional addresses:

1. Why I am not a Pacifist
2. Is Theology Poetry?
3. On Forgiveness
4. A Slip of the Tongue

As explained in Walter Hooper's Introduction, "Why I am not a Pacifist" was an address given by C. S. Lewis to a pacifist society in Oxford around 1940. The only extant copy of this address was given by Lewis to George Sayer and thence to Walter Hooper.

"Is Theology Poetry?" was a talk given by Lewis to the Oxford Socratic Club in 1944. It was originally published in *The Socratic Digest* in 1945 and later in Lewis' book *They Asked for a Paper* in 1962.

"On Forgiveness" was written by Lewis for the parish magazine of St. Mary, Sawston, Cambridgeshire at the request of Father Patrick Kevin Irwin. It was later given by the priest's family to the Bodleian Library, Oxford. It was first published by Walter Hooper in the collection entitled *Fern-seed and Elephants* in England in 1975.

"A Slip of the Tongue" was the last sermon preached by C. S. Lewis. It was delivered in the Magdalene College Chapel at Cambridge University in 1956. The sermon was originally published in *Screwtape Proposes a Toast and Other Pieces*. This was a book prepared for the press by Lewis himself, but not published until 1965.

The reader might be interested to know what the response was to Lewis' sermons, since *The Weight of Glory and Other Addresses* contains five of them. Fred Paxford, Jack's gardener, on whom Jack later modeled the character of Puddleglum in *The Silver Chair*, once wrote this about C. S. Lewis' preaching:

---

126 This summary of the history behind "Learning in War-Time" first appeared in my essay "Lewis in Oxford: The Later Tutorial Years (1939-1953)" published in *C. S. Lewis: Life, Works, and Legacy*, Volume I, Bruce L. Edwards, editor, Westport, Connecticut: Praeger, 2007, p. 174.

Mr. Jack should have been a clergyman. He would have made a great parson. When he preached at Quarry Church, it was always packed. He had a full clear voice which could be heard all over the church; and he nearly always brought a bit of humor into the sermons; and people seemed to like this. On a few occasions I had to drive him in to Oxford to preach in St. Mary's. As he always liked to be early, I parked the car and went to the service, and the church was always packed.[127]

---

127 David Graham, editor, *We Remember C. S. Lewis*, Nashville: Broadman & Holman, 2001, p. 127.

A C. S. LEWIS DISCUSSION GUIDE

Discussion Questions

1. In his sermon, "The Weight of Glory", C. S. Lewis says that he is, perhaps, trying to weave a spell to wake his hearers from the evil enchantment of worldliness, and he urges his hearers to remember their fairy tales. Do you hear Lewis, the writer of fairy tales, in this sermon? If so, how? In what ways does Lewis combine reason and imagination in this sermon?

2. If you had been a student sitting in the congregation on 22 October 1939 listening to C. S. Lewis preach "Learning in War-Time" how do you think you would have felt? What application does this sermon have to us, outside of its original setting?

3. In "Why I am not a Pacifist" we see displayed the expert reasoning skills of C. S. Lewis the philosopher and logician. Does he convince you of his argument? Why or why not?

4. In "Transposition" Lewis says that our natural experiences are like pencil lines on a flat piece of paper. If those experiences vanish in the risen life they will vanish only as pencil lines disappear when turning from a drawing to look at a real landscape. Does Jack Lewis, with his great gift for analogy, make concepts like the resurrection more believable to you? Why or why not?

5. How does Lewis answer the question: Is theology poetry? Lewis ends this address with one of his most famous statements: "I believe in Christianity as I believe that the Sun has risen, not only because I see it, but because by it I see everything else." Expand upon what Lewis means by this statement. Does Lewis convince us of the truth of Christianity in this lecture mainly by reasoned argument, or by poetic ability, or both?

6. In the sixth address in this collection Jack warns us against the alluring danger of the desire to be part of "the inner ring". What does he mean by "the inner ring"? Where does Jack illustrate this temptation in his fiction? Have

you experienced this temptation? How does Jack help us to overcome it? Do you think The Inklings was "an inner ring"? Explain your answer.

7. C. S. Lewis has been accused of not giving a very important place to the Church in his theology and writings. How does his address on "Membership" substantiate or mitigate this claim?

8. How does Jack's essay "On Forgiveness" help you in your understanding of this important topic? What do you find to be the hardest thing about applying Jack's teaching on this issue? Is it harder for you to accept God's forgiveness or to forgive others? How are the two related?

9. In his sermon, "A Slip of the Tongue", Jack argues for giving place to the eternal over the temporal, a constant theme throughout his writings. How does he make us want to give priority to the eternal through this sermon? How does he do it in his other writings?

10. Which one of C. S. Lewis' addresses in this collection is your favorite? Why? Which is your least favorite? Why? What ideas expressed in this collection do you have questions about? What ideas do you want to think further about? What ideas do you want to take action on in your life?

The Lion, the Witch and the Wardrobe

C. S. Lewis once said that the Narnian tales began with seeing pictures in his mind. At first the pictures did not form a story. *The Lion, the Witch and the Wardrobe* began with a picture of a Faun carrying an umbrella and parcels in a snowy wood. The picture had been in Jack's mind since he was about sixteen. Then one day when he was about forty, he said to himself: "Let's try to make a story about it."[128]

According to Roger Lancelyn Green, Jack began work on *The Lion, the Witch and the Wardrobe* at the end of 1939 shortly after receiving some child evacuees from London into his home outside of Oxford. Nine years later, in the summer of 1948, Jack made a casual remark to Chad Walsh indicating that he was desirous of completing a children's book he had begun, once he finished writing his autobiography, *Surprised by Joy*. By March 10, 1949, Jack was reading two chapters of *The Lion* to Green and had already read portions to Tolkien.[129] He finished writing the book shortly thereafter and *The Lion, the Witch and the Wardrobe* was finally published in the autumn of 1950.[130]

Why did Jack write *The Chronicles of Narnia*? As Paul Ford has pointed out, Aslan himself has answered that question for us.[131] At the end of *The Voyage of the Dawn Treader*, Aslan tells Edmund that he was brought to Narnia so that, by knowing him there, he might get to

---

128 Green & Hooper, pp. 237-238.
129 Ibid., pp. 238-241.
130 Paul F. Ford, *Companion to Narnia*, San Francisco: HarperCollins, 1980, p. 451.
131 Ibid., p. xxvi.

know him better in our world.[132]

So it seems that at least part of Jack's purpose in writing *The Chronicles* was to "baptize the imagination" of his child readers just as his own imagination had been "baptized" by reading George MacDonald's *Phantastes*.[133] It seems that Jack wanted to prepare his young readers to know and love Christ by first knowing and loving Aslan. But, as Jack himself once said, this was not at first a deliberate move on his part. In a letter to Sophia Storr, a schoolgirl, written on December 24, 1959, Lewis said that the Christian element in the books was neither unconscious nor at first intentional either. When he started writing *The Lion, Witch and Wardrobe* he did not foresee what Aslan was going to do and suffer. Aslan simply insisted on behaving in his own way.[134] Lewis was certainly not the first, nor the last writer to have one of his characters run away with the plot.

However, at this point, a qualification must be stated. Many people, in reading *The Chronicles*, have made the mistake of assuming that they are allegorical. Lewis emphatically stated on numerous occasions that they were not allegorical. In the same letter to Sophia Storr Lewis denied this allegorical element. Rather, Jack insisted, the Narnia stories were based upon a supposal. Supposing there was a world of talking beasts like Narnia. And supposing that world had gone wrong, like our world. Then what might God have done to rescue that world? The stories are Jack's answer.[135]

Therefore, we must be careful not to read too much into *The Chronicles*. We must not see in every character, place or event a representation of something in our world or an allegory of some Christian truth.

Judging by Jack's letters to children who read his Narnian Chronicles, he hit the mark he was trying to achieve–many

---

[132] C. S. Lewis, *The Voyage of the Dawn Treader*, New York: Macmillan, 1973, p. 216.
[133] See C. S. Lewis, editor, *George MacDonald: An Anthology*, New York: Macmillan, 1986, p. xxxiii.
[134] Walter Hooper & W.H. Lewis, eds., *Letters of C. S. Lewis*, San Diego: Harcourt, Brace & Company, 1993, p. 486.
[135] Ibid.

imaginations have been and continue to be "baptized" by Narnia. Jack was so effective, in fact, that one nine-year-old American boy named Laurence became concerned that he loved Aslan more than Jesus. Laurence's mother wrote to C. S. Lewis in care of Macmillan Publishing Company in April of 1955. Just ten days later, to her surprise and delight, she received an answer to her son's questions. Jack said, in part, "Laurence can't really love Aslan more than Jesus, even if he feels that's what he is doing. For the things he loves Aslan for doing or saying are simply the things Jesus really did and said."[136]

Why is it that *The Chronicles of Narnia* have had this kind of impact on children and adults alike? I think the reason is because these stories take people off their guard. In reading the real story in the Gospels the thought that one *should* feel a certain way actually inhibits the feeling.[137]

One of the joys of reading *The Lion, the Witch and The Wardrobe* as an adult is seeing how much Jack put of himself into the story. Clearly, the Professor is a type of Lewis, living in the country, away from London, and receiving child evacuees into his home. The Professor says just the types of things Lewis would say such as, "Why don't they teach logic at these schools?"[138] Then there is Mr. Beaver who smokes a pipe and drinks beer just like Jack did![139]

Excellent as *The Lion, the Witch and the Wardrobe* is, it is not without its defects. J. R. R. Tolkien was one of the most notable critics of *The Lion*. Tolkien, who prided himself on the sub-creation of completely different worlds, did not like the inconsistencies of *The Lion*.[140]

One of the most notable incongruities was certainly the inclusion of Father Christmas in the story. As an adult reader, one wonders, "How can Father Christmas exist in Narnia, where the birth of Christ has never taken place?" Despite the criticism, Jack kept Father

---

136 Lyle W. Dorsett & Marjorie Lamp Mead, *C. S. Lewis: Letters to Children*, New York: Macmillan, 1985, pp. 52-53.
137 See Clyde S. Kilby, *The Christian World of C. S. Lewis*, p. 136.
138 C. S. Lewis, *The Lion, the Witch and the Wardrobe*, New York: Macmillan, 1970, p. 45.
139 Ibid., pp. 69, 71.
140 Green & Hooper, p. 241.

Christmas in the story. One gets a hint at the reason from a letter which he wrote to an eleven-year-old American girl. Jack told her he wanted her to guess "Aslan's other name". Then he asked her whether she knew of anyone in our world who arrived at the same time as Father Christmas.[141] Apparently Jack kept Father Christmas in *The Lion* because he wanted to give his child readers a hint as to "Aslan's other name."

    C. S. Lewis wrote *The Lion, the Witch and the Wardrobe* primarily for children and it never seemed to bother him a great deal if adults didn't like the story as much. In fact, the inclusion of Father Christmas never bothered me when I read the story as a child, though it does bother me now that I am an adult. Perhaps it would be best if we all became like children again when reading *The Lion, the Witch and the Wardrobe* and were "taken off guard" by the Lion who is good, but never safe!

---

141 *Letters to Children*, p. 32.

Discussion Questions

1. Did you read *The Lion, the Witch and the Wardrobe* as a child? If so, what impact did it have on you then? How has your perspective on the book changed as an adult? If you have only read the book as an adult, how have you enjoyed reading "a story for children"? Do you think Lewis intended a message for adults in the book as well as for children? If so, what message?

2. Lewis once said that the idea for LWW began with a picture in his mind of a faun with an umbrella in a wood. LWW is filled with vivid images, some of which are intended to convey Christian truth. Which of the images are most meaningful to you and why?

3. When the Pevensie children first hear the name of Aslan mentioned, Lewis tells us that a very curious thing happened. None of the children knew who Aslan was, but the moment Mr. Beaver mentioned his name each of the children felt something jump inside them. How did you react when reading this passage? Have you ever had a similar experience? Explain.

4. While LWW does convey some powerful Christian concepts, Jack does little if any "preaching" through the story. However, the Professor tells the children that there are only three possibilities with regard to Lucy and her story about another world inside the wardrobe; either she is lying, or she is crazy or she is telling the truth. Does this remind you of anything Jack has said in one of his other books?

5. One of the sub-themes running throughout *The Chronicles of Narnia* is the suggestion that the educational system in England was none too good during the mid-20th century. The Professor repeatedly asks, "Why don't they teach logic at these schools?" From what you know of C. S. Lewis, what did he have against the educational system in England? How do you think he would view our educational system today?

6. What does Edmund's encounter and developing relationship with the White Witch teach us about temptation? How does this challenge you in your own life?
7. Do you find Jack's portrayal of Aslan as a lion who is "not safe, but good" an attractive one? Would you like to get to know Aslan? Why or why not?
8. Jack demonstrates his great love of nature and animals throughout LWW. Mr. Beaver suggests that the White Witch's reign will come to an end and all of nature will be put right when Aslan shows up. There is a faint echo here of the teaching in Romans 8:19-21, "The creation waits in eager expectation for the sons of God to be revealed. For the creation was subjected to frustration, not by its own choice, but by the will of the one who subjected it, in hope that the creation itself will be liberated from its bondage to decay and brought into the glorious freedom of the children of God." Do you think Jack would have joined in the contemporary environmental movement, were he alive today? Why or why not? Where might he have agreed with this movement and where might he have differed?
9. Of course, the climactic event of LWW is the killing of Aslan by the White Witch and his subsequent resurrection from the dead. Do you find this to be a compelling mythic portrayal of the death and resurrection of Christ? Why or why not? What effect did this part of the story have on you as a child, or on other children you have known who have read the story?
10. Obviously, Lewis believed that myth was an excellent means of communicating theology. He considered the imagination to be the organ for perceiving meaning. In what ways do you think Jack was more effective at communicating Christian experience through myth as opposed to his more straightforward apologetic works? What do you think are the weaknesses and dangers of communicating Christian truth through myth?

Prince Caspian

C. S. Lewis began writing *The Lion, the Witch and the Wardrobe* perhaps as early as the autumn of 1939. Like many of Jack's creations, the initial scribbles of LWW may have spent a good bit of time in a drawer, until they were taken out and polished up ten years later in 1949. Jack found it almost as hard to write a second Narnia tale. He began by exploring what had gone on before the White Witch's hundred year winter. How did the lamppost come to be standing in the middle of a wood?

Thus Jack began writing a story about a boy named Digory. In June 1949 he read a bit of it to Roger Lancelyn Green, his former student and friend, the one who had encouraged him so much in the writing of LWW. What came to be known as the Lefay fragment of *The Magician's Nephew* had its problems. So once again Jack set aside, for a time, what would eventually become a promising work.

The next idea which popped into Jack's mind was that in fairy tales people are often summoned by magic across time and space—but the summoning is always told from the perspective of the magician. What would it be like for the person being summoned? *Prince Caspian* was born as an answer to that question and it was originally titled *Drawn into Narnia*. This title was vetoed by the publisher, as authors' titles often are, and so was the second title Lewis came up with—*A Horn in Narnia*. Of course this second title reflected the fact that it was Queen Susan's magic horn which dragged the four Pevensie children, by magic, back into Narnia.

Jack initially scribbled some notes for a sequel to LWW. His surviving notations read as follows: "The present tyrants to be Men. Intervening history of Narnia told nominally by the Dwarf but really an abstract of his story which amounts to telling it in my own person."[142]

The manuscript of *Prince Caspian* was finished by December 1949. Green read and critiqued it, returning it to Lewis by the end of the year. On December 31, 1949 Lewis held a luncheon at Magdalen College, Oxford to meet Pauline Baynes and introduce her to some of his friends. Baynes was chosen to illustrate LWW because Jack liked her drawings for Tolkien's *Father Giles of Ham*.

By February 1950 the typescript of *Prince Caspian* was prepared. At this stage Green read the work again. In addition, it was read and enjoyed, at this point, by the children of one Professor Lawson.

Prince Caspian was finally published by Geoffrey Bles on October 15, 1951. It received the following excellent reviews:

> "Let no one suppose that this volume . . . is just pious precept. *Prince Caspian* is a first-rate story . . . The adventures carry suspense. The talking animals and dwarfs are good and bad in a thoroughly whole-hearted way, and their fate is exactly right for the necessary poetic justice." (*The Church Times, Christmas Book Supplement*, CXXXIV [30 November 1951], p. i.)

> "Boys and girls who enjoyed the first book will find here the same reward: a good plot, convincing characters, and the graceful working that distinguishes this writer." (*Saturday Review*, 34 [19 November 1951], pp. 70-1.)

> "The cuteness and archness that mar so many books written for children is blessedly lacking here. The story is for boys and girls who like their dwarfs and fauns as solid as the traffic policeman on the corner." (Chad Walsh, *The New York Times Book Review* [11 November 1951], p. 26.)

Personally I concur with these excellent reviews. *Prince Caspian* was, perhaps, my favorite Narnia story when I first read it. As a boy I loved the battle scene toward the end and the Telmarine head getting

---

142   *Companion & Guide*, p. 403.

lopped off! More than that, I relished the feeling of nostalgia at the beginning of the book with the Pevensie children returning to a half-remembered Cair Paravel, now in ruins.

Just as in the other Narnia tales, there is much spiritual food in *Prince Caspian*. Lewis once remarked that this story was about the "restoration of the true religion after a corruption".[143] But rather than tell in this place the spiritual themes I have discovered in *Prince Caspian*, let the reader discover those themes for himself or herself. The story should be enjoyed for itself, and as it is so enjoyed, either by child or adult reader, the spiritual themes will emerge to the reader's growing consciousness.[144]

---

143 See *The Collected Letters of C. S. Lewis*, Volume III, p. 1245.
144 Once one has read the stories: if assistance is desired in exploring the spiritual themes in the Narnia books, see Will Vaus, *The Hidden Story of Narnia*, Cheshire, CT: Winged Lion Press, 2010.

Discussion Questions

1. How is it different reading this book as an adult versus reading it as a child?
2. What bits of Lewis' own life experiences do you find interjected into the story? How does this affect your enjoyment of the book?
3. When the Pevensie children return to Narnia, they enter a world where many no longer believe in Aslan nor do they believe in the existence of Kings Peter and Edmund and Queens Susan and Lucy. Do you see any parallels to our own world? What do you think Lewis' message is in this to adults?
4. What do you think is the meaning of the writing on the Stone Table that had been worn away by ages of wind and rain and snow?
5. Trufflehunter, Trumpkin and Nikabrik all seem to represent different types of people that inhabit this new Narnia, a world filled with unbelief. How would you characterize each of their approaches to life?
6. What do you think Lewis intends by Lucy's comment that it would be dreadful if some day in our own world, human beings started going wild inside, but still looked human, so that you'd never know who the real humans were?
7. Lucy's character represents the predicament of believers living in an age of unbelief. How would you describe her predicament? What course of action do Aslan, and Jack, recommend for such believers?
8. What do you think of Aslan's statement to Lucy: "Every year you grow, you will find me bigger."?
9. What do you think Aslan's breath represents (the breath that causes a kind of greatness to hang about Edmund)?
10. What do you make of Trufflehunter's statement that Narnia is not a human country but it is a country for a human to

be King of? At the end of the story Caspian is pronounced King and it is stated that Narnia will henceforth belong to the Talking Beasts and the Dwarfs and Dryads and Fauns and other creatures quite as much as to the men. Do you think Lewis was an environmentalist?

11. What does Aslan mean when he says to Caspian that he is a descendant of Adam and Eve and that is "both honour enough to erect the head of the poorest beggar, and shame enough to bow the shoulders of the greatest emperor in earth."?

12. What do you think of the violence in *Prince Caspian*? Do you think it is good or harmful for children to read stories with this kind of violence?

13. What do you think of *Prince Caspian* as children's literature? Is it well written? Do you have a favorite line you would like to read? What is your favorite part of *Prince Caspian*? Why?

Mere Christianity

On February 7, 1941, Dr. James W. Welch, Director of Religious Broadcasting for the BBC, wrote to C. S. Lewis asking him if he would be willing to help them in their task of religious broadcasting. Welch had been very impressed with Lewis' *Problem of Pain*. Jack immediately wrote back accepting the invitation and suggesting a series of talks on objective right and wrong. Next, Jack heard from Eric Fenn, Dr. Welch's assistant, suggesting a series of four Wednesday evening talks in August or September of 1941.

Jack invited Fenn to lunch with him in Magdalen College, Oxford and they arranged for a voice test on microphone. It was the first time Jack had heard a recording of his own voice. He wrote to his friend Arthur Greeves after the event saying that he was unprepared for the total unfamiliarity of listening to his own voice.[145]

Jack eventually gave the first four talks live over the BBC airwaves in August 1941. The discipline of these 15-minute talks, no more, no less, must have developed his ability to boil down complex subjects into a few sparkling analogies and metaphors. The talks proved to be so popular that Jack was deluged with letters from both adoring and irate listeners. Thus he gave a further talk on "Answers to Listeners' Questions" which later became the chapter "Some Objections". This only served to fuel the fire under the letter writers and so began the vast correspondence Jack was to patiently endure for the rest of his life. Again, he wrote to Arthur Greeves, this time describing the letters he was receiving from listeners. Some letters, he said, were

---

145   See *The Collected Letters of C. S. Lewis*, Volume II, p. 486.

from lunatics, like the man who signed himself "Jehovah". Others were from women who wrote things like: "Dear Mr. Lewis, I was married at the age of 20 to a man I didn't love." However, Jack told Arthur that many of the letters were from serious inquirers to whom he felt duty-bound to respond.[146]

The first series of talks led to a second, delivered live in January and February 1942 on the topic: *What Christians Believe*. Jack asked four people from different Christian communions for critique of this second series of broadcast talks, prior to delivery, to see if there was any disagreement among them. He wanted to insure that what he was saying represented "mere Christianity" as much as possible. These two series of talks were published in July 1942 under the simple title: *Broadcast Talks*.

One famous passage from the broadcast talks, about Jesus being either "God or a bad man" was abbreviated in the subsequent book. In the original talk Jack had a very illuminating section in which he said:

> Of course you can take the line of saying He [Jesus] didn't say these things, but His followers invented them. But that's only shifting the difficulty. They were Jews too: the last people who would invent such a thing, the people who had never said anything of the sort about Moses or Elijah. That theory only saddles you with twelve inexplicable lunatics instead of one. We can't get out of it that way.[147]

Once again Jack was overwhelmed with responses to these talks. He asked the BBC to print some of his responses in their own periodical *The Listener* in order to lighten his own correspondence load. But nothing worked. The flood of mail continued.

In September and November of 1942 Jack gave yet another series of BBC talks, this time on the topic: *Christian Behavior*. These were published in 1943 under the same title. Then from February to April 1944 Jack gave his final series of BBC talks on Christianity. This series was published in October 1944 under the title: *Beyond Personality*. Most of these talks were delivered live; in fact, only one recording

---

146   Ibid., p. 504.
147   *C. S. Lewis Companion & Guide*, p. 308.

of Jack's BBC talks on Christianity still survives, on the topic of *The New Men*.

Jack's various broadcast talks, once they were published in book form, received many enthusiastic reviews. The following from *Time and Tide* was characteristic:

> Mr. C. S. Lewis has made the kind of public return to the ancient faith which infuriates other intellectuals. If only these undeniably intelligent laymen had kept quiet about their change of direction, they might have been endurable. But they have not kept quiet . . . An uncompromising, tonic little book.

It has been said that these war time talks over BBC radio made C. S. Lewis' voice the most recognizable in all of Britain during the war, second only to Winston Churchill. All of these talks were eventually revised, amplified and collected in the one volume entitled *Mere Christianity*, published in 1952.[148]

---

148 For a very thorough and entertaining history of C. S. Lewis' relationship with the BBC, see Justin Phillips, *C. S. Lewis at the BBC*, London: HarperCollins, 2002.

Discussion Questions

1. What is the main theme of *Mere Christianity*? What do you think was Lewis' purpose in writing the book, or in giving the original talks over the BBC?

2. Do you think Jack succeeded in presenting to the world "mere Christianity"? That is, has he succeeded in presenting what all Christians have believed at all times and in all places? Why or why not?

3. Do you think Lewis' argument credible – for the existence of God based upon the existence of the Moral Law? Why or why not?

4. What do you think of Lewis' statement that atheism is too simple? He says that if the universe has no meaning we should never have discovered the fact, just as if there wasn't such a thing as light, there wouldn't be creatures with eyes and therefore we should never know what dark was. The word "dark" would be without meaning.

5. At the end of his chapter on "The Shocking Alternative" Jack presents his famous trilemma: that Jesus was either lunatic, the Devil of Hell, or the Son of God. In examining the identity of Jesus of Nazareth, are Lewis' options the only ones open to us? If not, what other conclusions might one arrive at? Which option seems most credible to you and why?

6. In the chapter on "The Perfect Penitent" Lewis puts forward his own theory of the atonement. What do you think of it?

7. Many people today think that so long as they aren't hurting someone else they may do whatever they please. Why does Jack say that such a view of morality is incomplete? See the chapter on "The Three Parts of Morality".

8. What are the Cardinal Virtues? How does Lewis define each of these? What is the difference between developing these virtues in one's life and following a set of rules? Have you heard much talk about these virtues these days?

If not, why not, do you think? Or if you hear more about one than the others, why do you suppose that is the case?

9. What do you think of what Jack has to say about the relationship between morality and psychoanalysis?

10. Lewis says the old Christian rule regarding sexual morality is either marriage with complete faithfulness to one's partner, or else total abstinence. How is contemporary society faring with regard to this rule? Do you see Christians today wanting to change or bend this rule? If so, how? What negative effects stem from ignoring or changing this rule?

11. What do you think of what Jack has to say about Christian marriage? Do you agree there should be two different standards, one for Christians and one for everyone else in society? What do you think of what he says about headship?

12. Forgiveness, Lewis says, is central to Christianity. Which do you find harder, receiving forgiveness or granting it to others? Why?

13. Do you agree with Jack that pride is the great sin? If so, why? If not, which sin do you think is greater?

14. In his chapter on "Charity" Lewis reveals that charity is not primarily about developing certain feelings; it is all about acting a certain way whether one feels like it or not. How might following such a rule help us to forgive?

15. With regard to what Lewis says about the relationship between Faith and Works, do you think he comes out more on the Protestant side or the Catholic side? Or does he chart some middle course which might bring Protestant and Catholic together on this issue?

16. In his chapter on "Hope" Lewis says that if most people looked into their own hearts they would discover that they really desire something that cannot be had in this world. In this passage Lewis touches on the themes of heaven and unfulfilled longings, themes which appear over and over again in his writings. Do you think that

the unfulfilled longings which Lewis talks about prove that there is a heaven and that there is God? Why or why not?

17. In the final book of *Mere Christianity*, Jack articulates his understanding of the doctrine of the Trinity. Does he make this doctrine more understandable and believable to you? Why or why not?

18. In the chapter on "Time and Beyond Time" Lewis points out that God is outside of time. How does this concept help us better understand certain theological conundrums?

19. How does Jack's idea of "Good Infection" help the Christian to counteract mere moralism or legalism in the Christian life?

20. In the chapter entitled "Let's Pretend" Lewis says that there is a good kind of pretending to be done by every Christian. What is that? Does this idea help you get on with living the Christian life? Why or why not?

21. Lewis says that practicing Christianity is both harder and easier than most people think. In what ways is it harder, and in what ways easier?

22. Lewis was a master of the art of illustration, analogy and parable. What is your favorite illustration from *Mere Christianity* and why?

23. What is your favorite passage from *Mere Christianity* and why? Would you mind reading that passage to the group?

24. What affect, if any, has reading *Mere Christianity* had upon your personal life and your relationship with God?

25. N. T. Wright has said that he feels Book III, on *Christian Behavior*, is the most successful part of *Mere Christianity*. What do you think? Which part of the book is your favorite?

The Voyage of the Dawn Treader

Walter Hooper presents in his book, *C. S. Lewis: Companion & Guide* (p. 403), a rough sketch of *The Voyage of the Dawn Treader*, which he discovered in one of Jack's surviving notebooks. In that sketch Jack envisioned two children from our world somehow getting on board a ship of ancient build. He anticipated a story about a journey to various islands, like Homer's *Odyssey* or the legend of Saint Brendan. Jack wanted the beauty of the ship itself to cast a spell, as it were. He desired for this story to be "very green and pearly".

On the same sheet of paper Jack wrote down his idea of a magic picture. Initially he thought of one of the children getting through the picture into another world and one of the creatures of that world getting through the picture into our realm. Also delineated on this one sheet was Jack's idea for a sequel to *The Lion, the Witch and the Wardrobe*. He envisioned a story where the present tyrants in Narnia would be humans and the history of Narnia would be told by a dwarf.

Obviously these notes eventually worked their way into becoming separate stories—*Prince Caspian* as the sequel to *The Lion, the Witch and the Wardrobe* and then *Voyage of the Dawn Treader* following *Prince Caspian*. But this rough sketch from Jack's notebook reveals that he had aspects of *The Voyage* in mind at least as soon as he had finished writing *The Lion*.

Jack finished the manuscript of *The Voyage* by the end of February 1950 and gave it to his friend and former student, Roger Lancelyn

Green, to critique. This third Narnian book, which Jack said was about the spiritual life, especially in Reepicheep, was published in 1952.

Voyage received mixed reviews when it was first published. Louise Bechtel wrote in *The New York Herald Tribune Book Review*: "The strange symbolism will not often be understood, but it is well worth that place at the back of the child's mind where it will linger until suddenly it is clear." The book reviewer for the *New Yorker* called Voyage "A juvenile odyssey that in excitement and beauty surpasses even the preceding volumes." However, Chad Walsh, despite being a friend of Lewis, wrote in *The New York Times Book Review*: "My favorite was the first book of the trilogy – indeed it seems destined to become a modern fairy tale classic. The second was, by comparison, a let-down. The present book is better than its immediate predecessor, though perhaps not up to the very high level of *The Lion, the Witch and the Wardrobe*." Walsh is probably correct in his assessment from an adult, literary perspective, but I doubt that all children would share that perspective. As a child I think I liked *Prince Caspian* best. It took me a long time, and many readings before *The Voyage* held a very high place in my Narnian affections, but now I think it one of the Narnia books with some of the greatest spiritual lessons of all.

Discussion Questions

1. If the theme of *The Lion, the Witch and the Wardrobe* is redemption accomplished, and the theme of *Prince Caspian* is faith in an age of doubt, what do you think is the theme of *The Voyage of the Dawn Treader*? Why do you think so?

2. Why do you suppose Lewis has the action in this story take place largely on a small sailing vessel? What is the significance of the name of the ship?

3. Who do you think is the main character in *The Voyage of the Dawn Treader*? Why? What does this character teach us?

4. What do you think the children's enslavement on The Lone Islands is an image of? Why?

5. What do you think Eustace turning into a dragon is symbolic of? What about Eustace's attempts to remove his dragon flesh? And Aslan turning Eustace into a boy again? What message do you think Lewis is trying to convey through this part of the story?

6. What does the incident at Deathwater give us a picture of? What does the great and ancient book which Lucy found in the house of the old magician remind you of? Why?

7. In the chapter on "The Three Sleepers" what do you think the banquet table is symbolic of? Do the crimson cloth and the stone knife give you any clues? What is the significance of the fact that some people have fallen asleep at this table? Whose attitude toward the table do you think Lewis would want us to emulate? Why?

8. What is the biblical parallel to the Lamb's fish breakfast at the end of *The Voyage of the Dawn Treader*? Why do you suppose Lewis has the children meet a lamb who, a few moments later, turns into Aslan? What do you think the Lamb means when he says that there is a way into Aslan's country from all the worlds?

9. At the end of *The Voyage of the Dawn Treader* Aslan tells the children that in their world he has another name. "You must learn to know me by that name. This was the very reason why you were brought to Narnia, that by knowing me here for a little, you may know me better there." What do you think Aslan's other name is in our world? What does this statement from the lips of Aslan tell us about Lewis' purpose in writing *The Chronicles of Narnia*?

The Silver Chair

Amazingly, between the summer of 1948 and the spring of 1951 C. S. Lewis wrote five of *The Chronicles of Narnia*. Lewis' good friend and fellow writer, J. R. R. Tolkien, was, perhaps, a bit jealous of the ease with which Jack cranked out books, considering how long it took Tolkien himself to write *The Lord of the Rings*.

On page 404 of *C. S. Lewis: Companion & Guide* Walter Hooper tells us: "By 13 November 1950 Lewis had written several chapters of what was first called *Night Under Narnia*, and then *The Wild Waste Lands* and finally *The Silver Chair*, and when [Roger Lancelyn] Green saw Lewis again at the beginning of March 1951 he was able to read the rest of it. Green made notes for some possible alterations to *The Silver Chair*, and the letter Lewis wrote to Green on 6 March mentions exactly the sort of problem he occasionally ran into: 'You are quite right about a wood fire,' he said. 'Wood keeps on glowing red again in the places you have already extinguished – phoenix-like. Even the large webbed feet of a Marshwiggle couldn't do it. Yet it must be a flat hearth, I think. *Does* peat go out easily by treading? As an Irishman I ought to know, but don't. I think it will have to be a coal fire in a flat hearth. After all, Underland might well use coal, whereas wood or charcoal would have to be imported.'"

Despite these minor hurdles, *The Silver Chair* was published in the fall of 1953 and received good reviews like this one from *The Horn Book*, "Those who have accepted Mr. Lewis' three earlier Narnia stories as favorites will find this one equally entrancing and it may be introduced as a first to any lover of make-believe. Adults reading it aloud will appreciate its distinction of style – the deft characterizations, colorful descriptions and playful bits of satire."

Discussion Questions

1. What do you think of Lewis' description of Experiment House? What does this reveal about Jack's attitude toward 20th century education in England?
2. What spiritual truths do we learn from Jill's encounter with Aslan in chapter 2? How did you respond to reading of this encounter?
3. What do the Signs remind you of in our world? Why is it so important for Jill to remember the Signs?
4. Who does the Lady of the Green Kirtle remind you of in our world? What spiritual truth do you think Lewis means to convey by Rilian's and the children's first encounters with her?
5. What do you think of Puddleglum the Marsh-wiggle? What are his vices and virtues?
6. What effect does the Lady's telling about Harfang have upon the children and Puddleglum? What evil lure does this remind you of in our world? What do you think is the significance of the fact that the Lady of the Green Kirtle's realm is underground?
7. What do you think of Puddleglum's statement that there *are* no accidents when Aslan is their guide?
8. Do you see any significance behind the fact that Prince Rilian is in his right mind for only one hour every day?
9. What did you think of the scene where Puddleglum and Eustace free Prince Rilian from the silver chair?
10. What does the Queen of Underland's spell, which she casts over Rilian, Puddleglum and the children, remind you of in our world?
11. What do you think is the significance of the fact that Puddleglum has to *stamp out* the fire and Rilian and Puddleglum and Eustace have to *fight* the serpent? What is Lewis trying to say?

12. What do you think of Puddleglum's statement to the Queen that their play world licks her real world any day?

13. What spiritual truth do we learn from the fact that the Queen's kingdom crumbles after her death?

14. What is the importance of Rilian's choice to go and see his dying father rather than visit the land of Bism?

15. What is the biblical parallel to the Queen's promise to Rilian to make him king of her conquered territories one day?

16. Why do you think Jill could only think of her mistakes in Aslan's presence when he met the children at Cair Paravel? What did you think of Aslan's response?

17. How did the fact that Aslan wept over the dead King Caspian make you feel? Did it remind you of anything in the Bible?

18. What is the meaning behind Aslan's blood bringing Caspian back to life? Why do you think Caspian is young again when he is brought back to life in Aslan's country? How did reading this passage make you feel?

19. What did you think of the ending of the book? Why does Aslan only show his back to the students of Experiment House? Do you see any biblical parallel?

20. How would you summarize the theme of *The Silver Chair*?

The Horse and His Boy

The first mention of what would become *The Horse and His Boy* was made in the diary of Roger Lancelyn Green on 26 July 1950. As we have already seen, Green was the friend and former student of C. S. Lewis who read each of the Narnia stories in manuscript. Green's diary records: "spent most of the day reading Lewis' new story *Narnia and the North*, which is very enthralling—almost the best of the four."[149] Thus between March 1949 and July 1950 Lewis wrote: *The Lion, the Witch and the Wardrobe*, *Prince Caspian*, *The Voyage of the Dawn Treader* and *The Horse and His Boy*.

Much discussion went back and forth between Lewis and his publisher before settling on the title *The Horse and His Boy*. On 13 April, 1953 Lewis wrote to his publisher, Geoffrey Bles, suggesting the following possible titles: *The Horse and the Boy* (thinking it might attract the interest of the "pony-book" public), *The Desert Road to Narnia*, *Cor of Archenland*, *The Horse stole the Boy*, *Over the Border*, and *The Horse Bree*.[150] Bles replied with the winning idea of *The Horse and his Boy*, which of course suggests the equality of humans and talking animals in Narnia.[151]

In regard to the illustrations in *The Horse and His Boy* Lewis wrote in the same letter to Bles on 13 April with suggestions for Pauline Baynes. What Lewis wrote tells us much of how he conceived Calormen. He told Bles that Baynes could base her ideas of Calormene

---

149 Green & Hooper, p. 244.
150 Ibid., p. 245.
151 Ibid.

culture either on the *Arabian Nights* or on Babylon and Persepolis as conceived by Herodotus and/or the Old Testament.[152] Thus we know that Lewis' creation of Calormen was inspired, at least in part, by his reading of the *Arabian Nights*.[153]

On 21 January 1954 Lewis wrote to Pauline Baynes to compliment her on her drawings for *The Horse and His Boy*. He said it was delightful to find her doing the illustrations for each book a little bit better than the last. Jack especially liked the drawings of Lasaraleen in her litter, Shasta among the tombs, Rabadash hanging on the hook, Rabadash just turning into an ass, the Tisroc and Tashbaan. Lewis enjoyed discovering the full wealth of the Tashbaan picture by going over it with a magnifying glass.[154]

How did Miss Baynes view her collaboration with C. S. Lewis? Back in 1967 Pauline Baynes described her work on the Narnia books in this way:

> Dr Lewis and I hardly corresponded at all over the illustrations to his books: he was, to me, the most kindly and tolerant of authors who seemed happy to leave everything in my completely inexperienced hands! (Miss Baynes was 21 years old when she began illustrating Narnia.)[155]

The response to *The Horse and His Boy* when it was published in the fall of 1954 was entirely enthusiastic. Chad Walsh, writing in *The New York Times Book Review* is typical of reviewers at that time: "Children, surfeited on unimaginative tales of socially adjusted children learning socially useful processes, will welcome this story." Walsh's comment reflects the fact that prior to the publication of the Narnia stories the realistic children's story, or school story, was the most popular type of writing for children. Lewis' classic books

---

152 *The Collected Letters of C. S. Lewis*, Volume III, p. 322.
153 In conversation with Douglas Gresham on this point he agreed that Calormen may also have been inspired by Rudyard Kipling's picture of India. Kipling, though out of fashion even by the 1950's, had been a favorite author of the Lewis brothers.
154 *The Collected Letters of C. S. Lewis*, Volume III, pp. 412-413.
155 *C. S. Lewis: Companion & Guide*, p. 406.

changed all that. As evidenced by Harry Potter and the *Spiderwick Chronicles* among other books, fantasy books for children are still gaining an immense worldwide audience. We have Lewis to thank for opening the wardrobe door that has allowed children's imaginations to roam free ever since.

Discussion Questions

1. What would you say is the theme of *The Horse and His Boy*?
2. Does this story feel the same, or different, to you than the other Narnian tales? Why?
3. Who do the Calormenes remind you of in our world? Why?
4. Who does Tash remind you of? Why?
5. Why do you suppose Lewis portrays the Calormene nobility speaking to one another in such a high-flown manner?
6. What contrasts does Lewis draw in this story between the city and the country? Which do you think Jack liked better? Why?
7. What do you think of Jack's descriptions of nature in this story? Is there a passage you particularly like? If so, would you read it to the group?
8. What do you think of Lewis' statement that one of the worst results of being a slave is that when a slave gains his or her freedom he or she may have lost the power of forcing oneself to do what needs to be done?
9. What is it within Shasta that spurs him to go back and help Aravis and Hwin when they are being attacked by the Lion?
10. What do you think of Jack's statement that if one does one good deed the reward is to be set to do another and harder and better deed?
11. What do you think of the Hermit's statement to Aravis that in one hundred and nine winters he had never seen any such thing as luck?
12. What does the Hermit reveal to Bree that his problem has been all along?
13. How did you react to Shasta's meeting with Aslan? (p.

156 ff.) What does this encounter reveal about Aslan? What do you think of Aslan's statement to Shasta: "I tell no-one any story but his own."? What do you suppose was the "new and different sort of trembling" that came over Shasta toward the end of this encounter?

14. Shasta's meeting with the dwarfs in Narnia portrays a quality much loved by Lewis. How would you describe that quality?

15. What does the fight at Anvard reveal about Jack's attitude toward physical combat?

16. Jack says about Rabadash that though he could have faced torture by his enemies he could not bear being made ridiculous. Jack makes a similar comment about someone else in one of his books. Do you remember who?

17. What does Bree's denial of Aslan being a real lion correspond to in the Bible? Why do you suppose this was an important point for Lewis to make?

18. What do you think of Hwin's statement to Aslan that he is so beautiful that she wouldn't mind being eaten by him?

19. What do you think of Aslan's explanation to Aravis about his wounding of her?

20. What does Shasta's journey and discovery of his true family teach us? What might Lewis be giving us a picture of?

21. What do you think of Cor's statement that Aslan is "at the back of all the stories"?

22. What does Bree's attitude toward finally entering Narnia teach us about what our attitude often is toward serving God?

23. What do you think of the way Aslan deals with Rabadash and his handing him over to Tash, so to speak?

24. What do you think of King Lune's statement to Cor about the meaning of kingship?

English Literature in the Sixteenth Century

On 13 October 1922 C. S. Lewis, then an undergraduate at University College Oxford, had his first meeting with his English tutor, Frank Percy Wilson.[156] The relationship was destined to be life-long, and important, for F. P. Wilson was the man who would eventually invite Jack to write his magnum opus, *English Literature in the Sixteenth Century.*

As early as 1927, two years after beginning his work as an English tutor at Magdalen College Oxford, Jack conceived of writing a book about Sir Thomas More and Erasmus and the people of that time.[157] In March of 1928 he mentioned in a letter to his father that he was still working away at his studies in the sixteenth century, during mornings spent in the Bodleian Library.[158] Jack hoped to make a preliminary attempt at fleshing out his thoughts on this period of English literature in a course of lectures planned for 1929. That lecture series eventually included talks on Sir Thomas Elyot, Roger Ascham and Richard Hooker, three of the many authors Jack would write about more fully in future years.[159] At the time of his return to the Christian faith, in the autumn of 1931, Jack was reading the Poetical Works of John Skelton, another author from the same period.[160]

---

156 See *The Collected Letters of C. S. Lewis*, Vol. I, p. 600.
157 Ibid., p. 699.
158 Ibid., p. 749.
159 Ibid., p. 783.
160 Ibid., p. 974.

Thus Jack's special interest in sixteenth century English literature actually predated the invitation of F. P. Wilson to write the volume on that period for the *Oxford History of English Literature*. That invitation was extended in September 1935. At first Jack put Wilson off, suggesting that R. W. Chambers, Professor of English at University College, would be the better man for the job. But Wilson persisted and Jack finally relented.[161] The task of writing this volume was, however, so onerous, that Jack continually referred to the work by its initials: O.H.E.L. or "O HELL"![162]

Despite the formidability of the work, by 1938 Jack was able to report to Wilson that he had already treated the following subjects: Platonism, Douglas, Lyndsay, Tottel, Mulcaster's Elementarie, Sir Thomas More, Prayer-book, Sidney, Marlowe (non-dramatic), Nashe, Watson, Barclay, Googe, Raleigh (poems), Shakespeare (poems), Webbe, in addition to writing about Petrarch and Machiavelli as sources. Jack's lectures on *Prolegomena to Renaissance Poetry* served as a useful buttress to the writing of the book.[163] It has been said that in order to write *English Literature in the Sixteenth Century* Jack read everything published in English in that century. When one considers the thoroughness of the book, that claim is not too hard to believe.

One of Jack's major contentions in the book is that the Renaissance is an imaginary entity.[164] Since he came to believe that the Renaissance never occurred, at least in England, Jack wondered whether it was quite reasonable to entitle his lectures: *Prolegomena to Renaissance Literature*. But seeing no better alternative, he stuck by that title.[165]

On 2 February 1943, George Macaulay Trevelyan, Master of Trinity College, Cambridge, invited Jack to deliver the Clark Lectures for the academic year 1943-1944. These lectures, delivered in

---

161 *The Collected Letters of C. S. Lewis*, Volume II, pp. 167-168.
162 Ibid., pp. 221-222. Lewis' lectures on *Prolegomena to Renaissance Literature* were not only given at Oxford, but also at Cambridge, every Tuesday during Lent Term 1939.
163 Ibid., pp. 235-236.
164 Ibid., pp. 474-475.
165 Ibid., pp. 246-247.

April 1944, provided Jack with further opportunity to disseminate his ideas on sixteenth century English literature. Although these lectures formed only a small portion of what would become *English Literature in the Sixteenth Century*, Jack gave the resulting book the sub-title: *The Completion of the Clark Lectures, Trinity College, Cambridge, 1944*, out of respect for Cambridge University's most honorable invitation.[166] Jack continued to work on the book for several more years. In fact, he might never have completed the work had not Magdalen College given him a year off to do so, starting with the Michaelmas Term in the autumn of 1951.[167] With this time off from lectures and tutorials Jack was able to substantially complete the book by July of 1952.[168] I say "substantially" because there was still the task of going over the galley proofs, which work Lewis began to undertake during the Christmas holiday of that same year.[169] Jack continued to work on the galley proofs and the bibliography for OHEL throughout 1953. *English Literature in the Sixteenth Century Excluding Drama* was finally published by Oxford University Press on 16 September 1954 and Jack felt like an air balloon with its last sandbag dropped.

John Wain, reviewing Lewis' book for *The Spectator*, had this to say about its author: "Mr. Lewis is today the only major critic of English literature who makes a principle of telling us which authors he thinks we shall *enjoy*: this may not sound much, but most dons have moved a long way from any recognition that literature is something that people used to read for fun. Mr. Lewis, now as always, writes as if inviting us to a feast."[170]

---

166   Ibid., p. 552.
167   See *The Collected Letters of C. S. Lewis*, Volume III, pp. 112, 141 & 158.
168   Ibid., p. 215.
169   Ibid., p. 288. See also Don W. King, editor, *Out of My Bone: The Letters of Joy Davidman*, Grand Rapids: Eerdmans, 2009, pp. 138-139. Joy Davidman, who read the galley proofs during her Christmas holiday with the Lewis brothers, had this to say about the book in a letter to Chad Walsh: "The OHEL volume is going to make people sizzle; it's full of controversial stuff and reversals of conventional judgments."
170   See *C. S. Lewis: Companion & Guide*, pp. 507-508.

Lewis' biographer, George Sayer, has said: "On the strength of *The Allegory of Love* and of his *English Literature in the Sixteenth Century*, there can be no doubt of his greatness as a literary historian."[171] Sayers continues: "He is splendid on old favorites such as Edmund Spenser and Sir Philip Sidney and as fresh on Shakespeare's poems as if no one had written on them before. It is no exaggeration to say that there is wit and humor on every page…. Some Oxford tutors still warn their pupils that it is 'unsound but brilliantly written.' Nevertheless, or perhaps because of this warning, it outsells all the other volumes in the series."[172]

---

171 Sayer, *Jack*, p. 245.
172 Ibid., pp. 325, 326.

A C. S. Lewis Discussion Guide

Discussion Questions

1. In his Introduction, *New Learning and New Ignorance*, how does C. S. Lewis define Puritanism? Does what Jack has to say about the Puritans change your view of them at all? If so, how?
2. What does Jack mean by humanism? According to him, the humanists of the 16th century did two things, one good and one bad. What were those two things?
3. According to Jack, what did it feel like to be an early Protestant? Would you like to have been one? Why or why not?
4. Why does Lewis prefer not to use the term "Renaissance" to describe what was happening in the 16th century?
5. In the chapter on *The Close of the Middle Ages in Scotland* why, does Jack suppose, that poetical glory suddenly dies?
6. From which author of this period in Scotland does Lewis derive the title of one of his books? What is the book?
7. In the chapter on *The Close of the Middle Ages in England* whom does Jack say is the only poet of that age who is still read today for pleasure?
8. Lewis' chapter on *Religious Controversy and Translation* is probably the most appealing chapter in this book for those readers most interested in Lewis' theological works. In this chapter why does Jack use the term: *papists*?
9. Jack does not shy away from revealing some of his own religious opinions in this chapter. For instance, he conveys the fact that he prefers Dante's view of purgatory to that of Fisher or More. Why? What do you think of what Jack has to say on this point?
10. How does Lewis compare and contrast the writing of More and Tyndale? Why does Lewis say any sensible man will want both? What do you think?
11. In writing about religious translation in the sixteenth century Jack gives fascinating coverage of Bible

translations (leading up to the Authorized Version) and the Book of Common Prayer. He does not withhold his own comment on the matter, as in this statement about the Prayer Book: "…at its greatest it shines with a white light hardly surpassed outside the pages of the New Testament itself."[173] What new thing did you learn from this section of the book? What do you think of Lewis injecting so much of his own opinion into this work of literary history? Does it put you off, or keep you interested? Why?

12. What author of "Drab Age Verse" was responsible for supplying Lewis with the name of one of the most beloved Narnian characters? What was the name?

13. What do you think of Jack's wry sense of humor displayed throughout this book? Consider sentences such as this one about Henry VIII: "It is not clear that our poetry would be much the poorer if he had beheaded nearly every writer mentioned in this chapter."[174]

14. What do you think made *The Faerie Queene* one of Lewis' favorite literary works? If you have read *The Faerie Queene*, do you agree with Lewis? Why or why not?

15. As Spenser was one of Lewis' favorite imaginative writers from this period, why do you suppose Richard Hooker was his favorite theologian? Do you agree with Lewis in his judgment? Why or why not? What two aspects of Hooker's thought does Jack say we must understand in order to comprehend anything else about Hooker?

16. In the chapter on *Verse in the 'Golden' Period* what does Jack say chiefly differentiates the Golden poets from the Drab?

---

173 C. S. Lewis, *English Literature in the Sixteenth Century*, Oxford: Oxford University Press, 1973, p. 221. On one occasion when hearing a lecture from one of Lewis' agnostic colleagues about Lewis as a literary critic and historian, I witnessed that colleague being moved to tears by this passage. I believe this quote reveals how much Lewis the Christian shows through even in his work of literary criticism, and how much Lewis' Christianity still affects readers who may think they are "safe" when reading his works on English literature.

174 Ibid., p. 269.

What relevance or application might this judgment have had to poetry in Jack's own lifetime?

17. Why do you think Lewis prefers the sonnets of Shakespeare to those of Donne? Do you agree? Why or why not?

18. Lewis concludes this massive book by saying, "I do not suppose that the sixteenth century differs in these respects from any other arbitrarily selected stretch of years. It illustrates well enough the usual complex, unpatterned historical process; in which, while men often throw away irreplaceable wealth, they not infrequently escape what seemed inevitable dangers, not knowing that they have done either nor how they did it."[175] Is this a philosophy of history which could be embraced by Christian and non-Christian alike? Why or why not? Do you think this is a good summary of Lewis' philosophy of history? Why or why not?

19. In the course of reading this book what other authors has Jack enticed you to read, or read more of? Why?

20. How is Lewis' voice different or the same in this book as in his other works? Tolkien once said of this work that it was his friend Jack's only book which gave him unalloyed pleasure. Why do you suppose that was the case? Do you agree or disagree? Why?

---

175   Ibid., p. 558.

The Magician's Nephew

C. S. Lewis began writing *The Magician's Nephew* in 1949 shortly after completing *The Lion, the Witch and the Wardrobe*. The purpose of this story was to describe the creation of Narnia and explain how the Lamppost had come to exist in Lantern Waste. Lewis read two chapters of this new story to his friend and former student, Roger Lancelyn Green, on June 14 of that year. These chapters are referred to as The Lefay Fragment because Digory's godmother is called Mrs. Lefay in this early attempt at a sequel to LWW. In the Lefay Fragment, Digory lives with his Aunt Gertrude because his parents are dead. Furthermore, Digory has the ability to communicate with animals and trees; he befriends a large Oak in his garden and a squirrel named Pattertwig who lives in the tree.

Jack got mired down and was unable to go on with writing the story after the introduction of Digory's godmother, a woman who practices magic. He felt that the character of Mrs. Lefay didn't come off well and his friend Green agreed with him. Thus Jack decided to set aside this manuscript, but he incorporated some of the ideas from The Lefay Fragment into other Narnia stories.

Between the summer of 1949 and March 1950 Jack wrote five of the Narnia tales. Afterward he returned to a consideration of the creation of Narnia. He retained the names Digory and Polly from The Lefay Fragment and set the story in the days when Sherlock Holmes was still living in Baker Street and the Bastables were looking for treasure in the Lewisham Road—a nod of appreciation to one of his favorite children's authors: E. Nesbit.

Roger Lancelyn Green came to visit Jack at Magdalen College, Oxford from May 31 to June 1, 1951. During that visit he read about half of what would become *The Magician's Nephew*. Green visited again from October 31 to November 2 of the same year and read another quarter of the story. Green expressed displeasure over one section in which Digory visited Charn several times and stayed in a farm cottage with an old country gentleman called Piers and his wife. Jack was not convinced that he should cut out that part of the story but, nonetheless, he again set aside the writing of *The Magician's Nephew*, and instead turned his pen to writing the last of the Narnia stories—*The Last Battle*.

Jack wrote to his publisher, Geoffrey Bles, on March 11, 1953 to say that the last of the Narnian stories was finished. He then turned back to the task of revising *The Magician's Nephew*. Green read the manuscript in February 1954 and noted in his diary: "It seems the best of the lot . . . and is certainly vastly improved by the omission of the long section about Piers the Plowman—which I take some credit for persuading Jack to cut out. It's a single unity now, and irresistibly gripping and compelling."[176]

---

176   *Companion & Guide*, p. 405.

Discussion Questions

1. Do you notice anything significant about the time period in which this story is set?
2. How does Lewis teach morality through this book?
3. Does Jack make the supernatural realm believable in this story? If so how?
4. How is Digory like Jack?
5. Digory says of the wood between the worlds, "Nothing ever happens here. Like at home. It's in the houses that people talk, and do things, and have meals. Nothing goes on in the in-between places ..." Does this statement remind you of anything in any of Lewis' other books?
6. How would you describe Digory and Polly, using one adjective for each?
7. After reading this book, what would you guess was Jack's view of magic?
8. What view of kingship does this book present?
9. What do Jadis and Uncle Andrew have in common?
10. What does the situation with Digory's mother remind you of from Jack's life?
11. What do you think of Jack's account of the creation of Narnia? How does it compare to the biblical account of creation?
12. How might we judge each character in this story by their various reactions to Aslan?
13. What do you think Aslan means by the statement: "Evil will come of that evil, but it is still a long way off, and I will see to it that the worst falls upon myself."?
14. What do you think of Aslan's choice for the first King and Queen of Narnia?
15. What do you think of Aslan's response to Digory's request in chapter XII?

16. How do you respond to Jack's descriptions of scenery throughout this story?
17. How does Digory's temptation in the garden compare to the temptation in the Garden of Eden?
18. Do you think there is any connection between Jadis and the witches in the other Narnia stories?
19. How did you feel about the end of this story?
20. How would you summarize what this story is about?

Surprised by Joy

Shortly after his conversion to theism in 1929, C. S. Lewis wrote what might be called an early version of *Surprised by Joy*. His purpose was to explain how the experience of joy had led him to become a believer in God. This early manuscript consisted of sixty-two pages of a notebook and ten loose sheets which later came into the possession of Walter Hooper. Perhaps the reason why Jack did not finish this early manuscript was because he was still sorting out what he thought of Christianity.[177] It was not until two years later that Jack accepted Christ as divine.

We know from Warren Lewis' diary that the manuscript of Jack's final version of his autobiography was begun as early as March 1948. At that time Warren said of his brother's book that it "promises to be first rate–though of course there could hardly be anyone less competent to criticise the early chapters of such a work than I am."[178] Apparently Warren thought he was too close to the subject of the book to consider himself a proper judge of the book's merits.

After the publication of *Surprised by Joy* in 1955, Jack was asked by his publisher, Jocelyn Gibb of Geoffrey Bles Ltd, to write a more formal autobiography. Jack's response was as follows: "Oh no, but when I'm dead I suppose Roger [Lancelyn Green] will write my biography and Jock will publish it."[179]

---

177 Green & Hooper, p. 113.
178 *Brothers & Friends*, p. 219.
179 Green & Hooper, p. 7.

Though Jack probably had the title of the book and the theme of "joy" in mind as early as 1948, many people have supposed that he intended a double meaning, given the fact that the woman he married in 1956 was named Joy. This coincidence was not overlooked in Oxford at the time of Jack's marriage, when the clever thing to say was: "Do you know what's happened to C. S. Lewis? He's been surprised by Joy!"[180] The book, of course, is not about his marriage to Joy Davidman but about the experience of joy, variously called longing, desire, or "sehnsucht," which led Jack to belief in God and eventually in Christ as the Son of God.

Surprised by Joy was not without critics even among Jack's friends. Former student, long-time friend, and biographer, George Sayer writes: "For students of Lewis, it is a fascinating book, but as an autobiography it is unsatisfactory."[181] However, I think Sayer is unfair in his criticism at this point for it was not Jack's intention to write a strict autobiography. In his preface to the book Lewis makes clear,

> The book aims at telling the story of my conversion and is not a general autobiography, still less "Confessions" like those of St. Augustine or Rousseau. This means in practice that it gets less like a general autobiography as it goes on.[182]

As Jack explains, the net is drawn wide at the beginning of the story in order to include all those important elements which pertain to the subject of "joy." As he nears the telling of his conversion proper he eliminates all those biographical details which do not strictly effect his turn to theism and then his return to Christianity.

One of the key details of Jack's early life which is left out of the story is his relationship to Mrs. Janie King Moore, the mother of his friend Paddy Moore who was killed in World War I. Jack makes passing reference to this relationship at the beginning of his chapter entitled "The New Look" where he refers to "one huge and complex episode" that will be omitted. He claims he has no choice about this reticence. However, he does admit that as a result of this episode in

---

180   Ibid., p. 257.
181   Sayer, pp. 326-327.
182   C. S. Lewis, *Surprised by Joy*, New York: Harcourt Brace Jovanovich, 1955, p. vii.

his life all his "earlier hostility to the emotions was very fully and variously avenged".[183]

Why did Jack say that he had no choice about this reticence and that he was not free to tell the story? Perhaps this is due to the fact that Mrs. Moore's daughter Maureen was still alive and in active relationship with Jack at the time of writing. Just before her death, Maureen confided to George Sayer that Jack and her mother may have had a sexual relationship prior to Jack's conversion.

Warren Lewis comments on his brother's relationship to Mrs. Moore in his "Memoir of C. S. Lewis." He writes as follows:

> Mrs. Moore had lost her son; Jack had many years earlier lost his mother and now his father too seemed to have failed him emotionally. He may have felt also some sense of responsibility, a duty perhaps of keeping some war-time promise made to Paddy Moore. Be that as it may, Jack now embarked upon a relationship with Mrs. Moore which was almost of son and mother; and as soon as his first year as an undergraduate was over, instead of moving from college into lodgings, he set up a joint menage with her and her daughter Maureen. Having once embarked on this relationship with Mrs. Moore, it was not in Jack's nature later to abandon her, and the menage in fact continued in existence until her death in 1951.... The thing most puzzling to myself and to Jack's friends was Mrs. Moore's extreme unsuitability as a companion for him. She was a woman of very limited mind, and notably domineering and possessive by temperament. She cut down to a minimum his visits to his father, interfered constantly with his work, and imposed upon him a heavy burden of minor domestic tasks.... I dwell on this rather unhappy business with some regret, but it was one of the central and determining circumstances in Jack's life.[184]

Another question which George Sayer raises about the book has to do with Jack's account of his misery at school which takes up a third

---

183 Ibid., p. 198.
184 Hooper & Lewis, *Letters of C. S. Lewis*, pp. 32-33.

of the book. Why is it so exaggerated?[185] Jack partially answered this question in a letter to his friend Dom Bede Griffiths written on February 8, 1956. At that time he wrote:

> I feel the whole of one's youth to be immensely important and even of immense length. The gradual reading of one's own life, seeing the pattern emerge, is a great illumination at our age. And partly, I hope, getting freed from the past as past by apprehending it as structure.[186]

Warren Lewis believed that Jack's portrayal of the inferno of lusts at Malvern College was certainly exaggerated. Warren did not deny that the immorality existed but he believed it was less widespread than Jack made it out to be. Furthermore, on one occasion, Jack admitted Warnie's contention that sex was not the only topic of conversation in the college house.[187]

So why did Jack emphasize his school days and sexual lust so much in *Surprised by Joy*? Sayer maintains that Lewis wanted to be free of . . .

> . . . a near obsession with his school days and the memory of the sexual and sadistic obsessions that accompanied them. The way to freedom for him was through writing . . . it was very important that these obsessions be expunged from his imagination because he wanted it to be fresh and open, clear and clean for his work on the Narnia stories.[188]

Regardless of what one thinks about these portions of the story, *Surprised by Joy* remains a very compelling account of one man's journey to faith in Jesus Christ. Jack presents to us in this book some of his most superb prose. He enables us to feel, to see, to taste his own experience of "joy." And I think Jack does this in such a way that we cannot help but want to know the same source of joy which he himself came to know.

---

185 Sayer, p. 237.
186 Hooper & Lewis, pp. 452-453.
187 Ibid., p. 25.
188 Sayer, p. 327.

Discussion Questions

1. In the first chapter Jack tells us of his first experiences of "joy": seeing the toy garden, standing beside a flowering currant bush, reading *Squirrel Nutkin* and being entranced with the idea of autumn, reading *The Saga of King Olaf* and being uplifted by "Northernness". Have you ever had experiences like this? How might such experiences lead one to belief in God?

2. Jack describes the "loss of security" which he experienced following the death of his mother. How might one describe Jack's early life as a "search for security"? Do you think he found it?

3. Lewis says that it was during his "concentration camp" experience that he first became an effective believer. Fear played a dominant role in his early faith. How was this fear assuaged later on in Jack's life? Have you had a similar experience? Are you more fearful of God or drawn to him in love? Why do you think so?

4. It was at Cherbourg House (Chartres) in Malvern (Wyvern), England that Jack "ceased to be a Christian." What influenced him to become an atheist? Why was he "desperately anxious to get rid of his religion"? Have you ever had a similar experience?

5. What do you think of the fact that Jack describes, in some detail, the homosexual practices of Malvern College without condemning them? Does this make it easier or harder for you to listen to and appreciate Jack's journey to God? Why?

6. Jack notes that "spiritually speaking, the deadly thing was that school life was almost wholly dominated by the social struggle." What effect did this have on Jack's life? Did you ever experience this "social struggle" in your school days? What effect did it have on your life?

7. Lewis states that during his time at Malvern College he was angry with God for not existing and equally angry

with him for creating a world. Do you think other atheists experience this? Have you ever felt this way? Why?

8. One of the features of Jack's early life was a strained relationship with his father. How do you think this relationship influenced Jack's turn to atheism and later, back to Christianity?

9. In the middle portion of the book Jack describes two people who had a great influence upon him: his life-long friend, Arthur Greeves, and his tutor, William Kirkpatrick. How did these two people influence Jack? What role have other people played in your own spiritual journey?

10. One of the sub-themes of Jack's early life was his great desire to be "left alone." His great problem with Christianity was that there was a "transcendental Interferer" at the center of it. Do you think Jack's feelings on this subject are characteristic of many people? Why or why not?

11. Toward the end of Jack's time at Great Bookham he faced a great conflict between "joy" and his materialistic "faith." What was the conflict? How was this conflict eventually overcome?

12. Do you think the "dialectic of desire" is a powerful argument for theism? Why or why not?

13. In chapter 12 Jack writes that a person who wants to maintain his atheism needs to be careful of his reading. Two of the writers who had a dramatic impact on Jack's return to Christianity were George MacDonald and G. K. Chesterton. How did these writers affect him? What writers have been influential in your own spiritual pilgrimage?

14. How did Jack's Oxford friends (Jenkin, Barfield, Harwood, Coghill, Dyson and Tolkien) influence him toward embracing Christianity?

15. One of the most fascinating aspects of Jack's conversion to theism is the fact that he did not want to become a believer in God. Why was this true? Does this make Jack's story more or less credible to you?

16. What do you think of the fact that Jack immediately started attending his parish church once he became a theist even though churchmanship was "wholly unattractive" to him? Do you think there is anything we can learn from Jack in this regard?

17. The question which led Jack finally to accept Christianity was this: "Where has religion reached its true maturity?" Do you find Jack's answer to this question credible? Why or why not?

The Last Battle

The Last Battle, though it was the last of *The Chronicles of Narnia* to be published, was not the last Chronicle to be written. Jack completed writing *The Magician's Nephew* after *The Last Battle*. Roger Lancelyn Green, Jack's former student and friend who had encouraged him to complete work on *The Lion, the Witch and the Wardrobe*, read the first half of *The Last Battle* in February 1953. By the end of the same month, Jack wrote to Green and said, "I've nearly finished the last chronicle."[189]

On 2 March Jack wrote to his publisher, Geoffrey Bles, to say, "You will hear with mixed feelings that I have just finished the seventh & really last of the Narnian stories. That means there are 3 more. Are you still game? If so, tell me when to send you the next."[190]

In the end, Jack gave *The Magician's Nephew* and *The Last Battle* to John Lane, The Bodley Head, for publishing, and not to Geoffrey Bles who had published the first five Narnia tales. This apparently happened for a few different reasons. (1) When it came time for the last two Narnia stories to be published, Geoffrey Bles had retired from his own firm. (2) Jack wanted to do a good turn for The Bodley Head who had been so kind to him in his early years of writing when they published his science fiction trilogy. Jack wanted to share with them his newfound success through the Narnia stories. (3) Jack had by this time established himself with a literary agent, Spencer Curtis Brown, which agent obtained better financial deals for Jack in contracts for his books than what Geoffrey Bles had offered him in the past.

---

189 *Collected Letters*, Volume III, p. 297.
190 Ibid., p. 300.

Eventually Geoffrey Bles, Ltd. was purchased by William Collins & Sons. Lady Collins managed to get Jack's books out to more readers through her Fontana paperback series. Collins publishers eventually merged with Harper & Row to form HarperCollins, the second largest publisher in the world. HarperCollins, of course, now publishes all seven of *The Chronicles of Narnia*.

Before publication Jack toyed with a few different titles for his last Narnian chronicle. *The Last King of Narnia* and *Night Falls on Narnia* were in the final running. But *The Last Battle* won out and was published under that title on 19 March 1956.

In 1957 The Carnegie Medal (annually awarded by children's librarians since 1936 for the most outstanding book of the year for children and young people) was awarded to C. S. Lewis for *The Last Battle*. When the illustrator of the Narnia books, Pauline Baynes, wrote to Jack to congratulate him, Jack wrote back saying, "Is it not rather 'our' Medal? I'm sure the illustrations were taken into consideration as well as the text."[191]

Given the award of the Carnegie Medal, it should then come as no surprise that the first reviews of *The Last Battle* were glowing. That of Charles Brady, writing in *America* (27 October 1956) is typical, calling the whole series: "The greatest addition to the imperishable deposit of children's literature since the *Jungle Books*. Narnia takes its place forever now beside the jasper-lucent landscapes of Carroll, Anderson, MacDonald and Kipling ... The child will not respond to these values at once, though they will awaken in his memory when the time comes for full realization. He will respond immediately, however, to the narrative sweep; to the evocation of the heroic mood; to the constant eliciting of the numinous. Very possibly this latter service is the most startling one Lewis renders contemporary childhood. ... He touches the nerve of religious awe on almost every page. He evangelizes through the imagination."

---

191   Ibid., p. 850.

A C. S. LEWIS DISCUSSION GUIDE

Discussion Questions

1. What parallels do you see between the events in *The Last Battle* and the end-of-the-world events as described in the Bible? What do you make of the fact that there is no "second coming" of Aslan to Narnia in this story? Is there any significance to this?

2. Do the early chapters of *The Last Battle* build in you a sense of despair? Do you find the feeling bearable, or not?

3. Puzzle masquerading as Aslan, and Shift issuing commands in Aslan's name, raise the whole question: Are things good simply because Aslan commands them? Or must Aslan's creatures be able to see the intrinsic goodness in his commands in order to properly obey? What implications might the answers to these questions have for theology and our relationship with God in this world?

4. Throughout this story we see how the meaning of the statement: "Aslan is not a tame lion" can be twisted and distorted. What statements about God in our world, which may be true in some contexts, can have their meaning abused in another?

5. In this story the identities of Aslan and Tash are eventually amalgamated in the speech of the evil characters. What message is there for us in this about our understanding of God in our own world?

6. If you read *The Last Battle* as a child, how did you react then to this story? How did your enjoyment of it compare to your experience with the other Narnia books?

7. What do you think of the new worlds described at the end of *The Last Battle*? Do Jack's descriptions make you want to go there?

8. How did you respond to the dwarfs who refuse to be taken in? Of what do you think Jack is giving us a picture in them, or what message do you see in this vignette?

9. What did you think of Jack's description of the end of Narnia and the final judgment of all its creatures? Does the judgment seem just?

10. Did you like the way Jack brought all the chief characters back together from the earlier Narnia stories? What did you think of Susan not being there?

11. What did you think of Emeth? What is Jack trying to say through this character?

12. In the penultimate chapter Digory says, "It's all in Plato." What is in Plato? Compare and contrast the biblical and Platonic worldviews. Which do you think Jack is closer to representing in this book?

13. Do you have a favorite passage or statement in this story? If so, would you read it aloud to the group?

14. Which is your favorite of the Narnia stories? Why?

Till We Have Faces

Till We Have Faces is C. S. Lewis' re-telling of the story of Cupid and Psyche, first put on paper by the second century Roman writer Apuleius. Jack wrote the following about his adaptation of the original myth: "The central alteration in my own version consists in making Psyche's palace invisible to normal, mortal eyes—if 'making' is not the wrong word for something which forced itself upon me, almost at my first reading of the story, as the way the thing must have been. This change, of course, brings with it a more ambivalent motive and a different character for my heroine and finally modifies the whole quality of the tale."[192]

Jack wrote the following blurb for the flyleaf of the first English edition of *Till We Have Faces*: "This reinterpretation of an old story has lived in the author's mind, thickening and hardening with the years, ever since he was an undergraduate. That way, he could be said to have worked at it most of his life. Recently, what seemed to be the right form presented itself and themes suddenly interlocked: the straight tale of barbarism, the mind of an ugly woman, dark idolatry and pale enlightenment at war with each other and with vision, and the havoc which a vocation, or even a faith, works on human life."[193]

As the flyleaf of the first English edition goes on to say: "The author takes his title from the book itself. 'How can the gods meet us

---

192 From the back cover of the first edition: C. S. Lewis, *Till We Have Faces*, London: Geoffrey Bles, 1956.
193 From the flyleaf of the first edition.

face to face till we have faces?' asks Orual, in whose words the story is told; and it is the resolving of this question which forms the novel's theme."

Jack first read the myth of Cupid and Psyche while he was a student at Malvern College. Later, while he was an undergraduate at Oxford, he made at least three attempts at writing his own version of the story, first in couplets, next as a ballad, and finally as a play. However, Jack never felt that any of these attempts were successful and so he put the idea on a "back burner" for thirty-two years.

In the spring of 1955 during a weekend visit to the Kilns, Joy Davidman kicked around a few ideas with Jack for a new book; he was facing writer's block for the first time in his life. Joy felt that though she could not write one-tenth as well as Jack she could help him to write more like himself. The result of this brain-storming session was: *Till We Have Faces*. Jack wrote the first chapter the very next day; he submitted it to Joy for her criticism, then he re-wrote the first chapter, and following that he went on to write the rest of the book. Jack then submitted the manuscript to his editor, Jocelyn Gibb at Geoffrey Bles.

Jack's original title for the book was *Bareface*. This title reflected the fact that Orual is bare-face at the beginning of the story; then she puts on a veil for the rest of her life, until she goes bare-face before the gods at the end of the story. Gibb thought the title made the book sound like a Western and so Jack eventually suggested the alternative title: *Till We Have Faces*.

The book was published by Geoffrey Bles in England in September 1956 and by Harcourt Brace in January 1957 in the United States. At first the book sold very poorly even though it had received some favorable reviews. Nonetheless Jack thought it to be his best book, along with *Perelandra*. In more recent years a major reassessment of this book has taken place in critical circles, to the point where many Lewis scholars have come to agree with Jack in calling *Till We Have Faces* his best book, even, a masterpiece.

A C. S. Lewis Discussion Guide

Discussion Questions

1. If you are familiar with the myth of Cupid and Psyche, how does C. S. Lewis change the original story? What additions does he make?
2. If someone asked you what *Till We Have Faces* was about, what would you say?
3. If *That Hideous Strength* could be considered an illustration of *The Abolition of Man*, what Lewis book do you think *Till We Have Faces* is an illustration of?
4. How are the workings of storge, philia, eros and agape illustrated in *Till We Have Faces*?
5. What character or characters is Orual similar to in one of Jack's other books?
6. What do you think Orual's veil is symbolic of?
7. How does Jack develop the paired motifs of enlightenment and sacrifice in this story? What is Jack trying to teach us in this aspect of the story?
8. How does Jack develop the paired motifs of reason and imagination in this story? What do you think Jack is trying to tell us on this subject?
9. What do you think the god means when he tells Orual that she must "die before she dies because there is no chance after"?
10. Why is it that the gods cannot meet us "till we have faces"?
11. How does the relationship between Orual and Psyche after their encounters on the mountain illustrate Charles Williams's Way of Exchange?
12. What do you think of Orual's words: "I know now, Lord, why you utter no answer. You are yourself the answer."?
13. What did you think of Orual being made beautiful at the end of the story? How was it the fulfillment of her life-long desire?

14. How did you enjoy reading *Till We Have Faces* compared to reading Jack's other books? Was it harder or easier to read? Why?

Reflections on the Psalms

A number of scholars who have written about C. S. Lewis have pointed out that *Reflections on the Psalms* which was published in 1958 was Lewis' first new theological book after *Miracles*, which was published in 1947.[194] Scholars attribute this hiatus to the effect of Lewis' 1948 Socratic Club debate with Elizabeth Anscombe. Jack apparently said to friends after the debate that his argument for the existence of God had been demolished and that he could no longer write books like *Miracles*.[195] However, it is important to note that Jack's faith was not demolished. He simply felt that he could no longer keep up with current trends in philosophy. And so he turned to writing theological books of a more devotional character beginning with *Reflections*.

The idea for the book was suggested to Jack by his friend Austin Farrer, an Anglican priest and theologian. Much of the content was discussed with Farrer and with Joy Davidman during the summer of 1957. In November of that same year Jack wrote to his friend Arthur Greeves, "I have been writing nothing but academic work except for a very unambitious little work on the Psalms, wh. is now finished and ought to come out next spring."[196]

---

194 In between *Miracles* and *Reflections* Lewis did have *Transposition and Other Addresses* as well as *Mere Christianity* published. However, these were collections of things Lewis had written prior to *Miracles*. The flyleaf of the first edition of *Reflections on the Psalms* notes that Lewis in this book is not going "in for 'apologetics'" and that "This is the first religious book Professor Lewis has written for ten years."

195 Sayer, *Jack*, p. 307.

196 *Collected Letters*, Volume III, p. 900.

As things usually go in the publishing world, the process of getting the book out took longer than expected. Jack was correcting galley proofs in the spring of 1958 and the book was finally published in the autumn of that year. Jack's popularity as an author was so great at that time, that no less than 11,000 copies of *Reflections* were sold before publication in Great Britain, a very large pre-publication sale for a religious hardback in the 1950's in England.

Some reviewers criticized the book for not being more scholarly in its approach to the Psalms, despite Jack's introduction where he made it clear he was writing as one amateur to others. Interestingly enough, when I asked an Old Testament professor at Oxford for her opinion on *Reflections* during a visit in the summer of 2000, she said that she thought the book was very perceptive and insightful for a layman writing about the Psalms. Many other reviewers have agreed with the latter perspective. The reviewer for *The Church Times*, CXLI (12 September 1958), p. 5, wrote: "This is a brilliant book, not least in its powerful simplicity. The Psalms are not the easiest thing in the Bible to use or to understand. Here is a touch of magic interpretation ... which can do more than all the learned commentaries to make the reading of the Psalms an open door into the world of the Kingdom and the glory of the Lord."

One interesting result of writing this book was that Jack was invited by the Archbishops of Canterbury and York to join a committee being appointed for the purpose of revising the translation of the Psalms in the Book of Common Prayer. T. S. Eliot, Jack's old literary nemesis, was also on the committee. Meeting one another in this neutral setting, Eliot and Lewis found they had much in common and became fast friends. The result of their work *was The Revised* Psalter, published in 1963. However, that was not the end of Jack's work on biblical texts. He was also consulted about certain aspects of the New Testament translation for the New English Bible published in 1961. Jack enjoyed interacting with theologians and biblical scholars in these kinds of situations because he felt he had so much to learn from them. And he often passed on what he learned in conversation with friends.

Certainly, *Reflections on the Psalms* reveals what Jack gleaned about the Psalms from conversations with biblical scholars and theologians at Oxford and Cambridge, people like his friend Austin Farrer. But the greatest value in this book is Jack's perspective as a layman writing about his spiritual and intellectual wrestling with the Psalms and the applications he found for his own life. Due to his consistent attendance at college chapel as well as Sunday services at his parish church as well as his own private Bible reading, Jack was probably more familiar with the Psalms than any other book of the Bible. The richness of that lifelong familiarity comes through in this book. I think the reviewer for *The Downside Review*, 78 (September 1958), pp. 131-4, best summarized the experience of reading this book when he wrote: "C. S. Lewis' books are always delectable. One gets the impression as one reads them that he is sitting on the other side of the hearth and conversing familiarly and yet with great enthusiasm on some subject of inspiring interest. One listens, spell-bound, as he unravels one knotty problem after another, always in language understandable to those who do not possess a fraction of his learning, charmed by the flashes of wit with which he illuminates his meanings. *Reflections on the Psalms* forms the subject of one of the happiest of such conversations."

Discussion Questions

1. Some people have criticized C. S. Lewis for not being scholarly enough in his writing of *Reflections on the Psalms*. Do you think this is a fair criticism? Why or why not?
2. Jack proposes that the Jewish picture of God's judgment reflected in the Psalms is different from the Christian picture of God's judgment. What is the difference? How does Jack find the Jewish picture helpful? Do you agree? Why or why not?
3. What do you think of Jack's view of the cursing passages in the Psalms?
4. According to Jack, why did God not fully reveal the realities of Heaven and Hell to the Jews? How does this connect with the process of Jack's own spiritual development? How has the revelation of Heaven and Hell been important to your own spiritual development?
5. What do you think of what Jack has to say about joy in the Psalms? How do you think we can recover the joy of the Psalmists?
6. What do you think of what Jack has to say about the beauty of the Law? Do his comments make the Jewish view of the Law more understandable to you? Why or why not?
7. What do you think of what Jack has to say about the temptation to "connivance"? Do you ever try to avoid the company of certain people for the reasons he recommends?
8. What do you think of the Jewish response to Nature expressed in the Psalms? Should we seek to recover it? If so, how?
9. What is your response to Jack's thinking about praise?
10. Do you agree or disagree with Jack's view of the relationship between certain pagan myths and Christian truth? Why?

11. How would you describe Jack's view of Scripture? What do you think about it?
12. Do you think that the Christological second meanings that Christians like C. S. Lewis find in the Psalms are justified? Why or why not?
13. Do you have a favorite passage in this book? If so, would you read it aloud to the group?

The Four Loves

The seed of *The Four Loves* was planted when C. S. Lewis received a request, in January 1958, from the Episcopal Radio-TV Foundation of Atlanta, Georgia, to give some radio talks to be broadcast in the United States. The topic of the talks was left up to Jack to decide. He responded in a letter to the Foundation saying: "The subject I want to say something about in the near future in some form or other is the four loves – Storge, Philia, Eros and Agape. This seems to bring in nearly the whole of Christian ethics."[197]

Jack finished writing the scripts for these new broadcast talks in the summer of 1958 and recorded them in London on the 19th and 20th of August of that same year. One hour was devoted to each of the four loves.

However, Jack hit a snag with some of the bishops of the Episcopal Church. It was thought that his talk on Eros was far too frank to be broadcast to an American audience. (Oh, how the times have changed!) Jack was furious. "How can anyone talk about Eros without talking about sex?" he wondered. Jack refused to alter the scripts and so the end result was that these four talks on love were not broadcast as widely as originally planned at that time. Nonetheless, a number of years later the Episcopal Radio-TV Foundation began selling Jack's recordings of these talks, which are now available on CD.[198]

---

[197] *Collected Letters*, Vol. III, p. 941.
[198] To purchase the CDs visit http://episcopalonline.org/.

Jack asked the Foundation for permission to use the scripts for the recordings as the basis for a book. The Foundation gave Jack leave to do so and the result was *The Four Loves*, completed by mid-summer 1959 and published in March 1960. The blurb which Jack himself wrote for the fly-leaf of the first edition best sums up what the book is about:

> The four loves are, of course, Affection, Friendship, Eros and Charity. They have often been dealt with separately by authors as different as Ovid, St Bernard and Stendahl: and usually one or other of them is treated as the only love worth much consideration. Dr Lewis is more a map-maker than a partisan. He marks frontiers and trade-routes and tries to do justice to all.
>
> Three quotations used by the author indicate the principles that govern his survey: from St John, 'God is Love', from Donne, 'That our affections kill us not, nor dye' and from Denis de Rougemont, 'Love ceases to be a demon when he ceases to be a god'.
>
> On the three natural loves much demolition and reconstruction has proved necessary. Affection had to be disentangled from a suffocating over growth of sentimentality, and Eros from some misplaced solemnities. Friendship needed defence against modern neglect and even suspicion.

The Four Loves is, at points, as much biographical as it is theological or philosophical. In reading *The Four Loves* one can see the influence of Jack's relationship with Joy Davidman. The chapter Jack wrote on Eros could hardly have been the same if written before he met his wife. And the chapter on Friendship certainly reflects Jack's lifelong experience of that love—with Arthur Greeves, Owen Barfield, and especially in the context of the Inklings. All in all, the book serves as an excellent analysis of the loves depicted in another great Lewis work: *Till We Have Faces*.

The Four Loves, while not without its faults, is a real gem. Personally, I think Martin D'Arcy got it right in his review for *The New York Times Book Review* (31 July 1960), when he said that *The Four Loves* "deserves to become a minor classic as a modern mirror of souls, a mirror of the virtues and failing of human loving. Lewis combines a novelist's insights into motives with a profound religious understanding."

A C. S. LEWIS DISCUSSION GUIDE

Discussion Questions

1. What do you think of C. S. Lewis' distinctions between "need-love" and "gift-love", "nearness of likeness" and "nearness of approach"?
2. What do you think of Denis de Rougement's statement, "Love ceases to be a demon only when he ceases to be a god?"
3. What do you think of what Jack has to say about love of nature and saying your prayers in a garden early?
4. Do you agree with Jack's views on love of country in his chapter on "Likings and Loves for the Sub-Human"?
5. What do you think of what Jack has to say about rivalry between the loves in the chapter on "Affection"?
6. What positive and negative examples of Affection has Jack given us in his other works?
7. Does Jack introduce a new or deeper understanding of Friendship to you? Have you experienced this? If so, can you describe it?
8. What do you think of the contrast Jack draws between Eros and Friendship?
9. Do you agree with Jack's statement that we do not want to know our friend's affairs? Why or why not?
10. What do you think of what Jack has to say about friendship between men and women?
11. What do you think of Jack's statement about God choosing our friends for us?
12. What do you think of the minor place Jack gives to Eros in marriage?
13. Do you agree with Jack's attitude toward Venus? Why or why not?
14. And how about Jack's attitude toward the body – that the word "ass" is the exquisitely right word?
15. Where does Jack deal with sexual roles, masculinity and

femininity in his fiction? Do you agree with his views on these roles? Why or why not?

16. What do you think of Jack's comments on male headship in marriage?

17. Do you agree with Jack that Eros provides a nearness of likeness to Charity?

18. What do you think of Augustine's view of love versus Jack's view as expressed in the "no safe investment" paragraph?

19. What do you think of Jack's description of God's love for us where he says that: "God, who needs nothing, loves into existence wholly superfluous creatures in order that He may love and perfect them."?

20. There are many great statements in *The Four Loves*. Which is your favorite? Why?

Studies in Words

In *The Collected Letters of C. S. Lewis, Volume III* Walter Hooper tells us that C. S. Lewis began the Easter Term of 1956 at Cambridge University with a series of twice-weekly lectures entitled *Some Difficult Words*. His first lecture on April 19 was on the word "nature", and during the rest of the 1956 term and the Easter Terms of the next three years Jack lectured on the words: sad, wit, free, sense, simple, conscious and conscience. Furthermore, Hooper tells us that it seems to have been Jack's intention from the beginning to make a book of these lectures which were eventually published by Cambridge University Press in September 1960.[199]

In a letter on July 17, 1957 to Jocelyn Gibb, Jack's editor at Geoffrey Bles, Jack refers slightingly to his work on *Studies in Words*. "You couldn't find a duller, less saleable, more erudite, work."[200] And in a letter to Mary Willis Shelburne on December 25, 1958 Jack makes a similar comment. "I have let our correspondence get rather disgracefully behind on my side, not from ceasing to think of you, but from being very busy finishing a book (a dull, academic, technical one, tho' exciting to me) . . ."[201]

When asked by Cambridge University Press to "give a short description of your book in simple non-technical language which will be understood by salesmen and booksellers in all countries" here is what Jack wrote:

---

199 *Collected Letters of C. S. Lewis*, Volume III, p. 739.
200 Ibid., p. 871.
201 Ibid., pp. 1003-1004.

In how many different senses do you use the word wit or nature (or sense itself)? How many more senses of them have you found in old authors? How did such multiplicity of meanings come about? Do you always know which sense you are using yourself? These are the questions to which this book attempts an answer as regards seven words. They have been selected mainly for the light they throw on the history of thought and sentiment. But it is hoped that the study of them will have for the reader (as it has had for the author) a more than historical interest in increasing his awareness of what we are doing when we talk. It belongs on the same shelf as Pearsall Smith's *Four Words*, Owen Barfield's *Poetic Diction*, and Professor Empson's *Structure of Complex Words*.[202]

As indicated in Jack's comment above, the first edition of *Studies in Words* consisted of the following chapters:

1. Introduction
2. Nature
3. Sad
4. Wit
5. Free
6. Sense
7. Simple
8. Conscience and Conscious
9. At the Fringe of Language

Walter Hooper was responsible for adding three additional chapters written by Jack to the book in the second edition printed in 1967. Those chapters are entitled "World", "Life" and "I Dare Say". In a personal e-mail to me Walter Hooper had this to say about that work:

> The additional chapters were amongst the papers Warnie had given Paxford to burn. There was not much work to do to get them ready for the Second Edition of the book, and in doing this I followed a course I believe Lewis already had in mind. I remember working too on the Index, and as I look back on it I wish I had made the index more

---

202 Ibid., p. 1183.

complete. Great writers like Lewis almost never produce good indexes. But I think I drew back from making any more changes than I did.

If nothing else, *Studies in Words* displays to every reader willing to take it on why those who knew C. S. Lewis in his lifetime thought him the best read man of his generation. In this book Jack quotes nearly every major writer from the canon of Western literature from the author(s) of Genesis down to John Henry Newman. However, typical of his time and place, Jack quotes few if any of the great authors of the twentieth century (other than making reference to G. K. Chesterton's Father Brown series)[203]. One must remember that in Jack's day at Oxford the English department covered literature only up through the nineteenth century and Jack had a special personal antipathy for twentieth century poetry as represented by T. S. Eliot.

Nonetheless, *Studies in Words* is a remarkable tour de force. Only someone with a photographic memory like Jack, and someone who had read both broadly and deeply from the Bible (in the original Greek for the New Testament and in numerous translations for the Old Testament), Greek and Latin classical literature, the great works of the Middle Ages, as well as the length and breadth of English literature from Beowulf on down, could come up with the examples of changes in the meaning of words with the seeming ease that he does it. I believe we can see in this book what makes all of C. S. Lewis' books so great. Jack had an immense vocabulary, understanding and deep acquaintance with the English language as well as all of English literature. In short, as a reader, literary critic, amateur theologian and writer of fiction, Jack lived in a very large world. Consequently the reader of Jack's works seldom feels cramped. Rather, to read C. S. Lewis is to have one's mind and heart, not only educated, but enlarged and enthused.

---

[203] See C. S. Lewis, *Studies in Words*, Cambridge: Cambridge University Press, 1991, p. 178.

Discussion Questions

1. In his Introduction C. S. Lewis explains his method in *Studies in Words*, a method which results in this philosophical reflection: "There is something, either in the structure of the mind or in the things it thinks about, which can produce the same results under very different conditions."[204] What do you think of this?

2. On page eleven Jack makes a statement about the etymology of the word "candlestick" which reveals he was thinking like a philologist from a rather young age. What other examples from Jack's life and writing can you think of which display his desire to define words precisely?

3. In this book, as in many of his works, Jack adopts a conversational tone. For example, on page twenty-one he writes: "When I was a boy—a *bourgeois* boy—it was applied to my social class by the class above it; *bourgeois* meant 'not aristocratic, therefore vulgar'". Do you find Jack's tone off-putting or inviting? Why? What other examples of this tone have you come across in his writing?

4. Out of all the words Jack could have chosen for this study why do you think he has chosen the words which he has?

5. Does Jack's chapter on "Nature" remind you of a particular one of Lewis' other books? Consider especially what he says on page thirty-seven.

6. What similarities, in general, do you see between this book and Jack's other writings?

7. Jack's lifelong friend and lawyer, Owen Barfield, once wrote about *The Five C. S. Lewises*. The five he had in mind were: Lewis the original literary critic, the highly successful author of fiction, the writer and broadcaster of popular Christian apologetics, and Lewis both before and after conversion. Despite the fact that we can all

---

204 *Studies in Words*, p. 6.

easily identify five different Lewises there was something, Barfield maintained, which united them all. He called it "presence of mind". Barfield wrote, "somehow what he [Lewis] thought about everything was secretly present in what he said about anything." (*Owen Barfield on C. S. Lewis*, p. 122.) Do you think that is a true assessment? And if so, how is that truth borne out in *Studies in Words*?

8. One can see in this book, as much as in *The Abolition of Man*, Lewis as the great believer in and defender of the concept of Natural Law. In fact he almost argues for this, however subtly, in the use of one great quote, and that not even from Holy Writ, but from Sophocles' *Antigone*. (See p. 59.) What do you think of this?

9. Jack's interest in the levels of meaning in a word like "sad" may not have been purely academic. Do you think it merely coincidental that Jack should choose to write and lecture about the meaning of this word at the very time when he was enduring the greatest sadness of his own life, namely his own wife's battle with cancer and subsequent death?

10. On pages 131 and 132 Jack writes about a number of words which have fallen victim to what he calls "verbicide". What other words can you think of which have undergone the same fate? How can we avoid committing verbicide in the future?

11. Which chapter of *Studies in Words* did you like the best? Why?

12. Do you have a favorite quote or passage from this book? If so, would you read it aloud to the group?

13. What new thing did you learn from Jack in this book?

The World's Last Night and Other Essays

The World's Last Night and Other Essays contains seven essays previously published by C. S. Lewis in various periodicals. The publication of this book came about as follows.

John McCallum, of Harcourt, Brace & World, approached Jack in early 1959 about publishing an essay collection. McCallum originally wanted to include in the volume: "The Efficacy of Prayer", "On Obstinacy in Belief", "Religion and Rocketry" and "The World's Last Night". Jack suggested adding "Lilies that Fester" which originally appeared in *The Twentieth Century*, CLVII (April 1955). However, Jack declined to include one of McCallum's choices: "Prudery and Philology" which had appeared in the *Spectator*. Another one of Jack's additions to the collection was "Good Work and Good Works" which also appeared in *The Catholic Art Quarterly*, XXIII (Christmas 1959). Jack wanted to include in this volume his essay "On Three Ways of Writing for Children" which originally appeared in a Librarian's magazine. But apparently McCallum didn't think this piece suited the rest of the collection. Jack wanted to title the book: *Essays in Reaction*.[205] However, as publishers often do, Harcourt, Brace & World opted for a different title to which Jack agreed.[206]

The title essay, "The World's Last Night", originally appeared as "Christian Hope: It's Meaning for Today" in *Religion in Life*, 21 (1951-1952).[207] The editor of *HIS* magazine had, apparently without

---

205 *Collected Letters*, Vol. III, pp. 1037-1038.
206 Ibid., p. 1053.
207 Ibid., p. 424.

Lewis' knowledge, taken this essay and reprinted it as "The World's Last Night" in *HIS* XV (May 1955).[208]

The essay entitled "Religion and Rocketry" originally appeared in the *Christian Herald*, LXXXI (April 1958) as "Will We Lose God in Outer Space?" [209] Jack did not like the title given to this essay by the *Christian Herald* and so he re-titled it.

"The Efficacy of Prayer" originally appeared in *The Atlantic Monthly*, CCIII (January 1959). And "On Obstinacy in Belief" originally appeared in *The Sewanee Review*, LXIII (Autumn 1955).

"Lilies that Fester" was the only one of the essays on which Jack did any significant editing prior to inclusion in this collection. This was due to Jack's running debate with E. M. Forster on the meaning of Humanism.[210]

The final essay to be added to this collection was "Screwtape Proposes a Toast". The original *Screwtape Letters*, while being Jack's most popular work (before Narnia), was his least favorite to write. Jack said that the act of projecting himself into the mindset of a devil almost smothered him before he was finished with the work.[211] Nonetheless, over the years, as the horrible memory of writing *Screwtape* grew weaker, ideas which demanded "Screwtapian" treatment kept popping into Jack's mind. Then *The Saturday Evening Post* invited Jack to publish an essay in their magazine and that "pressed the trigger".[212] "Screwtape Proposes a Toast" appeared in the 19 December 1959 edition of *The Saturday Evening Post*.

The World's Last Night and Other Essays was published only in the United States for a number of reasons. (1) The project was initiated by Harcourt, Brace & World for the American reading public. (2) Jack didn't think the English reader would be much interested in buying a collection of essays on different subjects. (3) Jack wanted his English publisher, Geoffrey Bles, to get on with publishing *The Four Loves*. And (4) Jack was afraid that such a collection of essays

---

208 Ibid., p. 891.
209 Ibid., p. 921.
210 Ibid., p. 1054.
211 C. S. Lewis, *The Screwtape Letters*, New York: Macmillan, 1977, p. xiv.
212 Ibid., pp. xiv-xv.

would be viewed as "old work" by the English public.[213] Perhaps all of these reasons suggest how much more popular Lewis' work was in America in the late 50's. American readers were ready to gobble up anything written by Lewis at the time, British readers less so.[214] Thus *The World's Last Night and Other Essays* was published by Harcourt, Brace & World of New York City on 10 February 1960.[215]

---

213 *Collected Letters*, Vol. III, p. 1062.
214 However, Jack's editor at Geoffrey Bles, Jocelyn Gibb, disagreed with him on this whole matter and very much wanted to publish a collection of Jack's essays. (See *Collected Letters*, Vol. III, p. 1247.) Therefore Bles eventually published *They Asked for a Paper*, a much more scholarly collection of essays, in 1962. But perhaps Jack was correct in his understanding of both the American and British reading publics; *They Asked for a Paper* is now out of print in Great Britain, whereas *The World's Last Night* continues to sell in America.
215 Ibid., p. 1132.

A C. S. Lewis Discussion Guide

Discussion Questions

The Efficacy of Prayer

1. How does C. S. Lewis answer the question: "What sort of evidence would prove the efficacy of prayer?" Do you agree with his answer? Why or why not?
2. Jack says that assurance of answered prayer can't come on the basis of scientific experiment, but only on the basis of personal relationship. What does he mean by this? What do you think?
3. What does Jack have to say about the question: *Does prayer work?* How do you respond to the same question?
4. How would you summarize what Jack says in this essay?

On Obstinacy in Belief

1. What does Jack say that Christian faith, at least initially, is based upon? Do you agree? Why or why not?
2. Why does "wish fulfillment" not explain faith? Jack deals with this topic in other places. Do you remember where? What light do his comments elsewhere throw on this topic?
3. How would you summarize the point of this essay?

Lilies That Fester

1. What does Jack mean by the statement: "Lilies that fester smell far worse than weeds."
2. Given what Jack says here about the meddlesome nature of rulers what would you gather his overall political outlook was?
3. Why does Jack say that sanctity and culture should not be dictated from above?
4. How would you summarize this essay?

Screwtape Proposes a Toast

1. In one word, to what quality would you say Screwtape is proposing a toast?
2. What did Screwtape see as the plusses and minuses of sin in Western society at the end of the 1950s? How might Screwtape view this same issue today? What issues might Screwtape touch upon, and what would his viewpoint be on those issues, if he were proposing a toast at the Tempter's Training College in our time?
3. Why do you think Jack chose to add this "Screwtapian" reflection to the canon?

Good Work and Good Works

1. According to Jack, what kind of work does God want us to be doing for our occupation, if it is within our choice? What are we to do if it is not within our choice?
2. Which do you think is more important, doing "good work" or "good works"? Why?
3. Why is it important that our "good works" of charity and our occupational work be done well?

Religion and Rocketry

1. How are the points in this essay illustrated in Jack's *Cosmic Trilogy*?
2. How does Jack answer the question "Will we lose God in outer space?" Do you agree with his answer? Why or why not?

The World's Last Night

1. What does Jack say are the two reasons for modern embarrassment over the doctrine of the Second Coming of Christ? How does he answer these objections?
2. How would you compare and contrast what Jack has to say on this doctrine compared to some of the popular

theology of today on this point (for example: the *Left Behind* series)?

3. Do you find Jack's approach to this doctrine helpful? Why or why not?
4. Which one of Jack's essays in this collection is your favorite? Why? Which is your least favorite? Why?
5. What ideas expressed in this collection do you have questions about?
6. What ideas do you want to think further about?
7. What ideas do you want to take action on in your life?

A Grief Observed

A Grief Observed was written by C. S. Lewis following the death of his wife Helen Joy Davidman Gresham in July 1960 from cancer. As Jack himself says in chapter IV of *A Grief Observed* the book was written as a "defense against total collapse, a safety valve."[216] Douglas Gresham, Lewis' step-son, tells us that Jack did not originally intend to publish his jottings about his experience of grief. However, upon reading through his journal sometime later Jack changed his mind and thought that his writing about grief might be helpful to others going through a similar experience.[217]

Jack originally published *A Grief Observed* under the pseudonym of N. W. Clerk and it was only after his death that the executors of his literary estate decided to publish the book under Jack's own name. N. W. are the initials for "Nat Whilk" which is the Old English for "I know not whom." "Clerk" is the Old English word for "scholar." Thus the pseudonym means "I know not what scholar."

Walter Hooper tells us that Jack originally submitted the manuscript to his literary agent Spencer Curtis Brown under the name *Dimidius* which is the Latin for "halved," a revealing statement about the one-flesh nature of marriage and how Jack felt truncated after Joy's death. Curtis Brown, in order to maintain Jack's anonymity, sent the manuscript to Faber, who had not previously published any of Lewis'

---

216 N. W. Clerk, *A Grief Observed*, Greenwich, CT: The Seabury Press, 1963, p. 47.
217 Douglas H. Gresham, Foreword to *A Grief Observed*, New York: HarperCollins, 1994, p. 12.

books. T.S. Eliot, who was working for Faber at that time and who knew Lewis, immediately recognized the writing. It was Eliot who suggested that a plausible English pen name be used. Jack selected the name "N. W. Clerk," combining "Nat Whilk," a pen name he had used before, with Clerk. Jack also uses the letter "H," being the first initial of his wife's first name, to refer to his spouse in order to preserve his and her anonymity.

Hooper says that the reason Jack used a pseudonym was so as not to embarrass or upset his friends, many of whom did not approve of the marriage or attend Joy's funeral.[218] Chad Walsh traces the reason for using a pseudonym to Jack's characteristic delicacy.[219] Jack was certainly reticent to talk or write about his personal life. In one sense the issue goes back to what Jack wrote in *The Personal Heresy*: "The poet is not a man who asks me to look at him; he is a man who says 'look at that' and points; the more I follow the pointing of his finger, the less I can possibly see of him ... I must make of him not a spectacle but a pair of spectacles."[220] Even Jack's autobiography, *Surprised by Joy*, leaves out many personal items of interest from his life which would normally be included in an autobiography.

It has been debated whether or not *A Grief Observed* is autobiographical. In an essay entitled "C. S. Lewis and C. S. Lewises" Walter Hooper suggests that the book was not, strictly, autobiographical. "Lewis told me how he intended the book to be understood. 'The structure of it,' he said, 'is based on Dante's *Divine Comedy*. You go down and down and down. Then, as in Dante, when you hit bottom and pass Lucifer's waist you go *up* to defense of God's goodness.' Lewis went on to say that, while he had to make it sound like straight autobiography if the book was to help the average sufferer, he took various precautions to prevent *anyone* thinking it was by him or about his grief."[221]

---

218 *Companion & Guide*, pp. 194-195.
219 Chad Walsh, Afterword to *A Grief Observed*, New York: Bantam, 1976, p. 149.
220 *The Personal Heresy*, pp. 11-12.
221 Walter Hooper, "C. S. Lewis and C. S. Lewises", in *The Riddle of Joy*, Grand Rapids: Eerdmans, 1989, pp. 44-47.

On the other hand, Douglas Gresham has written the following about the autobiographical nature of the book: "*A Grief Observed* is true and therefore it is valuable to all who read it. It cost Jack great pain and yet rewarded him with deeper understanding. I find it hard, even to this day, to read, for I was there when he wrote it and I was a part of his agony and he a part of mine.[222]

One false notion about Jack which Douglas Gresham corrects is the idea that Jack had never known any real pain until the death of Joy, the idea that in writing *The Problem of Pain* Jack was merely acting as an "arm-chair theologian." This false view of Lewis is suggested in the Anthony Hopkins version of the movie "Shadowlands" with screenplay written by William Nicholson. Gresham gets closer to the truth when he writes about Lewis that:

> . . . pain was not an experience with which he was unfamiliar. He had met grief as a child, he lost his mother when he was nine years old. He had grieved for friends lost to him over the years, some lost in battle during the first World War, others to sickness.
>
> He had written also about the great poets and their songs of love, but somehow neither his learning nor his experiences had ever prepared him for the combination of both the great love and the great loss which is its counterpoint.[223]

Jack knew pain before the death of his wife, though the pain after her death was certainly greater than any he had ever experienced. The amazing thing about C. S. Lewis was that he was able to turn his own personal pain into a source of help and hope for many others who have trod the way of grief.

---

222 Douglas H. Gresham, *Lenten Lands*, New York: HarperCollins, 1988, p. 131.
223 Gresham, Foreword to *A Grief Observed*, pp. 5-6.

A C. S. LEWIS DISCUSSION GUIDE

Discussion Questions

1. With his wife's death, the intensity of C. S. Lewis' love and grief brought on emotional and spiritual struggles that almost made his earlier faith seem simplistic. Do you see this as a weakness of faith, or does the honest expression of his struggles—unafraid to voice even his most severe doubts–show a profound trust in God?

2. In the first chapter of *A Grief Observed* Jack wrote that he was not in much danger of ceasing to believe in God but that he was in danger of coming to believe dreadful things about him. What dreadful things was Jack in danger of believing as a result of Joy's death? Have you ever felt this way about God?

3. With his well developed theology of suffering, why do you think Jack had such great difficulty accepting God's hand in his own bereavement? Were his earlier views inadequate to confront real grief? Was he previously writing "beyond his own ability to believe"? Is proper theology ever sufficient by itself?

4. Jack wrote about his love-relationship with Joy that it left "no cranny of heart or body unsatisfied." He then went on to argue that: "If God were a substitute for love we ought to have lost all interest in Him." What do you think he meant by this statement? Do you think his argument for the existence of God is a convincing one? Why or why not?

5. Jack says that it is difficult to bear with people who say there is no death or that death does not matter. Have you noticed yourself or others trying to side-step the reality of death? How? What effect do you think this has on those who are grieving the death of a loved one?

6. If you have experienced the loss of a spouse, or someone else close to you, do you identify with what Jack says in this book? In what way? How has Jack's writing helped you to cope with grief?

7. Jack suggests that all the supposedly Christian imagery of family reunions on the further shore is not biblical but rather stems from poor hymns and lithographs. What do you think he means by this statement? Do you agree with him? Why or why not?

8. What do you think of Jack's concepts of Purgatory and prayers for the dead as expressed in this book?

9. After reading *A Grief Observed* do you think that Jack lost his faith in God after the death of his wife? And if so, did he regain faith? Why or why not?

10. What do you think of Jack's statement that your belief either in God or not in God will not be very serious if nothing much is staked on it.?

11. In chapter III Jack states that in the matter of suffering a perfectly good God is hardly less formidable than a "Cosmic Sadist." What do you think he means by this? Do you think he is right? Why or why not?

12. Jack uses the analogy of a drowning man to describe the frantic reaching out for God performed by the person going through grief. The drowning man and the frantically grieving man cannot be helped because they clutch and grab. Do you find this analogy helpful? Encouraging? Or discouraging? Why?

13. What do you think of Jack's view that bereavement may not be the truncation of the growing marriage relationship but one of its phases, not the interruption of the dance, but the next figure?

14. What do you make of Jack's experience that the less he mourns Joy the nearer he seems to her? If you have lost a loved one was this the case for you or for other bereaved people you know?

15. In the final chapter of the book Jack says that grief is like a long, winding valley where each curve may show forth a wholly new landscape. What new landscapes or insights has *A Grief Observed* revealed to you about C. S. Lewis, about grief, about God, about yourself?

16. At the end of the book Jack takes Plato's cave analogy and applies it, in his own words, to the situation of grief. What does Jack learn through the contemplation of this idea in his situation? What hope does it offer?

17. Jack says that God is the great iconoclast. What does he mean by this? How does this transform his view of grief?

An Experiment in Criticism

*I*n the months following his wife's death in July 1960, C. S. Lewis wrote what his biographer, George Sayer, called one of his best books of literary criticism, *An Experiment in Criticism*.[224] The idea for the book arose from conversations Jack had been having with literary friends for years. He was seeing an increasing problem among his students, namely that they viewed great literature "wholly through the spectacles of other books."[225] Then Jack thought he saw a way out of this debacle: to look at books from the reader's point of view. For example, according to Jack a good reader is one who re-reads books and has his life enriched and ennobled by the experience.

Jack wrote *An Experiment in Criticism* quickly. By 25 January 1961 his Belfast friend, Arthur Greeves, was reading the proofs of the book.[226] The book was published by Cambridge University Press on 13 October 1961.

Jack anticipated that his book would be very unpopular. But on the contrary the book initially elicited some "fan mail" from a few Cambridge undergraduates. Jack took this as a hopeful sign that perhaps the tide in literary criticism was turning at last.[227]

Christopher Derrick's review of *An Experiment in Criticism* well summed up both the inherent danger seen in this book and its great

---

[224] Sayer, *Jack*, p. 398.
[225] C. S. Lewis, *An Experiment in Criticism*, Cambridge: Cambridge University Press, 1961, p. 128.
[226] *Collected Letters*, Volume III, p. 1229.
[227] Ibid., pp. 1287-1288.

value. Derrick writes that this book "is a plea for a resolutely low-church attitude to criticism, and already it has drawn some angry gunfire from representatives of the high and powerful priesthood which it threatens. The point is that this cultural priesthood not only offers . . . something rather like a surrogate religion, but also creates in its observants an habitual attitude of anxious prickly suspicion towards books, and even towards life and the universe at large. Dr Lewis insists that this is a bad thing, that imaginative literature offers an immensely valuable 'enlargement of our being' . . . he is wonderfully right; for those in favour of happiness but distrustful of politics and the elevated disapproving mind, his book is a charter and a liberation."[228]

---

228 Hooper, *C. S. Lewis: Companion & Guide*, p. 523.

Discussion Questions

1. How would you define what C. S. Lewis' "experiment" in criticism actually is?

2. In Chapter I Jack articulates four key differences between "the few" and "the many" readers. What are those differences? Do you agree with the way Jack classifies readers? Why or why not?

3. In Chapter II Jack notes that in some supposedly literary families the only real literary experience may be occurring where a young boy is reading *Treasure Island* by flashlight under his bedcovers. What does Jack mean by this? What do you think?

4. In Chapter III Jack draws a comparison between the way the few and the many use books and the way the few and the many use other forms of art like pictures and music. He says that the many "use" art while the few "receive" it. What does he mean by this distinction? Do you find this distinction valuable? Why or why not?

5. In Chapter IV Jack delineates five characteristics of the unliterary reader. What are they? What do the unliterary most want out of their reading? Jack distinguishes three main types of this thing the unliterary long for in their reading. What are those three types? Do the literary enjoy these same things in reading? If so, what is the difference here between the literary and the unliterary reader?

6. In Chapter V Jack defines six characteristics of myth. What are these? What does he say is the difference between the person who enjoys myth and the person who reads only for the "Event"? Jack maintains that great myth can be communicated through poor writing. What favorite author of Jack's is an example of this?

7. In Chapter VI Jack defines the meanings of fantasy. What is a literary fantasy? What are the three meanings of fantasy as a psychological term? What does Jack say is the difference between Egoistic and Disinterested Castle-building? What would be an example of the latter

from Jack's own life, which moved into the realm of the literary?

8. In Chapter VII Jack describes two different types of literary realism. What are they? Do they ever function independent of one another? What does Jack say was the dominant taste in 1961? How about today? In this chapter Jack says, "Not to acquire a taste for the realistic is childish in the bad sense; to have lost the taste for marvels and adventures is no more a matter for congratulation than losing our teeth, our hair, our palate, and finally, our hopes." What do you think of this?

9. According to Chapter VIII how do literary people sometimes misread?

10. At the beginning of Chapter IX Jack sums up the five points he has been trying to make so far in the book. What are they? Why does Jack suggest that school children should not engage in literary criticism?

11. According to Chapter X what is the significance of the fact that less and less of the literary and hardly any at all of the unliterary read poetry? What does Jack suggest is the difference between reading older poetry and newer poetry? Do you agree or disagree? Why? According to Jack, what errors do the literary often commit in reading poetry?

12. In Chapter XI how does Jack want to define good literature? What are the three advantages he notes which go along with this definition? Would you agree with his definition of good literature? Why or why not? Which types of literary criticism does Jack find helpful? Which kind does he not find helpful? Why?

13. In the Epilogue how does Jack answer the question: "Why should we read at all?" What do you think of his answer?

Letters to Malcolm: Chiefly on Prayer

C. S. Lewis attempted to write a book on prayer as early as 1953. This is indicated in one of his Latin letters (January 5, 1953) to Don Giovanni Calabria, founder of the Congregation of the Poor Servants of Divine Providence in Verona, Italy. Jack invited Calabria's prayers concerning a book he was trying to write on private prayer for the use of lay people, especially recent converts to the Christian faith who, as yet, had no "sustained and regular habit of prayer". Jack took on the job of writing this book because he found so few books on prayer for those who were still "babes" in the Faith. However, Jack found writing the book difficult and so he was unsure if God wanted him to continue or not.[229]

Jack mentioned the book on prayer to Calabria once again, on 17 March 1953.[230] However, by 15 February 1954 he wrote to another correspondent, Sister Penelope, to say that he had to give up the book on prayer because it was clearly not for him.[231]

Only a forty five page manuscript of this early attempt at a book on prayer still survives. One thing is clear from this early manuscript: Jack did not want to come off looking like he was teaching other people about prayer. He felt like he was still in the learning stages himself. Why then, did Jack think he should write a book about prayer at all? As he put it in that early manuscript: there are many things which we all learn in school which are most successfully explained to us, not by a

---

229 *Collected Letters*, Volume III, pp. 275-277.
230 Ibid., p. 307.
231 Ibid., p. 428.

teacher, but by another student. Sometimes one fourth grade student can help another fourth grader understand what an adult cannot help him or her to comprehend at all. The two students "speak the same language and have the same difficulties." There are certain kinds of help best provided by someone who is just a little bit ahead in their understanding than you are. That, Jack claimed, was his "only excuse for writing a book on prayer."[232]

Jack's main problem in writing the book had to do with finding a suitable form for what he wished to say. His early attempt came off too "preachy", at least from his own perspective. Then in the spring of 1963 the right form suggested itself: an imaginary correspondence between himself and a friend, Malcolm, about prayer. With that format in mind the book flowed from Jack's pen in March and April of 1963. Thus, on 22 April he was able to write to Mary Willis Shelburne: "I've finished a book on Prayer. Don't know if it is any good."[233] And on 16 May Jack was able to tell his editor at Geoffrey Bles, Jocelyn Gibb, that the book was with the typist.[234] When Gibb received the manuscript a few weeks later he wrote back to Lewis: "Respect and admire you as I do, this *Letters to Malcolm* . . . has knocked me flat. Not quite; I can just sit up and shout hurrah, and again, hurrah. It's the best you've done since *The Problem of Pain*. By Jove, this is something of a present to a publisher!"[235]

Gibb asked Jack to write something for the blurb on the flyleaf of the book, but Jack always struggled with what he called "blurbology". Still, a couple of Jack's suggestions did make their way on to the flyleaf of the first edition:

> Malcolm is a friend of C. S. Lewis' to whom he writes these letters: twenty-two of them. Prayer is the theme; not corporate but private prayer. It could be a delicate subject but Mr. Lewis, as we would expect, does not treat it as anything strange or awkward. He simply asks his readers to imagine themselves being allowed to listen to two very ordinary laymen discussing the practical and speculative

---

232 Hooper, *Companion & Guide*, pp. 378-379.
233 *Collected Letters*, Vol. III, p. 1423.
234 Ibid., p. 1427.
235 *Companion & Guide*, p. 380.

problems of prayer as these appear to them: the last thing he would claim is to be teaching.

Some passages are controversial, but this, he tells us, is almost by accident. The wayfaring Christian cannot altogether ignore recent Anglican theology when it has been built as a barricade across the high road. The book ends with a haunting passage of speculation about the Resurrection of the body.

Witty, sometimes gay, sometimes serious, Mr. Lewis has shown once again that he has no equal. His sane, imaginative approach to Christianity, lucidity of expression and richness of metaphor are qualities which bring him respect and admiration from the whole world over.

Since the book was first published, down to this day, readers have wondered who Malcolm really was. That "wondering" only betrays the reality that C. S. Lewis was just as good at imaginative letter-writing in 1963 as he was when he wrote Screwtape in the early 1940s. But sadly, this was to be the last of Jack's imaginary letter-writing, or for that matter, the last of any writing from his pen. For he died on November 22, 1963, the same day as the assassination of President John F. Kennedy and the death of Aldous Huxley, author of *Brave New World*.

An early edition of portions of this book (letters 15-17) was published under the title *Beyond the Bright Blur* on 25 December 1963 by Harcourt, Brace & World of New York City. This limited edition was intended to be a New Year's greeting from Jack to his readers in the United States. *Letters to Malcolm: Chiefly on Prayer* was published in England by Geoffrey Bles on 27 January 1964 and in the United States by Harcourt, Brace & World on 12 February of the same year.[236] The reviewer for *The Times* spoke for many readers when he said, "Only Screwtape will be glad that Mr. Lewis has written his last letter."[237]

---

236 Ibid., p. 809
237 Ibid., p. 392.

A C. S. Lewis Discussion Guide

Topical Index by Letter

Letter	Topic
1.	Corporate Prayer/Liturgy
2.	Ready-made & Home-made Prayers
3.	Asking Prayers of the Saints
	When & Where to Pray
	The Role of the Body in Prayer
4.	Why pray when God knows all?
	What should we pray about?
5.	Festoons to The Lord's Prayer
6.	Religion & Guilt
7.	Petitionary Prayer
8.	The Serious Business of Prayer
9.	Does prayer change God?
10.	Prayer: Part of the Tapestry of Providence
11.	The Prayer of Faith
12.	Levels of Prayer
	Intercessory Prayer
13.	The Soliloquy of Prayer
14.	Practicing The Presence of God
15.	Breaking Through The Fourth Wall
16.	The Use of Images
17.	Thanksgiving & Adoration (Looking At & Looking Along)
18.	Penitential Prayer
19.	Holy Communion
20.	Forgiveness
	Prayers for the Dead
	Purgatory
21.	The Duty of Prayer
22.	"Liberal Christians"
	Heaven
	Resurrection of the Senses

Discussion Questions

1. What do you think of C. S. Lewis' statement about liturgy in the first letter, that it is our job as lay people to "take what we are given and make the best of it"? How about what he has to say about his desire that the liturgy of the church should be "always and everywhere the same"?
2. After reading letter two, which manner of prayer do you think Jack valued most and why: ready-made or home-made prayers? Which do you value most? Why?
3. In letter three, what do you think of what Jack has to say about asking prayers of the saints?
4. What do you make of Jack's comment in letter four that people who haven't learned to ask God for childish things will be less ready to ask God for great things?
5. Which of Jack's festoons on The Lord's Prayer in letter five do you find most helpful? Why?
6. In letter six Jack writes that he often prays only for the amount of self-knowledge he can handle at that moment. How might this practice help one deal appropriately with the "vague sense of guilt" we all feel from time to time?
7. Why does Jack say in letter seven that we cannot properly remove petitionary prayer from Christianity? Do you agree with him? Why or why not?
8. What do you think of Jack's statement in letter eight that the "hiddenness" of God may press most painfully on people who are nearest to God? Have you ever experienced this?
9. In letter nine what do you think of Jack's answer to the question: "Does prayer change God?" Do you agree with his answer? Why or why not?
10. In letter ten Jack writes that if providence exists at all then everything that happens is providential and every providence is a special providence. Do you believe that God is involved in all events? Why or why not?

11. In letter eleven Jack writes that Jesus' prayer in Gethsemane is the model prayer for most of us: "Thy will be done." He says that praying for mountains to be removed can wait. What do you think?

12. In letter twelve Jack suggests there is a certain ease in intercessory prayer that we ought to be wary of. For example: it's easier to pray for a bore than to visit him or her. Which is easier for you — praying for yourself or for others? Why? Where do you most need to grow in prayer?

13. What do you think of Jack's concept, in letter thirteen, of prayer as soliloquy, God speaking to God through human beings?

14. In letter fourteen Jack writes that we may ignore God but we cannot evade God for God is present everywhere. God walks everywhere *incognito* but in a way which is not hard to detect. Our real job is to remember God, to attend to God's presence. In fact, Jack says, our task is to wake up and stay awake. How does Jack's concept of *practicing the presence of God*, which he borrows from Brother Lawrence, transform the practice of prayer? Has this ever worked for you?

15. In letter fifteen what does Jack have to say about "putting himself in the presence of God"? Does his practice of remembering the "stage set" and seeking to address the "Author of the play" help you in any way?

16. In letter sixteen Jack says that mental images play an important part in his prayers but that he must "kiss them as they fly." What part do mental images play in your own prayers? Do you find certain images helpful? Are some not helpful? Explain.

17. What do you think of Jack's practice (explained in letter seventeen) of making every pleasure into a channel of adoration? Have you ever done this? Has this helped you to make prayer more a part of your moment-by-moment existence?

18. In letter eighteen Jack says that the wrath of God and the pardon of God are both analogies, but they are both concepts we need to keep in mind when it comes to prayer because such concepts are important to every personal relationship. What do you think? Does Jack's reasoning in this letter help you to engage more effectively in petitionary prayer?

19. In letter nineteen Jack writes that in Holy Communion he finds the "veil between the worlds" most "thin and permeable to divine operation". He says that in Communion a hand from the hidden country touches not only our souls but also our bodies. What does he mean by this? Do his thoughts make Holy Communion more meaningful to you? Why or why not?

20. In letter twenty what do you think of Jack's concepts of praying for the dead and Purgatory? Do you agree with him? Why or why not?

21. In letter twenty-one Jack writes that just because prayer is painful that doesn't mean it isn't something we weren't created to do. Once we are perfected, prayer will be a delight and no longer just a duty. In the mean time we must simply get on with praying. What do you think of this? Does this encourage you in your prayer life? Why and how?

22. In letter twenty-two what do you think of Jack's concept of "the resurrection of the senses"? What does he mean by this? Do you agree with his view? Why or why not?

The Discarded Image

As C. S. Lewis explains in the Preface to *The Discarded Image* this book is based upon a course of lectures which he taught more than once at Oxford.[238] In 1931 Jack lectured for the first time on "Prolegomena to Medieval Poetry". In 1939 he did the same for Renaissance Poetry. In 1944 he lectured on Renaissance Literature more generally. Then in 1954 his last series of lectures at Oxford was entitled "Prolegomena to Medieval Literature". These lectures were repeated at Cambridge during his years there as Professor of Medieval and Renaissance English Literature. It seems likely that Jack began compiling *The Discarded Image* shortly after giving a series of lectures on medieval poetry in the winter of 1961.[239] By July 1962 he was writing the Preface to the book, thus indicating that his work of putting the lectures into book form was complete.[240]

One of Jack's former students, Arthur Lewis (no relation), once told me he felt that C. S. Lewis was the best lecturer at Oxford in the 1930s and early 1940s. Arthur Lewis explained that part of the attraction in Jack's lectures was his style. Jack would invite his students to listen to what he had to say without taking notes. Then he might stop and dictate something very specific for his students to write down. Then Jack would invite his audience to simply listen again.

---

238 C. S. Lewis, *The Discarded Image*, Cambridge: Cambridge University Press, 1964, p. ix.
239 *Collected Letters*, Vol. III, pp. 1361-1362.
240 *Discarded Image*, p. x.

Jack was also a master of time management. He would often begin his lectures while still making his way into the lecture hall itself. Then he would invariably borrow a watch from a student in the front row. (He once explained that the reason he didn't wear a watch himself was that he could never keep it going; he was very poor at handling anything of a mechanical nature!) One of those students in Jack's early lectures from whom he would borrow a watch was Roger Lancelyn Green, later a friend and biographer. When Jack was coming to the end of his talk he would gather up all his papers, return the borrowed watch to Green, and finish his lecture just as he strode out the back door of the hall. Given this background it appears most appropriate that Jack eventually dedicated *The Discarded Image* to none other than Roger Lancelyn Green.[241]

On 28 December 1962 Jack wrote to Colin Eccleshare of Cambridge University Press because Eccleshare had asked him for information that would be helpful in the promotion of *The Discarded Image*.[242] Jack was concerned that his book would be viewed as merely following after the pattern set by E. M. W. Tillyard's *The Elizabethan World Picture*. In fact, Jack explained, the situation was the reverse. His own lectures on "Prolegomena to Medieval Poetry" at Oxford had given Tillyard the idea of doing the same thing for Renaissance studies.

Jack communicated to Eccleshare that he hoped his book would have a three-fold appeal. First, he thought the chapters on "Selected Materials" might have some things of interest to other scholars like himself. Second, he viewed the main body of the book as being directed to students of medieval literature. And third, he hoped that the general reader would find his treatment of the middle ages to be of "larger interest". Jack desired that his readers would find the discarded worldview of the medieval period to be of interest for its "emotional and aesthetic impact". He felt strongly that all people should consider the character of *all* worldviews including their own.[243]

---

241 See my essays on Jack's years at Oxford and Cambridge in *C. S. Lewis: Life, Works, and Legacy*, Vol. I., pp. 174, 199.
242 *Collected Letters*, Vol. III, p. 1397.
243 *Collected Letters*, Vol. III, pp. 1397-1398.

Jack worked on correcting a proof copy of *The Discarded Image* during the spring of 1963. He delivered that corrected copy to Cambridge University Press on 15 May of that year.[244] The book was published posthumously on 7 May 1964.[245]

Derek Brewer, one of Jack's former students, reviewed the book for the *Birmingham Post* and said, "The best in the man and his books was more than generous; it was noble. It does you good to read his learned books, not because you are preached at, but because to read them is for the mind what a walk over fine, sometimes rough, country, in good weather is for the healthy body." And Helen Gardner, one of Jack's colleagues, wrote a review for *The Listener* in which she summed up the impact of Jack's life and work on herself: "Whether we were his pupils in the classroom or no, we are all his pupils and we shall not look upon his like again."[246]

---

244 Ibid., p. 1427.
245 Ibid., p. 1362.
246 Hooper, *Companion & Guide*, p. 548.

Discussion Questions

1. What are the chief characteristics of the "Medieval Situation"? How do these differ from the chief characteristics of our own age?
2. What "Reservations" does Jack state in Chapter II concerning his "Model" of the middle ages?
3. What sources are most necessary for a student of medieval literature to read? Why does Jack not expound upon these sources?
4. What sources from the classical period does Jack focus upon? Which one of these classical sources directly influenced one of Jack's own books? Which book?
5. What does *The Discarded Image* reveal about the scope and depth of Jack's own reading?
6. What did Pagans and Christians have in common during "the seminal period"?
7. How did knowledge of Plato differ in the medieval and Renaissance periods? Why?
8. Who is the second greatest author of the seminal period? What key idea did Jack borrow from him which was vitally important to Jack's own philosophy and theology?
9. After reading the chapter on "The Heavens" do you think Michael Ward's thesis in *Planet Narnia* is more or less believable?
10. What are the chief differences between the manner in which a medieval person and a modern person looks at "the heavens"?
11. What are the Longaevi and the four theories in regard to their origin and identity?
12. What was the purpose of the mappemounde?
13. How does our educational system today differ from that of the middle ages?
14. How were medieval people like Tolkien's Hobbits?

15. What was the great vice and what was the great virtue of medieval literature?
16. What was the typical activity of the medieval author?
17. What was the chief characteristic of medieval art?
18. How were medieval books like the cathedrals?
19. Do you have a favorite quote from this book? If so, would you read it to the group?
20. How do you think knowledge of medieval literature impacted Jack's own writing? How was he like the medieval writers? How was he different?
21. According to Jack, how are we to regard all "Models"?
22. What did you learn from reading this book?

Poems

Poems was the first posthumous collection of C. S. Lewis' writing edited for publication by Walter Hooper, Jack's secretary during the summer of 1963. Jack had previously published two collections of poetry in book form: *Spirits in Bondage* and *Dymer*. (This collection excludes those poems.) In addition, over the years Jack had published numerous short poems in *Punch*.

As Walter Hooper explains in the Preface to this volume, Jack began collecting some of his poetry as early as 1953 with the intention of publishing another volume of poetry to be entitled: *Young King Cole and other Pieces*.[247] For some reason Jack never had this volume published, perhaps because he knew his style of poetry was out of fashion at the time. This collection, originally prepared by Jack, was edited and added to by Hooper.

Readers interested in Jack's development as a poet might have preferred that these poems had been arranged in this volume in chronological order. However, such an arrangement proved difficult if not impossible for Hooper to achieve since he often had nothing more to date these poems by than Jack's handwriting. In addition, Jack was continually revising his poems and he certainly would have preferred the revised versions to be published as opposed to his earlier versions of the same poems. Perhaps it is best that these poems have been arranged topically as this leads the reader to focus more on what

---

247 Walter Hooper, ed., *Poems*, San Diego: Harcourt, Brace & Company, 1992, p. vii.

the poems say rather than on the development of the person writing them.

Hooper's Appendix is quite helpful to the reader interested in tracking the first appearance of Jack's previously published poems in this volume. In addition, Hooper's Appendix indicates which poems have been revised by Jack. Hooper's only contribution to some of the poems has been the titles, for Jack often didn't give a title to some of the pieces in this collection.

Initial reviews of this collection were mixed. The review by American academic, Thomas Howard, was glowing: "This is the best—the glorious best—of Lewis." However, the reviewer for *The Times Literary Supplement* said "Lewis's verse is not without talent or dexterity, and certainly not without feeling; but it is written in a variety of obsolescent modes . . . His real talent was not here—it was for narrative, in which he is always immensely skillful and happily at home."[248] The individual reader of course will have to decide for himself or herself. While most readers will probably not find this collection of poetry to be their favorite volume in the Lewis canon, true Lewis fans will still value many of the gems included here.

---

248 Hooper, *Companion & Guide*, p. 177.

Discussion Questions

1. Which one is your favorite poem? Why? Would you read it to the group?

2. What do you think of Jack's poem *The Planets*? Would the line "winter passed/and guilt forgiven" ever have suggested to you a connection with *The Lion, the Witch and the Wardrobe*? Or a connection between LWW and Jupiter? What do you think of Michael Ward's theory expressed in *Planet Narnia*? As you read this poem do you see any connection between any of the other planets and the Narnia books?

3. Young Jack's great desire was to be an epic poet, along the lines of Milton or Spenser. For those who have read Jack's only published epic poem, *Dymer*, what do you think of his ability as an epic poet? How does his epic poetry compare to his lyric poetry?

4. Jack's first publication was *Spirits in Bondage*, a cycle of lyric poems. What significance do you see in the fact that Jack was first published as a poet and only later as a writer of prose? How do you think Jack's skill as a poet affected his prose?

5. What do you think of the poems included here from *The Pilgrim's Regress*, namely *Caught, Deception, Divine Justice, Dragon Slayer, The Dragon Speaks, Footnote to All Prayers, Forbidden Pleasures, Lilith, The Naked Seed, Nearly They Stood, Posturing, Virtue's Independence, When the Curtain's Down* and *Wormwood*? Do these poems have as much meaning here as they do in the context of *The Pilgrim's Regress*? Which is Jack better at: arranging cut flowers (stand alone lyric poems) or cultivating an entire garden (poetry in the context of a wider prose story)?

6. Why do you think Jack included less poetry in his prose works as he grew older?

7. Why do you think Jack continued to publish poetry after becoming a successful prose writer? And why do you think he published most of his poetry under a pseudonym?

8. Why do you think Jack did not like the poetry of T. S. Eliot? Consider Jack's poem *A Confession* when giving your answer. For those who have read both Eliot and Lewis, whose poetry do you like better? Why?
9. Is there a poem in this collection which you have a question about?
10. Did you find the reading and understanding of Jack's poetry harder or easier than comprehending his prose works? Why do you think that is the case?
11. Jack maintained in *The Personal Heresy* that it was unnecessary to understand a poet's biography in order to comprehend his poetry. In fact, he felt it was dangerous and misleading to read poetry through the lens of the poet's biography. Do you agree with him? Why or why not? Does understanding something of Jack's life enhance your reception of such poems as *The Five Sonnets, As The Ruin Falls* and *To Charles Williams*? If so, how?
12. For those who have read *Spirits in Bondage*, do you think Jack's return to Christian faith made him a better poet? If so, how? You may wish to consider the following poems when giving your answer: *On Being Human, The Apologist's Evening Prayer, Footnote to All Prayers* and *Love's as Warm as Tears*.

Letters of C. S. Lewis

According to Walter Hooper, the idea for publishing the letters of C. S. Lewis may have begun with Jack himself. During the last year of Jack's life, his brother Warnie kept on his desk a letter from Jack written in the summer of 1962 when Jack was in the Acland Nursing Home and Warnie was in Drogheda, Ireland. Jack was afraid that in the event of his death Warnie might be left with insufficient financial support. Therefore, in the letter, he urged Warnie "to keep the wolf from the door by collecting his *letters spirituelles* and 'making a book of them'".[249]

After Jack's death in November 1963 this is what Warnie proceeded to do. When Walter Hooper got to know Warnie in January 1964 Warnie had already been seeking copies of Jack's letters from various correspondents and re-typing them on his typewriter. Warnie's letter to Hooper from Ireland written on 8 February 1964 reveals what kind of book he was creating: "When I get back I intend to see what sort of a hand I make at a 'Life and Letters' of dear Jack. Not exactly an L. & L. in the usual sense, for of course I shall not use anything he has himself told us in *Surprised by Joy*. It will be more what the French 17th Cent. Writers used to call *Memoires pour Servir* etc . . ."[250]

When Warnie returned to The Kilns he began writing the early chapters of the book, combining his own memories of Jack's childhood

---

249 Hooper, Walter & Lewis, W. H., editors, *Letters of C. S. Lewis*, San Diego: Harcourt, Brace & Company, 1993, p. 15.
250 Ibid., p. 14.

with some of the early family letters. Despite his continuing battle with alcoholism Warnie finished the book rather quickly. By the second week of October 1964 Warnie's 230,000 word manuscript was ready for a copy to be made and sent to the editor, Jocelyn Gibb of Geoffrey Bles, Ltd. According to Hooper, toward the end of 1964 Warnie dictated a letter to him to be sent to his literary agent giving the publisher "rights *carte blanche* to do whatever he wants" with the book.[251]

Nonetheless, when Jocelyn Gibb sent Warnie an advance copy of the book in the spring of 1966 Warnie was furious. In his diary Warnie wrote:

> To begin with, I think, I should have been sent proofs for me to give the book a last *nihil obstat* instead of being confronted with a *fait accompli*. Definitely it is no longer my book at all, for this busybody Derrick[252] has performed the most ruthless surgery on it; and some of it inexplicable. Why on earth has he cut out the dedication? Then all the early years have vanished, and J comes on the stage within a few weeks of his sixteenth birthday! This in spite of fact well known that in a work of this sort nearly everyone finds the earlier portion the most interesting. But this isn't D's worst outrage. I had deliberately refrained from asking contributions from Barfield because I suspected they would be philosophical, or in other words unintelligible to the ordinary reader. This busy fool has obtained them, and sprinkled them generously throughout my material, and they prove to be exactly as I feared—unintelligible. This is bound to choke off the casual book buyer. Imagine myself for instance going into Blackwell's for something to read, and the book, to paraphrase Lamb, instead of opening on some pleasant walking tour, landing me bolt on some withering discourse on the nothingness of the utterness or some similar topic! I should do as many potential buyers no doubt will do—close the book with a shudder and move on in search of more palatable fare. But this not to

---

251 Ibid., pp. 14-15.
252 Christopher Derrick, a former pupil of Jack's, had been hired by Jocelyn Gibb to edit Warnie's manuscript.

say that I think it a bad book; I regret the omissions (and inclusions) but what has been retained seems readable. I wrote to Jock giving my criticisms much to this effect, but in milder terms than I have permitted myself here.[253]

Thankfully, Warnie's original "Life and Letters" of his brother is still available to read at the Marion E. Wade Collection of Wheaton College, Wheaton, Illinois.

Thus the original version of *Letters of C. S. Lewis* was published in England by Geoffrey Bles and in the United States by Harcourt, Brace & World in 1966 and retains a brief "Memoir of C. S. Lewis" written by W. H. Lewis. A revised version of this book, edited by Walter Hooper, was published in 1988. Though the complete *Collected Letters of C. S. Lewis* are now available in three massive volumes of over one thousand pages each, the revised version of *Letters of C. S. Lewis* is still in print and perhaps provides the most accessible, while still varied, introduction to Jack's letters for the first-time reader.

---

253   *Brothers & Friends*, pp. 256-257.

A C. S. Lewis Discussion Guide

Discussion Questions

1. Consider Jack's letter of 7 March 1916 to his friend Arthur Greeves. Warren Lewis calls Jack's reading of *Phantastes* by George MacDonald a major turning-point in his brother's life. How did reading *Phantastes* affect Jack? How did George MacDonald become a major influence upon Jack's thought and work?
2. Read Jack's letters of 7 December 1916 and 28 April 1917 to his father from Oxford. How do you think being educated at Oxford affected Jack's life and work? What affect did World War I have on him?
3. Read Jack's telegram to his father from 15 November 1917. How did Albert Lewis' misunderstanding of this telegram and failure to see Jack off from Southampton affect their future relationship? What do you make of Jack's relationship to Mrs. Moore based upon all of his published letters?
4. Notice Jack's diary entry for 27 May 1926. What do you think it would have been like to have C. S. Lewis as a tutor in English literature?
5. Read Jack's cable to his brother sent on 27 September 1929. What influence do you think Albert's death had on Jack's subsequent conversion and future life as a Christian?
6. Consider Jack's letters to Arthur from 22 September and 18 October 1931. What do you think of Jack's account here of his return to Christian faith? How does it compare to his account in *Surprised by Joy*?
7. Read Jack's letter to his brother Warnie from 11 November 1939. How do you think Jack's relationships with the members of the Inklings shaped his life and writings?
8. Read Jack's letter to his brother from 21 July 1940. What do you think of his account of the genesis of *The Screwtape Letters*?
9. Read Jack's letter to Sister Penelope from 15 May 1941. What does this letter convey about Jack's attitude toward his speaking on the BBC and at the RAF bases?

10. Read Jack's letter to his friend Owen Barfield written on 18 May 1945 concerning the death of Charles Williams. What does this letter tell you about Jack's relationship to Williams? What does it say about the loss Jack felt over Williams' death when compared to the loss he felt at his mother's or father's death?

11. Read Jack's letter of 17 April 1951 to Sheldon Vanauken. Many of Jack's letters, like this one, were written to people who wrote to him asking questions about Christianity. Many wrote to Jack because he helped to lead them to Christian faith, either through his books, BBC talks, or personal relationship. What do you think of both the quantity and quality of Jack's letters of this type?

12. Consider Jack's attitude toward the death of Mrs. Moore on 12 January 1951 as expressed in his letter to Sister Penelope on 10 January 1952. What does this letter reveal about Jack's attitude toward Mrs. Moore, unbelievers in general, and prayers for the dead?

13. Jack did not often write about his own work. However, in a letter to the Milton Society of America written toward the end of 1954 he commented on his own perception of his work. What do you make of Jack's assessment of the variety in his own writing?

14. Read Jack's letter to Dorothy Sayers written on 25 June 1957. What does this letter reveal about Jack's relationship with Joy Davidman and what he learned through that relationship?

15. Read Jack's letter to Sister Penelope from 17 September 1963 and his letter to Miss Jane Douglass from 31 September 1963. What do these last letters from Jack's pen reveal about his attitude toward his own death?

16. Is there another one of Jack's letters which you found especially meaningful? If so, would you read it aloud to the group and comment on it?

Christian Reflections

As it says on the fly-leaf of the first edition of *Christian Reflections*, "C. S. Lewis was a prolific writer and when he died he left many pieces behind which had not appeared in book form. Here is a further selection of them, fourteen in number, which were written during the last twenty years of his life. Once again they show the wide range of his mind. As the editor, Walter Hooper, says in his preface, Lewis' defence of pure Christianity was always colourfully varied, adapting his tactics of exposition to suit his audience and this collection of religious pieces gives ample evidence of his skill and versatility."[254]

This collection of Jack's essays offers what I think are two indispensible pieces: "The Poison of Subjectivism" and "Modern Theology and Biblical Criticism". This collection also reveals, in pieces like "Petitionary Prayer: A Problem without an Answer", how Jack worked through various theological problems over a period of time. Jack's final answer to this problem is revealed in *Letters to Malcolm: Chiefly on Prayer*. However, when Jack originally delivered this paper to the Oxford Clerical Society on 8th December 1953, he was still working his way through to a solution, and in fact, seeking the help of the clergymen to whom he addressed the paper. *Christian Reflections* also offers in the essay "On Church Music", what may be to some readers, a humorous insight into how Jack almost thoroughly disliked church music of almost every kind. In fact, he most usually attended the early service of Holy Trinity Church, Headington Quarry, because that service did not have music!

---

254 Hooper, Walter, ed., *Christian Reflections*, London: Geoffrey Bles, 1967, from the fly-leaf.

Christian Reflections was originally published by Geoffrey Bles in England and by Eerdmans in the United States in 1967.

Summary

Jack's essay on *Christianity and Literature* is about the Christian approach to literature, about the principles of Christian literary theory and criticism. The main points are these: modern literary criticism speaks of creativity whereas in the New Testament the art of life itself is the art of imitation. Therefore an author should never conceive himself as bringing into existence beauty or wisdom which did not exist before, but simply and solely as trying to embody in terms of his own art some reflection of eternal Beauty and Wisdom. According to Jack, the Christian should take literature a little less seriously than the cultured non-Christian, for literature itself is not ultimate.

In *Christianity and Culture* Jack asks what the Christian's attitude toward culture should be. He points out in this essay that the New Testament displays a cold attitude toward culture. Culture may be innocent but it is not important. Then he goes on to analyze the thought of both Pagan and Christian thinkers on the subject of culture. After that he lays out the major points of his own view: (1) Provided that there is a demand for culture, and that culture is not actually deleterious, literary critics such as Jack and others in the various cultural disciplines, are justified in making their living by supplying that demand, if they are not fit for anything else. (2) Christians must resist the abuse of culture. (3) Culture can provide good pleasure; therefore we may enjoy those pleasures and teach others to enjoy them. (4) Some of the values of culture may be sub-Christian but they may also prepare a person for conversion, as they did in Jack's own life.

In *Religion: Reality or Substitute?* Jack explores whether the Christian religion is a substitute for the real well-being we have failed to achieve on earth. He explores what he knows about realities and substitutes in other areas of life. From this examination he draws the conclusion that introspection is of no use at all in deciding which of two experiences is a substitute or second best. All our knowledge depends upon authority, reason and experience.

It is often asserted that the world must return to Christian ethics in order to preserve civilization, or even in order to save the human species from destruction. In *On Ethics* Jack disagrees with this view because it is based upon faulty presuppositions. After defining Christian ethics as a body of injunctions he goes on to point out the faulty presuppositions: (1) that Christian Ethics is one among several alternative bodies of injunctions; (2) that we to whom the disputants address their pleadings, are for the moment standing outside all these systems in a sort of ethical vacuum.

In *De Futilitate* Jack asserts that we live in a state of cosmic futility and that there are only three lines one can take about this futility: (a) consistent pessimism (Bertrand Russell), (b) denial of the scientific picture of the universe (Western Idealism; Oriental Pantheism; Judaism; Islam; Christianity), (c) accept the scientific picture and try to do something about it. Jack goes on to show why we cannot adopt the position of total skepticism about human thought. If there is a relation of truth between thought and objective reality then thought is not alien to the nature of the universe. Reason is not merely human but cosmic. If Reason is merely human then saying that the universe is futile has no meaning. If Reason is cosmic then saying that the universe is futile means that there is a way the universe is supposed to be and it has veered off that path.

In *The Poison of Subjectivism* Jack shows why Subjectivism, the belief that reason is merely the product of chemical or electrical events in the human cortex, is untenable. He maintains that the whole attempt to jettison practical reason (i.e. traditional values and morals) as something subjective and to substitute a new scheme of values is wrong because (1) the human mind cannot invent a new value and (2) every attempt to do so consists in selecting one maxim of traditional morality, isolating it, and raising it above the rest. There are only two choices. Either we must accept traditional morality as the result of practical reason, or else have no values at all. Jack goes on to prove his case that there has only been one morality common to all cultures and that accepting this unmovable standard is the only route to true progress. Jack also answers the Christian objections to his view of Natural Law.

In *The Funeral of a Great Myth* Jack pronounces a funeral oration over the myth of Evolutionism. He distinguishes between the biological theorem of Evolution and Evolutionism, by which he means the idea that the world is moving in a direction of greater and greater improvement. He shows how this myth came on the scene before Darwin's *Origin of the Species*. He also reveals how this myth is self-contradictory.

In *On Church Music* Jack starts from the assumption that nothing should be done or sung or said in church which does not aim directly or indirectly either at glorifying God or edifying the people or both. What he calls "learned" music in church may not always edify a congregation with more simple tastes, but neither will the more popular hymns always edify. Jack argues for fewer, better and shorter hymns, especially fewer! He thinks the case for abolishing all Church Music is stronger than the case for abolishing the trained choir and just letting the congregation sing their "favorites". Jack sets forth his belief that there are two musical situations upon which we can be confident that God's blessing rests: (1) where a priest or organist sacrifices their own trained tastes and gives the people the humbler fare they want, and (2) the situation where the untrained layman humbly accepts the trained music offered to him which he cannot fully appreciate.

In *Historicism*, Jack shows why he thinks wrong the belief that human beings can, by the use of their natural powers, discover an inner meaning in the historical process. He maintains that the philosophy of history is a discipline for which human beings lack the necessary data.

In *The Psalms* Jack notes how the spirit of the Psalms often feels alien to him. But for him the fact that many of the Psalms display a vindictive and vengeful human spirit reveals just what God can do, by his grace, through an incorrigible group of people. According to Jack, we can learn something even from a psalm like 109 which is full of maledictions. We can learn that whenever we have wronged a fellow human being we have tempted that person to be such a one as could write Psalm 109. Therefore, we should not eliminate any of the Psalms. We need to be steeped in this book in which our Lord was also steeped. Jack goes on in the second part of this essay to show the differences between the Jewish and the Christian attitude toward judgment.

In *The Language of Religion* Jack points out that there is no specifically religious language. The language of religion tends to be the same sort we use in everyday conversation or the same sort we use in poetry. Religious language often functions in a similar fashion to poetic language which often expresses emotion not for its own sake but to inform us about the object which aroused the emotion. In this essay Jack does not try to prove religious language true, but merely significant, if the reader meets such language with good will and a readiness to find meaning.

In *Petitionary Prayer: A Problem without an Answer* Jack outlines two patterns of petitionary prayer. Pattern A is when we pray, "Thy will be done." Pattern B is commanded in Matthew 21:22: "And whatever you ask in prayer, you will receive, if you have faith." Are not these two patterns in conflict? Which pattern are we to follow?

In *Modern Theology and Biblical Criticism* Jack addresses priests of the Anglican Church (shepherds) with his bleats as a layperson (sheep) in regard to this subject. His first bleat is that modern theologians and biblical critics ask him to believe that they can read between the lines of the old texts but they display an obvious inability to read the lines themselves. Jack's second bleat is that all theology of the liberal type involves the claim that the real behavior and purpose and teaching of Christ came very rapidly to be misunderstood and misrepresented by his followers, and has been recovered or exhumed by modern scholars. This, to Jack, seems highly unlikely. Thirdly, Jack finds in these theologians a constant use of the principle that the miraculous does not occur. But this is a philosophical presupposition brought *to* the texts of Scripture not derived *from* the texts themselves. Fourthly, Jack maintains that all this sort of criticism attempts to reconstruct the genesis of the texts it studies, but this is quite impossible given that we have little or no reliable information outside of the New Testament itself to help us construct the genesis of these texts.

In *The Seeing Eye* Jack responds to the statement from the Russian cosmonauts that they did not find God in outer space. He concludes that this is not sufficient proof of the non-existence of God; rather it may be proof of the fact that the Russian cosmonauts lacked the requisite apparatus for detecting God. Jack maintains that space-travel really has nothing to do with proving or disproving God's existence. To some people, God is found everywhere; to others God is found nowhere. Whether God is discovered or not all depends upon what Jack calls "the seeing eye."

Discussion Questions:

1. What implications does Jack's essay on *Christianity and Literature* have for originality in various forms of art? Do you agree with him that the Christian should take literature a little bit less seriously than the non-Christian? Why or why not?

2. H. Richard Niebuhr once outlined five different relationships between Christ and Culture: (1) **Christ Against Culture** (as exhibited in portions of the monastic tradition and the Amish), (2) **Christ of Culture** (whereby Christ is identified with what human beings conceive to be their noblest institutions; this position was espoused by theologians like Schleiermacher and more recently in feminist theology), (3) **Christ Above Culture** (the aim of people adopting this position is to correlate the fundamental questions of culture with the answers of Christian revelation; synthesis is the key word), (4) **Christ and Culture in Paradox** (this position is essentially dualistic since the Christian is said to belong to two realms, the temporal and the eternal, and must live in the tension of fulfilling responsibilities to both), (5) **Christ the Transformer of Culture** (people who adopt this position attempt to convert the values and goals of culture to the service of the kingdom of God). After reading Jack's essay on *Christianity and Culture* which position would you say he espouses? Why? Which position do you think you hold to?

3. Why is introspection of no use at all in deciding whether religion is real or a substitute? Do you agree with Jack's answer? Why or why not?

4. Before reading Jack's essay *On Ethics* would you have said that we need to return to Christian ethics in order to preserve our culture? If so, after reading the essay is your mind changed at all? If so, how?

5. Do you agree with Jack's assessment that we live within a state of cosmic futility? Why or why not? If you agree,

which response do you take to this situation? Why? Are there any options other than those outlined in the essay *De Futilitate*?

6. Do you agree with Jack's assertion in *The Poison of Subjectivism* that either we must accept traditional morality as the result of practical reason, or else have no values at all? Why or why not?

7. What do you think of what Jack has to say about Evolution and Evolutionism in *The Funeral of a Great Myth*? Based upon this essay do you think that he accepted some of the basic tenets of biological evolution? Why or why not? Where do you stand on this issue and why?

8. What do you think of what Jack has to say in his essay *On Church Music*? Did any of it surprise you? Do you share his attitude toward church music? Why or why not?

9. Do you agree with Jack where he says in *Historicism* that we cannot find an inner meaning in the historical process using our natural powers? Why or why not? If we cannot discover meaning in history using our natural powers is there another way? Explain.

10. What do you think of what Jack has to say in his essay on *The Psalms*? Have you ever been bothered by some of the same things in the Psalms? Does Jack's approach to reading and taking the Psalms on board help you at all? If so, how?

11. Does what Jack says in *The Language of Religion* cause you to look at religious language differently? If so, how?

12. Have you ever wrestled with the same problem as Jack in regard to petitionary prayer? If so, does his essay encourage you in any way? If you remember his answer to this problem from *Letters to Malcolm* what do you think of it?

13. Have you ever wrestled with reading modern theology and/or biblical criticism as Jack did in his essay? If so, do you find his approach to these fields of study helpful? Why or why not?

14. Does Jack's conclusion in "The Seeing Eye" reduce religion to a merely subjective phenomenon? Why or why not?
15. Which essay is your favorite? Which essay is your least favorite? Why?

Letters to an American Lady

In his book *C. S. Lewis: The Man and His Achievement* John Peters wrote:

> Lewis' influence spread far beyond the confines of Oxford and Cambridge Universities where he spent the whole of his professional and working life. There were many reasons for this. In the first place there was the effect of his teaching and lecturing. Secondly, there was the publication of his scholarly works, articles, reviews, sermons, religious volumes, science fiction, and of the Narnia Chronicles. A third factor, though not so widely appreciated, was his vast correspondence with adults — of all ages, temperaments, cultures, religions and backgrounds — and children throughout the world. Letters addressed to him arrived relentlessly at Magdalen [Oxford], Magdalene [Cambridge], and 'The Kilns', and were all dealt with as soon as he possibly could, his replies being written in his own handwriting. Since his death on 22nd November 1963 in Oxford, three volumes of his letters have been published: (1) *Letters of C. S. Lewis*, edited by W. H. Lewis (1966); (2) *Letters To An American Lady*, edited by Clyde S. Kilby (1969); (3) *They Stand Together: The Letters of C. S. Lewis to Arthur Greeves 1914-63*, edited by Walter Hooper (1979).[255]

---

[255] Peters, John, *C. S. Lewis: The Man and His Achievement*, Exeter: The Paternoster Press, 1985, p. 100.

It should also be noted that since the publication of Peters' book, other volumes of Jack's letters have been published: *Letters To Children*, edited by Lyle W. Dorsett and Marjorie Lamp Mead, *The Latin Letters of C. S. Lewis*, translated and edited by Martin Moynihan, and *The Collected Letters of C. S. Lewis*, edited by Walter Hooper and published in three huge volumes.

Peters goes on to write about *Letters to an American Lady* that it:

> ...contains more than a hundred letters written between 26th October 1950 and 30th August 1963 (within three months of his death). They were written to a woman who died in 1978. These letters are as good an indication as any of his almost saintly willingness to answer even the most trivial of enquiries. Some of the letters are very brief indeed, or as he put it, 'just a scrape of the pen', and it is apparent that this lady wrote to him with great (some would say obsessive) regularity and without any real appreciation of the demands on his time. Her letters followed him everywhere, even on holiday, as one of his replies headed 'Somewhere in Eire' (dated 18th August 1956) shows.[256]

Who was this American lady and how did she come in contact with Jack? Her name was Mary Willis Shelburne of Washington, D.C. She was put in contact with Jack in 1950 by some other correspondents of his, Mr. and Mrs. Kilmer, also of Washington, D.C. The Kilmers had eight children and Jack dedicated *The Magician's Nephew* to the Kilmer family. Many of Jack's letters to the Kilmer children can be found in *Letters to Children*.[257]

Clyde Kilby once described Mary Willis Shelburne as follows:

> A widow four years older than Lewis, she was described by one friend as "very charming, gracious, a southern aristocratic lady who loves to talk and speaks well." Once financially independent, she had fallen upon privation and, what was worse, serious family problems....About the time the correspondence began she turned from the Episcopal Church to the Roman Catholic. Twice she has

---

256   Ibid., p. 101.
257   *Companion & Guide*, p. 760.

been so near death that the last rites of the church were administered.... She is a writer of reviews, articles, poems and stories.²⁵⁸

What was the character of Mary Willis Shelburne and her letters? Walter Hooper tells us that:

> Her own letters were filled with complaints about her family and friends, but Lewis, who thought her 'a very silly, tiresome, and probably disagreeable woman' knew she was also 'old, poor, sick, lonely, and miserable.' For this reason he always took time to answer each of them with letters that are perfect gems in their way. ²⁵⁹

John Peters agreed with this assessment when he wrote:

> Humanity, common sense, honesty all shine through his [Lewis'] letters; they reveal him as a courteous person who would, for example, take the trouble to explain at some length why he had left a lady's [Mary Willis Shelburne's] letter unanswered ... The lady in question wrote frequently and, perhaps, even pestered him so that his forbearance and patience are all the more commendable.²⁶⁰

In addition to the letters, Jack assisted Shelburne financially, arranging through his American publishers a small stipend for her which continued until her death.²⁶¹ Jack also encouraged the Kilmers to minister to her needs.²⁶²

What is the value of these letters to the study of C. S. Lewis and his work? Jack's letters in general, and specifically those to Mary Willis Shelburne, give us great insight into Lewis the man. John Peters said of Jack's letters:

> Taken together with his published works, they may be regarded as part of that 'special mission' Lewis performed

---

258   Kilby, Clyde S., editor, *Letters to an American Lady*, Grand Rapids: Eerdmans, 1967, pp. 8-9.
259   *Companion & Guide*, p. 91.
260   Peters, p. 106.
261   Kilby, p. 9.
262   *Collected Letters*, Vol. III, p. 1240.

for those who were 'slowly finding their way towards some sort of Christian orthodoxy'.... These letters may also be regarded as 'parallel autobiography', preserving as they do much detail about Lewis' life. Their importance appears in the extensive use made of them by Roger Green and Walter Hooper in the official biography. The letters offer deep insights into the character, temperament, and personality of a remarkable man of God.[263]

Finally we must ask: Why did Jack write these letters? In his later years he loathed letter writing. With all his other duties and activities Jack could easily have justified pitching such letters as those from Mary Willis Shelburne into the waste bin. So why did he write some 136 letters to an American lady whom he would never meet? Clyde Kilby answers that question as follows:

> The main cause was that Lewis believed taking time out to advise or encourage another Christian was both a humbling of one's talents before the Lord and also as much the work of the Holy Spirit as producing a book. John Wesley somewhere in his journal during the days when vast crowds were hearing him says that on a given night he preached to only one poor sinner at the inn. Lewis had the same dedicated attitude, the belief that one's days and his talents are given him not for private expenditure but to be used in all lowliness within the will of God. Though the flesh abhorred it, he mortified the flesh.[264]

---

263 Peters, p. 113.
264 Kilby, p. 7.

Discussion Questions

1. Green and Hooper write in their biography of C. S. Lewis, "Even the actual recipient of his *Letters to an American Lady* (1967) is less believable than the imaginary Malcolm with whom his creator argues and shares reminiscences, and whom he sometimes needs to comfort."[265] Do you agree with this assessment? How do the letters to Malcolm and those to the American lady compare and contrast? Which did you enjoy reading more? Why?

2. Consider Jack's letter of November 10, 1952. What do you think Jack means by this statement about those at the center of various Christian denominations being closer to one another? What about those at the center of theistic religions? Do you agree? Why or why not.

3. Read Jack's letter of July 10, 1953 in which he reveals something of his attitude toward the monarchy. What do you think Jack means by this statement? Does this in some way make the monarchy necessary or helpful to our understanding of our relationship to God? How is this mitigated, or not, by the present state of the British monarchy?

4. What do you think of Jack's comments on the devotional life in his letter of February 20, 1955?

5. What do you think of his comments on suffering in his letter of April 26, 1956?

6. What do you think of Jack's insight about forgiveness in his letters of April 15, 1958 and July 21, 1958? What has your experience of God's forgiveness been like?

7. What do you think of his comments about old age and the resurrection in his letter of September 30, 1958? How about his comments about death in his letter of June 7, 1959?

---

265 Green & Hooper, *C. S. Lewis: A Biography*, p. 233.

8. What do you think of what Jack says about grief in his letter of September 24, 1960? How does this compare to what he says in *A Grief Observed*?
9. What do you think of his thoughts on poverty in his letter of December 10, 1962?
10. What other insights have these letters given you into C. S. Lewis the man?
11. Do you have a favorite letter, or portion of a letter, from this collection? If so, would you read it to the group?

God in the Dock

God in the Dock is a collection of essays and a few letters written by C. S. Lewis, spanning from the 1940s right up until his death in 1963. These essays deal, for the most part, with theological and ethical topics. This collection was gathered and edited by Walter Hooper, Jack's secretary for a short while in 1963. *God in the Dock* was first published in 1970. The title of the book is taken from Jack's essay by the same title, in which he says that human beings in ancient times approached God, or the gods, as an accused person approaches a judge. In modern times the roles have reversed. Humanity is the judge: God is "in the dock", on trial. Human beings are kindly judges, Jack maintains. If God should have a reasonable defense for allowing war, poverty and disease then human beings are willing to listen to that defense. The trial may even end in God's acquittal. However, the important thing to recognize is that human beings sit on the judge's bench and God is in the dock.[266]

---

266 *God in the Dock*, p. 244.

A C. S. Lewis Discussion Guide

Discussion Questions

1. How would you answer Jack's argument against Naturalism on page 21 of the first essay?
2. How would you answer Jack's question in the second essay on page 31: What is one to make of people who admit miracles but deny the Virgin Birth?
3. In "Answers to Questions on Christianity" what do you think of Jack's perspective on the relationship of faith and works? (See page 55.) Do you think he comes down more on the Protestant or the Roman Catholic side of this question? Why?
4. What do you make of Jack's statement in "The Grand Miracle" that the Christian story is precisely the story of one grand miracle? (See page 80.)
5. Do you agree or disagree with Jack's assertion in "Christian Apologetics" that what is needed in publishing is not "more little books about Christianity, but more little books by Christians on other subjects – with their Christianity *latent*?" (See page 93.) Do you think Jack followed his own advice? How or how not?
6. At the end of "Some Thoughts" Jack insists that because Christians love something else more than this world they love even this world better than those who know no other world. (See page 150.) What do you think of this?
7. At the end of his essay, "What are we to make of Jesus Christ?" Jack says that there is no question of what we can make of Jesus; the real question is what Jesus intends to make of us. We must accept or reject the story about him. (See page 160.) How do you respond to this?
8. What do you think of Jack's "Rejoinder to Dr. Pittenger"? (See especially page 182.) Do you enjoy Jack's dry sense of humor that he often uses to make a point?
9. In "The Decline of Religion" Jack asserts that conversion

requires an alteration of the will which doesn't occur without the intervention of the supernatural. (See page 221.) What do you think of this?

10. How would you summarize Jack's argument against priestesses in the Church? (See pages 234-239.) Do you agree or disagree with his argument? Why?

11. Do you think Jack's analysis about God being "in the dock" today is correct? (See page 244.) How has this situation changed since Jack's time?

12. In "Cross Examination" what do you think of Jack's analysis of his own conversion, that he was "decided upon"? (See page 261.)

13. What do you think of Jack's statement in "The Sermon and the Lunch" that after the fall no organization or way of life has a natural tendency to go right? (See page 284.)

14. Do you agree or disagree with Jack that we have "no right to happiness"? (See pages 317-322.) Why? Does a supposed "right to happiness" justify divorce? Why or why not?

15. What do you think of Jack's belief expressed in his letter entitled "Mere Christians" that what unites the Evangelical and the Anglo-Catholic against the 'Liberal' or 'Modernist' is thoroughgoing supernaturalism, a common belief in the creation, the fall, the Incarnation, the Resurrection, the Second Coming, and the four last things? (See page 336.)

16. Do you have a favorite passage from this collection which we have not touched upon? If so, would you read it aloud to the group and comment?

Letters to Children

C. S. Lewis: Letters to Children is a collection of Jack's letters to his godchildren and to other children who wrote to him with questions or comments about the Narnia stories. The letters were selected from Jack's voluminous correspondence by Lyle Dorsett and Marjorie Mead of the Wade Collection at Wheaton College, one of the major repositories of Lewis' letters in the world. The collection contains a treasure of a Foreword by Douglas Gresham, Jack's step-son, as well as a fine introduction, a delightful chapter about Jack's childhood, and a helpful Annotated Children's Bibliography to C. S. Lewis. The book is not only suitable for young readers of the Narnia stories but for C. S. Lewis fans of all ages. In fact, next to the Narnia stories themselves this is one of my favorite volumes of Lewisiana. *Letters to Children* was originally published by Macmillan in the United States and by Collins in the United Kingdom in 1985.

Discussion Questions

1. What do you think of Jack's advice to his goddaughter Sarah about making her first Communion? (See letter of 3 April 1949.)
2. How would you describe Jack's attitude toward children (how he treated them) as expressed in these letters? Do you think Jack understood children well or not?
3. What do you think of Jack's view of stories as expressed in his letter of December 18, 1953? Do you agree? Why or why not?
4. In a letter written on May 9, 1954 Jack explained the difference between allegory and what he was trying to do with the Narnia stories. So what is the difference between allegory and Jack's "supposal"? (See also his letter of 11 September 1958.)
5. What do you think of Jack's advice to Laurence, the boy who was concerned that he loved Aslan more than Jesus? (See letter of 6 May 1955.)
6. What do you think of Jack's advice to Joan about writing on 26 June 1956? Do you think he followed his own advice?
7. In his letter of January 3, 1959 Jack gives some simple advice about literary criticism. This advice ties in to what he called "the personal heresy," trying to figure out what was going on in the author's life that led him to write what he did. Jack applied this same rule to New Testament criticism, suggesting it is difficult, if not impossible, to get behind the texts themselves. Do you agree with Jack on this point? Why or why not?
8. Which is your favorite letter in this collection? Why?
9. How do these letters compare to Jack's letters to adult correspondents? Or to his fictional letters to Malcolm? Or the letters from Screwtape to Wormwood?

Books About C. S. Lewis

Jack: A Life of C. S. Lewis by George Sayer

Jack: A Life of C. S. Lewis was written by George Sayer, a former pupil of C. S. Lewis at Oxford University, and later friend and sometime participant in the Inklings. This biography was originally published by Harper & Row in 1988 and was re-issued by Crossway in 1994. *Jack* has been hailed by many Lewis scholars as the best biography of C. S. Lewis to date. This is probably true for at least five reasons:

1. It is written by someone who knew Lewis rather intimately, first as a student, and later as a friend. And so we have in this book an eyewitness account of the life and times of this great Oxford scholar and author. Through first-hand accounts Mr. Sayer not only introduces us to C. S. Lewis but also to many of Lewis' friends and colleagues: Mrs. Janie King Moore, J. R. R. Tolkien, Charles Williams, Joy Davidman, Ruth Pitter, and many others.

2. At the same time, *Jack*, has a certain level of objectivity which is not as much present in the official biography written by Roger Lancelyn Green and Walter Hooper. The original edition of the Green/Hooper biography was published in the early 1970s. Sayer brings together a number of resources and insights which were not available to Green and Hooper when they first wrote the official biography of Lewis. *Jack* is obviously the product of very careful and accurate research as well as first-hand knowledge.

3. As a teacher of English for many years at Malvern College

Sayer obviously developed his own excellent prose style. This book is as much a joy to read for itself as it is, through it, to learn more about C. S. Lewis.

4. Mr. Sayer was raised, and lived his entire life, in a similar atmosphere to that of C. S. Lewis. Sayer knows the places of Lewis' life as well as the people. He understands the times and the milieu in which Lewis came to worldwide recognition and he is able to communicate that sense of place and time to the reader.

5. Finally, while Mr. Sayer is sympathetic in his portrayal of Lewis as teacher and friend, he does not write without a discerning eye with regard to Lewis' life and work. Here is no haphazard book of hagiography, but a carefully considered assessment of the life and work of one of the most popular Christian authors of all time.

A C. S. Lewis Discussion Guide

Discussion Questions

1. How did you find Mr. Sayer's personal relationship with C. S. Lewis impacting this biography?
2. How did Jack's family background and upbringing affect the man that he became?
3. Why do you think Mr. Sayer entitled chapter 3 "Into Bondage"? What effects did Jack's early schooling at Wynyard, Cherbourg, Campbell and Malvern have on the direction of his life?
4. What events do you think most contributed to Jack becoming an atheist?
5. Why do you think Jack's days at Great Bookham were such a highlight of his early life?
6. How do you think Jack's service during WWI was similar to or different from the experience of other young men his age? What life-long marks do you think this war left upon his life?
7. What do you make of Jack's relationship with Mrs. Moore?
8. How do you see Jack's love of philosophy during his early years at Oxford coming out in his later writings?
9. What impact do you think Jack's years of poverty and struggle to get a job had on his later life and writing?
10. How do you think Jack's life as a fellow and a tutor shaped his life and writings?
11. How did Jack's return to Christian faith affect his outlook on his job? What people, events and discoveries were influential in Jack's return to Christian faith?
12. How do you see Jack's love of nature and walking coming out in his books?
13. What led to the formation of the Inklings? What affect do you think this group had on the literary output of the individual members? What do you think we can

learn from the Inklings about the importance of true friendship?

14. Why do you think Jack wrote his cosmic trilogy? Do you think he succeeded in accomplishing what he set out to do?

15. What impact do you think WWII had on the writing and success of Jack as a Christian author?

16. How do you think Jack's BBC talks and his lectures to the RAF affected his style of writing?

17. What was the response of Jack's colleagues to the expression of his faith through popular books and broadcasting? What do you think we can learn from Jack's life in this regard?

18. How do you think Jack's writing of *Miracles* and his debate with Elizabeth Anscombe at the Socratic Club affected the future course of his writing? Do you agree or disagree with Sayer's view on this subject? Why?

19. Why do you think Jack wrote *The Chronicles of Narnia*? Do you agree with Mr. Sayer that these books will be the best and most long-remembered of all Jack's writing? Why or why not?

20. What affect do you think Jack's tortuous relationship with Mrs. Moore and his brother's alcoholism had upon him personally and upon his writing?

21. What do you make of Jack's life-long friendship with Arthur Greeves? Why do you think Jack kept up his contact with Greeves?

22. What do you think of Jack's relationship with Joy Davidman Gresham? How is the relationship portrayed in *Jack* similar or different than that portrayed in the movie *Shadowlands*?

23. What influence do you think Joy had on Jack's mature writing?

24. Do you think Jack lost his faith after the death of his

wife? Do you think that he wanted to die or found it difficult to go on living?

25. How do you think reading and writing helped Jack through some of the difficult times in his life?

26. In what ways do you think Jack grew in his Christian faith from 1931 until his death in 1963?

27. What new insight did this book give you into the man, C. S. Lewis?

Lenten Lands by Douglas Gresham

Lenten Lands, while not strictly a biography of C. S. Lewis, gives many insights into the last ten years of his life. As it says in the sub-title, this book is the story of Douglas Gresham's childhood with Joy Davidman, Gresham's mother, and C. S. Lewis, his step-father. However, the book offers much more than that. It also gives us eye-witness glimpses into the lives of William Lindsay Gresham (Douglas' father and author of the bestselling book *Nightmare Alley*), C. S. Lewis' brother Warren Hamilton Lewis, as well as a whole host of characters floating in and out of Lewis' home, The Kilns, not the least of which is Fred Paxford (Lewis' gardener on whom the Narnian character Puddleglum the Marsh-wiggle was modeled).

The book begins, unusually, with the funeral of C. S. Lewis, a critical juncture in the life of then eighteen-year-old Douglas Gresham, who had to endure in his teen years, not only the death of his step-father, but also his mother and father. The author then flashes back to the beginning of his life and upbringing in New York. The book is beautifully, sometimes hauntingly written, as the story winds its way from Staatsburg, in upstate New York, to Oxford, England to Australia and Tasmania. The one draw-back to *Lenten Lands* is that it ends on an incomplete note. I imagine another whole book could be written about Douglas and Merrie Gresham's marriage and family life and their thirteen year ministry in Ireland at Rathvinden House. (The couple now lives on the island nation of Malta in the Mediterranean Sea.) Thankfully, Gresham has written an Afterword to the original edition of *Lenten Lands* which tells briefly of his commitment to follow

Christ beginning in the early 1990s and something of his life from 1988 to 2004. Still, I imagine many readers long to know a bit more of this man who is now one of only two living heirs of C. S. Lewis.

However, the heart of this book deals not so much with Gresham but with his own eyewitness account of the relationship between his mother, writer Joy Davidman Gresham, and his eventual step-father, C. S. Lewis. As it says on the back cover of my copy of *Lenten Lands*, "There has probably not been a less likely couple: she, an American divorcee and the mother of two young boys; he, an Oxford don and confirmed bachelor who inhabited an eccentric household with his brother, a retired Royal Army major. Yet the relationship of C. S. Lewis and Joy Davidman, as told here by her son Douglas Gresham, was destined to become one of this century's most deeply moving love stories."[267] In fact, Douglas Gresham acted as a consultant to the second *Shadowlands* movie with Anthony Hopkins and Debra Winger, thus adding touches of realism to the screen story which only an eyewitness could bring.

The reviewer for *The Bookstore Journal* said of *Lenten Lands*: "Gresham is a brilliant writer in his own right....With his literary acumen and exposure to Lewis, [Gresham] will give Lewis fans more accurate, penetrating insight into the philosopher than any other biographer—a perspective that is long overdue." While *Lenten Lands* may not, in the end, provide *more* accurate and penetrating insight into Lewis than *any* other biography, it nonetheless provides a very valuable perspective on Jack from the pen of one of the only living people who actually lived in the home of C. S. Lewis, seeing him in both public and private situations over the course of the last ten years of his life. For that reason alone, if for no other, *Lenten Lands* is, and should remain, a treasured volume amidst the ever-growing corpus of secondary literature on C. S. Lewis.

---

267 Gresham, Douglas, *Lenten Lands*, New York: HarperCollins, 1994.

Discussion Questions

1. What do you think is the meaning and significance of the title *Lenten Lands*?
2. How did you respond to the opening of the first chapter, with the funeral of C. S. Lewis?
3. What did you think of Gresham's portrait of his mother? How does it compare to the portrait given in the movie *Shadowlands*?
4. How does Gresham portray Warnie? How did you feel about Warnie after reading this book?
5. How did you respond to Gresham's physical description of Jack? Is it what you expected or not? Why?
6. What new insights into Jack's life and character has this book given you?
7. What did you think of Jack and Joy's relationship as Douglas portrayed it?
8. In what ways, if any, is the relationship different from that portrayed in the movies or other biographies on Jack which you have seen or read?
9. What did you think of Doug's encounter with God in the churchyard?
10. How did you respond to Doug's descriptions of life at the Kilns and on vacation with his mother and step-father? Did it make you want to be there?
11. What was the price for Douglas of living through such "glory days"?
12. How did you feel about Doug's descriptions of his life at boarding school?
13. What did you think of Jack and Doug's relationship after Joy's death? Do you think they helped one another through the grieving process?
14. Do you think this book would be helpful to someone experiencing grief?

15. Doug obviously knew a lot of pain in his young life — his parent's divorce, the deaths of his mother, father, and step-father along with Warnie's alcoholism. In the book, how do you see Doug responding to that pain?

16. What did you think of the chapters on Doug's life following Jack's death? How about the ending to the book?

17. In the preface to the book Doug says that one of the reasons why he wrote it was as a therapeutic procedure. He says that through the process of writing the book he came to see his childhood not as a time of testing and torment, but as a time of privilege and education. What do you think?

18. What do you gather was the overall impact of C. S. Lewis' life on the life of Douglas Gresham?

Surprised by Joy
An Introductory Class on C. S. Lewis

One way to explore the life and work of C. S. Lewis in a small group, Sunday school class or book discussion group is to do a six week overview of Lewis' life and work, meeting for one hour each week. I would suggest utilizing the video documentary of Lewis' life: *Through Joy & Beyond* narrated by Walter Hooper with Peter Ustinov supplying the voice of C. S. Lewis.[268] The group may watch about ten minutes of the documentary each week and then spend the rest of the hour discussing the questions in this guide. You might also wish to set aside time at the end of the six weeks to watch Richard Attenborough's *Shadowlands* (133 minutes) and discuss the movie after the showing.

<u>Overall Class Description:</u> In this class we will explore the life and writings of Clive Staples Lewis: Oxford don, Cambridge professor, literary scholar, Christian apologist, and writer of fantasy books for children and adults alike. Lewis was the author of nearly 40 books with more than 200 million copies in print today in numerous languages, making him the best-selling Christian author of all time, outside of the Bible. The class will be divided into six, one-hour sessions as follows:

1. BOXEN & THE SINKING OF ATLANTIS (1898-1908). We will explore Lewis' family background and upbringing in Belfast including the death of Lewis' mother when he was 9 years old.

---

[268] Other helpful DVD resources include: *The Magic Never Ends* and *The Life of C. S. Lewis* produced by The Day of Discovery.

2. THE TASTE OF JOY (1908-1918). We will take a look at Lewis' school experiences and developing atheism beginning with his "concentration camp" experience in England, encompassing his private tutelage under William Kirkpatrick in Surrey, his entrance into Oxford, and subsequent army service during World War I.

3. MOVING TO CHECKMATE (1919-1931). We will examine Lewis' relationship with Mrs. Janie King Moore, mother of Lewis' friend Paddy Moore who died in the First World War, his declining relationship with his father, and his failed attempts at becoming a successful poet. This class will conclude with an investigation into Lewis' return to Christian faith in 1931.

4. THE INKLINGS (1932-1942). We will explore Lewis' developing relationships with members of the Inklings: J. R. R. Tolkien, Charles Williams, and others. These were the years of Lewis' first Christian writing: *The Pilgrim's Regress*, *Out of the Silent Planet*, *The Problem of Pain*, and his most successful, *The Screwtape Letters*. This was also a time of great scholarly achievement followed by popular notoriety through his RAF lectures, BBC talks, and founding of the Socratic Club in Oxford.

5. INTO THE WARDROBE (1943-1951). We will traverse Lewis' most prolific years of writing which saw the publication of: *Christian Behavior*, *Perelandra*, *The Abolition of Man*, *Beyond Personality*, *That Hideous Strength*, *The Great Divorce*, *Miracles*, *The Weight of Glory*, and culminating with *The Lion, the Witch and the Wardrobe*. We will explore Lewis' fascination with fantasy as well as the conclusion to that "huge and complex episode": his relationship with Mrs. Moore, who died in 1951.

6. THROUGH JOY & BEYOND (1952-1963). We will inquire into Lewis' relationship with Joy Davidman, whom he met in 1952, married in 1956, and lost to cancer in 1960. We will examine Lewis' move from Oxford don to Cambridge professor as well as briefly surveying Lewis' mature writings: *Surprised by Joy*, *Till We Have Faces*, *Reflections on the Psalms*, *The Four Loves*, *A Grief Observed*,

and *Letters to Malcolm: Chiefly on Prayer*. Finally, we will consider the literary and spiritual impact of Lewis' life and writings.

"Boxen & the Sinking of Atlantis"
1898-1908

Discussion Questions

1. How did you become acquainted with the life and writings of C. S. Lewis?

2. What books have you read by Lewis? What did you get out of those books? If you have read several, which book or books did you think the best?

3. Which aspect of Lewis' writings do you find most helpful– his apologetic works, his fantasy works, essays on ethics, or his candid and agonizing account of his struggles with grief?

4. What aspects of Lewis' thought do you find most challenging? What do you want to study in depth?

5. Did you read *The Chronicles of Narnia* as a child? What was your reaction to them at that time?

6. Based upon this introduction to C. S. Lewis what influences of early events and relationships do you see in his books? Do you see any connection between Lewis' Boxen and his later development of Narnia? What are the similarities and/or differences?

7. Lewis compared his mother's death to the sinking of Atlantis. He says that with his mother's death all settled happiness disappeared from his life. How do you think Lewis' response to his mother's death may have contributed to his later adoption of atheism? Have you had any similar grief in your life which led to a subsequent loss of faith?

8. How was the experience of "joy" important in the life of the young C. S. Lewis? Have you ever had a similar experience? If so, what impact has this experience had upon your life?

A C. S. LEWIS DISCUSSION GUIDE

"The Taste of Joy"
1908-1918

Discussion Questions

1. C. S. Lewis says that it was during his "concentration camp" experience at Wynyard School at the age of ten that he first became an effective believer. Fear played a dominant role in Lewis' early faith. Have you had a similar experience? Are you more fearful of God or drawn to God? Why?

2. It was at Cherbourg House in Malvern, England that Lewis "ceased to be a Christian". What influenced Lewis to become an atheist? Why was he "desperately anxious to get rid of his religion"? Have you ever had a similar experience?

3. In his autobiography Lewis describes, in some detail, the homosexual practices of the students at Malvern College, but he does not condemn them. In fact, Lewis' lifelong friend, Arthur Greeves, was a homosexual. These early experiences may well have shaped Lewis' view of homosexuality as "pitiful" rather than abominable. What do you think of Lewis' view in light of Scripture? How well do you think the Church today is treating homosexuals and the issue of homosexuality?

4. Lewis writes in *Surprised by Joy* that "spiritually speaking, the deadly thing was that school life was almost wholly dominated by the social struggle." What effect do you think this had on Lewis' life? Did you ever experience this "social struggle" in your school days? What affect did it have on your life?

5. Lewis states that during his time at Malvern College he was angry with God for not existing and equally angry with God for creating a world. Do you think other atheists experience this? Have you ever felt this way? Why?

6. One of the features of Lewis' early life was a strained relationship with his father. How do you think this relationship may have influenced Lewis' turn to atheism?
7. In the middle portion of *Surprised by Joy* Lewis tells of two people who had a great influence upon him: his life-long friend, Arthur Greeves, and his tutor, William Kirkpatrick. How did these two people influence Lewis? What role have other people played in your spiritual journey?
8. In 1915 Lewis happened to pick up a copy of George MacDonald's *Phantastes* in a train station. Lewis later said that reading this book "baptized" his imagination; he later called George MacDonald his mentor. What was the new quality that was introduced into Lewis' life through this book? Why do you think this writer would become so influential in Lewis' later return to the Christian faith?
9. In 1917 Lewis entered the army even though he was exempt from military service as an Irish citizen. He also made a vow to look after his friend Paddy Moore's family should Paddy be killed in the war. Both of these incidents point out the value of honor in Lewis' young life. What do you think of these two decisions in Lewis' life? How do you see the theme of honor played out in his writings?

A C. S. Lewis Discussion Guide

"Moving To Checkmate"
1919-1931

Discussion Questions

1. One of the sub-themes of Lewis' early life was his great desire to be left alone. Lewis' great problem with Christianity was that there was a "transcendental Interferer" at the center of it. Do you think Lewis' feelings on this subject are characteristic of all people? Why or why not?

2. During the end of Lewis' time in Great Bookham he faced a great conflict between joy and his materialistic faith. What was the conflict? How was this conflict eventually overcome? Do you think that the dialectic of desire is a powerful argument for theism? Why or why not?

3. In chapter twelve of *Surprised by Joy* Lewis writes, "A young man who wishes to remain a sound Atheist cannot be too careful of his reading." Two of the writers who had a dramatic impact on Lewis' turn to Christianity were George MacDonald and G. K. Chesterton. How did these writers affect Lewis? What writers have been influential in your spiritual pilgrimage?

4. How did Lewis' Oxford friends (Jenkin, Barfield, Harwood, Coghill, Dyson & Tolkien) influence him toward embracing Christianity? What people has God used in your life to move you closer to Christ?

5. One of the most fascinating aspects of Lewis' conversion to theism is the fact that he did not want to become a believer in God. Why was this? Does this make Lewis' testimony more or less credible to you?

6. What do you think of the fact that Lewis immediately started attending his parish church once he became a theist even though churchmanship was wholly unattractive to him? Do you think there is anything we can learn from

Lewis on this point?

7. The question which led Lewis finally to accept Christianity was this: "Where has religion reached its true maturity?" Do you find Lewis' answer to this question credible? Why or why not?

8. What do you make of Lewis' relationship to Mrs. Moore? What lessons in Christian charity, honor and witness might we learn from this relationship?

9. Do you think it is at all significant that Lewis' father died the same year that Lewis became a theist? Why or why not?

"The Inklings"
1932-1942

Discussion Questions

1. Through the writing of his science fiction trilogy Lewis learned that any amount of theology could be smuggled into people's minds under the guise of fantasy. What do you think about Lewis' method of pre-evangelism? What impact have Lewis' fantasy books had on your own life?

2. What influence did Lewis' friends, like J. R. R. Tolkien, have in leading Lewis back to the Christian faith and sustaining him in that faith? How has the Lord used other people in your life to lead you closer to him?

3. Most readers find Lewis' first Christian book, *The Pilgrim's Regress*, difficult to understand. By the time of writing *The Screwtape Letters* and delivering his broadcast talks, Lewis was able to communicate the Christian faith much more simply. What do you think may have enabled Lewis to grow into a more effective communication style? Do you find Lewis' writing difficult or easy to understand, or both at different times? Why?

4. What do you think of Lewis' ability to simultaneously write scholarly works, popular Christian books, carry on

a heavy load of work as an Oxford don, lecture at RAF camps during WWII, form the Socratic Club and care for a family, all in the same decade? What do you learn from this decade of Lewis' life?

5. Lewis said of writing *Screwtape*: "Though I had never written anything more easily, I never wrote with less enjoyment." Why do you think this was the case? What do you make of Lewis' concept of evil being the absence of good? Do you agree with this? Why or why not?

6. Do you think Lewis succeeded in presenting to the world mere Christianity? That is, has Lewis succeeded in presenting what all Christians have at all times and in all places believed? Why or why not?

7. In *Mere Christianity*, Lewis presented his famous trilemma, that Jesus was either a lunatic, the Devil of Hell or God. In examining the identity of Jesus of Nazareth are Lewis' options the only ones open to us? If not, what other conclusion might one arrive at? Which option seems most credible to you and why?

"Into The Wardrobe"
1943-1951

Discussion Questions

1. Why do you think Lewis was critical of the educational system in England as reflected in such books as *The Abolition of Man*? From what you know of Lewis, what do you think he would say about our educational system in the United States today?

2. In some ways Lewis found poetic language best suited for theology and considered imagination the organ for perceiving meaning. Contrast this with more traditional approaches to theology, such as systematic theologies and church doctrinal statements. In what ways are poetry and fantasy better able to communicate God and Christian experience? What are its weaknesses and dangers?

3. According to Lewis a Christian novelist must be true to his craft and not engage in any unnecessary sermonizing. Do you think Lewis was right or do you think, for the Christian writer, a clear Christian message outweighs other literary considerations?
4. In his preface to *The Great Divorce* Lewis basically says that all roads do *not* lead to to heaven. What do you think? Why?
5. Read the vignette about the man and the lizard from *The Great Divorce*. What did you think of this vignette? Did this story fill you with any desire for heaven? Why or why not?
6. What is your reaction to Lewis' vast correspondence in the midst of a very busy life? Is there anything we can learn from Lewis' example?
7. Read Lewis' "confirmation" letter to his God-daughter Sarah from *Letters to Children*. What do you think of this letter?
8. Why do you suppose Lewis was so effective in writing stories for children when he never had any children himself?
9. If you have read the Narnia stories which is your favorite and why?

"Through Joy & Beyond"
1952-1963

Discussion Questions

1. With Joy's death, the intensity of Lewis' love and grief brought on emotional and spiritual struggles that almost made his earlier faith seem simplistic. Do you see this as a weakness of faith, or does the honest expression of his struggles–unafraid to voice even his most severe doubts–show a profound trust in God?

2. With his well-developed theology of suffering, why do you think Lewis had such great difficulty seeing God's hand in his own bereavement? Were his earlier views inadequate to confront real grief? Was he writing beyond his own ability to believe? Is proper theology ever sufficient by itself?

3. If you had the opportunity to converse with Lewis, what would you want to discuss? What questions would you have for him?

4. In Lewis' inaugural address at Cambridge University he referred to himself as a dinosaur. What do you think he meant? Lewis also said: "to study the past does indeed liberate us from the present, from the idols of our own marketplace . . . it liberates us from the past too." Discuss each claim that he makes in this provocative sentence.

5. Regarding *Till We Have Faces*, Reflections on the Psalms, *The Four Loves*, *A Grief Observed*, or *Letters to Malcolm: Chiefly on Prayer*, what differences do you see between these and Lewis' earlier writings? Which do you like better? Why?

6. What has been the literary and spiritual impact of C. S. Lewis on your life? What do you think his impact has been on the world?

7. What is one insight you have gained from this class that you want to take with you? What areas of Lewis' life and writings do you want to further explore?

Planning a C. S. Lewis Tour

Journeying on a C. S. Lewis tour of Ireland and England is a wonderful way to grow in one's knowledge of Jack the man and the background to his writing life. This can be done with a group. A simple internet search will reveal some groups leading tours. Or you can go on your own, which is most often the least expensive option. Another way to approach the project would be to attend a summer class at The Kilns, Lewis' former home now operated by the C. S. Lewis Foundation of Redlands, California.[269]

I have traveled to England and Ireland and explored the places related to the life of C. S. Lewis on numerous occasions, even leading some tours of my own for other interested parties. Each time I have returned home richer for having had the experience.

The first time I went on a "C. S. Lewis Pilgrimage" the only book I had to guide me was Clyde Kilby and Douglas Gilbert's *C. S. Lewis: Images of His World*. Now, at least two very helpful guides to the places of Lewis' life have been written.

Touring C. S. Lewis' Ireland & England by Perry C. Bramlett and Ronald W. Higdon was the first book of its kind to be written, originally published by Smyth & Helwys in 1998. Bramlett and Higdon's book tells the reader something about numerous sites related to the life of C. S. Lewis in both England and Northern Ireland with a special focus on three key cities: Belfast, Oxford and Cambridge. The book also has a section on sites in England beyond Oxford and Cambridge. It gives much helpful background about each site as well as telling you how to find each one. Useful maps, itineraries and bibliography are included. I used this guide on a recent trip to Oxford in order to find all the houses Lewis lived in throughout his many

---

269   For more information visit their web site: www.cslewis.org.

years as an Oxfordshire resident. It was a delightful time of search and discovery.

In 2006 Ronald W. Bresland's book, *Travel with C. S. Lewis*, was published by Day One Publications. This book tells not only of places of interest to visit, it also provides contact information for various sites and helpful web site information. Like Bramlett and Higdon's book, this one also provides maps and travel guides. However, the real plus of this guide is that it contains over 150 color photos. When planning a trip and trying to decide what places I want to visit beforehand I always find color photos to be a most encouraging guide. The problem with these photos is that they will make you want to visit every place mentioned in the book which could take as many as four weeks to do right! Bresland's narrative on the life and work of Lewis is more extensive than Bramlett's. In fact, this book is much more than a travel guide; it is a delightful book on C. S. Lewis even for the "armchair traveler". If I had to recommend only one book as a C. S. Lewis travel guide Bresland's book would be the one.

I am often asked for suggestions of what to see on a Lewis tour of Ireland and England. If you are planning your own tour without a tour group, here is my suggested itinerary. Either Bramlett's or Bresland's book will give you detailed information about how to get to each site....

Day 1:
- Fly to Belfast, Northern Ireland.

Day 2:
- Arrive in Belfast. Rent a car and proceed to The Old Inn, Crawfordsburn, where C. S. Lewis would usually spend the first week of his summer holidays, and where he brought his wife Joy for a belated honeymoon in 1958. Make this, the oldest inn in Ireland, your lodging place during your stay in the Belfast area.
- After lunch at The Old Inn, drive or walk by Silver Hill, the adult home of Lewis' life-long friend Arthur Greeves.

- Drive by St. John's Church, Helen's Bay. This is the church where Lewis would worship while in Crawfordsburn.
- Go for a walk in Crawfordsburn Country Park down to the beach.
- Enjoy dinner at The Old Inn.

Day 3:

- Breakfast at the Old Inn.
- Tour St. Mark's Church, Dundela, Belfast where Lewis' maternal grandfather was the first Rector and where Lewis was baptized. (Call the church in advance to arrange for a tour. Or else visit a Sunday service.)
- Drive by Little Lea, the Lewis family home from 1905-1929.
- Tour Campbell College where Jack spent the autumn term of 1910 as a boarder. (Call in advance to arrange for a tour.)
- Drive by Dundela Villas (now Dundela Flats), Jack's birthplace.
- Lunch on own in Belfast.
- Go for a drive up the coast road to Ballycastle where the Lewis family spent some summer holidays when Jack was young. Continue along the Antrim Coast to visit the Carrick-a-rede Rope Bridge and Giant's Causeway.
- Return for dinner at The Old Inn, Crawfordsburn.

Day 4:

- Breakfast at the Old Inn.
- Fly from Belfast to London. (An alternative would be to take the ferry from Belfast to Liverpool.)
- Rent a car and drive to Great Malvern, where Jack attended school from ages 12-15.
- Check-in and enjoy dinner at the Foley Arms Hotel where Jack and Warnie often had a meal together in their adult years when they would visit Malvern on holiday.

Day 5:

- Breakfast at the Foley.
- Tour Cherbourg House and Malvern College. (Call the college in advance to arrange for a tour.)
- Lunch on own. You might want to visit the Unicorn Pub across the street from the Foley. This was a favorite spot for Jack and Warnie.
- Tour the Priory Church after lunch.
- Drive up to the British Camp, and then hike to the top of the hill. This was one of Lewis' favorite walks in Malvern.
- Have dinner at the Foley Arms.

Day 6:

- Breakfast at the Foley Arms.
- Depart Malvern for the "dreaming spires" of Oxford.
- Tour the Bodleian Library.
- Lunch at the Eagle and Child pub.
- Tour St. Mary the Virgin Church in Oxford, where Lewis delivered his famous sermon "The Weight of Glory".
- Tour Magdalen College and stroll around Addison's Walk where a very important conversation with J. R. R. Tolkien and Hugo Dyson led to Jack's return to Christian faith.
- Check-in to the Eastgate Hotel. After dinner go for an evening stroll around the back streets of Oxford or drive out to the Trout Inn at Godstowe, another of Jack's favorite pubs.

Day 7:

- Breakfast at the Eastgate.
- Take the morning to enjoy shopping in Oxford or punting on the Cherwell River.

- If you go punting, be sure to stop for lunch at the Cherwell Boathouse.
- In the afternoon, drive out to Headington Quarry and visit Holy Trinity Church and Lewis' grave. Call the church in advance in order to see the inside of the building.
- Tour the Kilns, Lewis' home for over 30 years, by arrangement with the C. S. Lewis Foundation. (Call in advance.)
- Drive by 10 Old High Street, former home of Joy Davidman.
- Visit the Oxford Crematorium where Joy Davidman's ashes are interred.
- Drive out to Horton-cum-Studley for dinner at the Studley Priory Hotel, a favorite of Jack and Joy.

Day 8:

- Breakfast at the Eastgate.
- Drive to Cambridge; check-in at the University Arms.
- Dinner at the University Arms. Stroll around Cambridge after dinner.

Day 9:

- Breakfast at the University Arms.
- Tour Magdalene College where Lewis was Professor of Medieval and Renaissance English Literature.
- Lunch at the Pickerel Pub across the street from Magdalene College.
- Tour King's College Chapel Cambridge.
- In the afternoon drive out to Grantchester for tea at The Orchard. There is a lamppost in a wood not too far away!
- Return to King's College Chapel for Evensong.
- Try the Café Rouge for dinner.

Day 10:

- Depart for London.
- See the changing of the guard at Buckingham Palace.
- Tour Westminster Abbey.
- Lunch at the Hard Rock Café.
- Check-in to any one of many fine hotels or B&B's in London. I highly recommend The Rembrandt in the Knightsbridge district.
- Shop at Harrod's or visit the Victoria & Albert museum not far from the Rembrandt Hotel.
- Dinner at your hotel.

Day 11:

- Breakfast at hotel.
- Tour the Tower of London.
- Then head to St. Paul's Cathedral and enjoy lunch in the Crypt (yes, in the Crypt!) before touring the rest of the Cathedral.
- Enjoy dinner at a pub of your choice then enjoy a night ride on the London Eye.

Day 12:

- Depart London for home.

Postscript

In his essay "Meditation in a Toolshed[270]," C. S. Lewis wrote about the difference between "looking at" and "looking along." One can look at a sunbeam and get one perspective, or one can look along the sunbeam back up to its source—the sun. To do the first is often interesting, but to do the second is truly important.

In this book, we have looked a lot *at* C. S. Lewis, what he wrote and how he lived. It is my hope that you have found this exploration interesting. However, it is my prayer that you will also look *along* the life and writings of C. S. Lewis to the Son of God of whom he spoke so eloquently, make that Son your Lord, one to walk in his light all your days, just as Jack did.

May God bless you and keep you *looking at* and *looking along*.

Will Vaus
Monterey, Virginia
Easter 2011

---

[270] *God in the Dock*, pp. 212-215

A Select Bibliography

Barfield, Owen. *Owen Barfield on C. S. Lewis.* edited by G. B. Tennyson. Middletown, Connecticut: Wesleyan University Press. 1989.

Barkman, Adam. *C. S. Lewis & Philosophy as a Way of Life.* Hamden, CT: Zossima Press, 2009.

Bramlett, Perry C. and Higdon, Ronald W. *Touring C. S. Lewis' Ireland & England.* Macon, Georgia: Smyth & Helwys. 1998.

Bresland, Ronald W. *Travel with C. S. Lewis.* Leominster, UK: Day One Publications. 2006.

Burson, Scott R. & Walls, Jerry L. *C. S. Lewis & Francis Schaeffer.* Downers Grove, Il.: InterVarsity Press. 1998.

Carpenter, Humphrey. *The Inklings.* London: HarperCollins. 1997.

Christensen, Michael J. *C. S. Lewis on Scripture.* Waco, Texas.: Word Books. 1979.

Como, James, ed. *C. S. Lewis at the Breakfast Table.* New York.: Harcourt Brace. 1992.

Cording, Ruth James. *C. S. Lewis: A Celebration of His Early Life.* Nashville: Broadman & Holman. 2000.

Derrick, Christopher. *C. S. Lewis and the Church of Rome.* San Francisco: Ignatius, 1981.

Dorsett, Lyle W. *And God Came In.* New York: Ballantine. 1984.

Dorsett, Lyle W. *Seeking the Secret Place*, Grang Rapids: Brazos Press, 2004.

Downing, David C. *The Most Reluctant Convert.* Downers Grove, Il.: InterVarsity Press. 2002.

Gibson, Evan K. *C. S. Lewis: Spinner of Tales.* Washington, D. C.: Christian College Consortium. 1980.

Gilbert, Douglas and Kilby, Clyde S. *C.S. Lewis: Images of His World.* Grand Rapids: Eerdmans. 1977.

Glaspey, Terry W. *Not a Tame Lion: The Spiritual Legacy of C. S. Lewis.* Elkton, MD: Highland Books. 1996.

Glyer, Diana Pavlac, *The Company They Keep.* Kent, Ohio. Kent State University Press, 2007.

Goffar, Janine, compiler. *The C. S. Lewis Index.* Wheaton.: Crossway Books. 1998.

Graham, David, ed. *We Remember C. S. Lewis, Essays & Memoirs.* Nashville.: Broadman & Holman. 2001.

Gresham, Douglas H. *Lenten Lands.* San Francisco.: HarperCollins. 1988.

Green, Roger Lancelyn and Hooper, Walter. *C. S. Lewis: A Biography.* Glasgow.: Collins. 1980.

Harwood, Lawrence, *C. S. Lewis, My Godfather.* Downer's Grove. IL: Intervarsity Press, 2007.

Hooper, Walter, ed. *All My Road Before Me.* Orlando.: Harcourt, Brace, Jovanovich. 1991.

Hooper, Walter, ed. *C. S. Lewis Collected Letters.* Vols. I-III. London: HarperCollins. 2000, 2004, 2007.

Hooper, Walter. *C. S. Lewis Companion & Guide.* New York.: HarperCollins. 1996.

Hooper, Walter & Lewis, W. H., eds. *Letters of C. S. Lewis.* San Diego.: Harcourt, Brace & Company. 1993.

Hooper, Walter. *They Stand Together: The Letters of C. S. Lewis to Arthur Greeves.* New York.: Macmillan. 1979.

Howard, Thomas. *The Achievement of C. S. Lewis.* Wheaton: Harold Shaw. 1980.

Kilby, Clyde S. *Images of Salvation.* Wheaton, Ill.: Harold Shaw Publishers. 1978.

Kilby, Clyde S. *The Christian World of C. S. Lewis*. Grand Rapids, Mich.: William B. Eerdmans Publishing Company. 1964.

Kilby, Clyde S., and Mead, Marjorie Lamp, eds. *Brothers & Friends, The Diaries of Major Warren Hamilton Lewis*. San Francisco.: Harper & Row Publishers. 1982.

King, Don, editor, *Out of My Bone: The Letters of Joy Davidman*. Grand Rapids: Eerdmans, 2009.

Kreeft, Peter. *Between Heaven & Hell*. Downers Grove, Il.: InterVarsity Press. 1982.

Kreeft, Peter. *C. S. Lewis for the Third Millennium*. San Francisco.: Ignatius Press. 1994.

Lawlor, John. *C. S. Lewis: Memories and Reflections*. Dallas: Spence Publishing Company. 1998.

Lindskoog, Kathryn. *Finding the Landlord*. Chicago: Cornerstone Press. 1995.

Lewis, C. S. *A Grief Observed*. London: Faber and Faber. 1961. (Under the pseudonym N. W. Clerk).

-----------. *A Preface to Paradise Lost*. London: Oxford University Press. 1942.

-----------. *A Mind Awake*. edited by Clyde S. Kilby. London: Geoffrey Bles. 1968.

-----------. *An Experiment in Criticism*. Cambridge: Cambridge University Press. 1961.

-----------. *Arthurian Torso*. London: Oxford University Press. 1948.

-----------. *Boxen*. edited by Walter Hooper. London: Collins. 1985.

-----------. *Christian Reflections*. edited by Walter Hooper. London.: Geoffrey Bles. 1967.

-----------. *Dymer*. London: J. M. Dent. 1926.

-----------. Editor. *George MacDonald: 365 Readings*. New York: Macmillan. 1986.

-----------. *God in the Dock*. edited by Walter Hooper. Grand Rapids, Mich.: Eerdmans. 1970.

----------. *English Literature in the Sixteenth Century.* Oxford: Clarendon Press. 1954.

----------. *Letters to an American Lady.* edited by Clyde Kilby. Grand Rapids, Mich.: Eerdmans. 1967.

----------. *Letters to Children,* edited by Lyle W. Dorsett and Marjorie Lamp Mead. New York.: Macmillan. 1985.

----------. *Letters to Malcolm: Chiefly on Prayer.* London: Geoffrey Bles. 1964.

----------. *Mere Christianity.* London: Geoffrey Bles. 1952.

----------. *Miracles.* London: Geoffrey Bles. 1946.

----------. *Narrative Poems.* edited by Walter Hooper. London: Geoffrey Bles. 1969.

----------. *Of Other Worlds.* edited by Walter Hooper. London: Geoffrey Bles. 1966.

----------. *Of This and Other Worlds.* edited by Walter Hooper. London: Collins. 1982.

----------. *Out of the Silent Planet.* London: John Lane The Bodley Head. 1938.

----------. *Perelandra.* London: John Lane The Bodley Head. 1943.

----------. *Poems.* London: Geoffrey Bles. 1964.

----------. *Prince Caspian.* London: Geoffrey Bles. 1951.

----------. *Present Concerns.* edited by Walter Hooper. London: Collins. 1986.

----------. *Reflections on the Psalms.* London: Geoffrey Bles. 1958.

----------. *Rehabilitations and Other Essays.* London: Oxford University Press. 1939.

----------. *Selected Literary* Essays. edited by Walter Hooper. Cambridge: Cambridge University Press. 1979.

----------. *Spenser's Images of Life.* edited by Alastair Fowler. Cambridge: Cambridge University Press. 1967.

----------. *Spirits in Bondage/a Cycle of Lyrics,* London:

William Heinemann, 1919.

-----------. *Studies in Medieval and Renaissance Literature.* Cambridge.: Cambridge University Press. 1966.

-----------. *Studies in Words.* Cambridge: Cambridge University Press. 1960.

-----------. *Surprised by Joy.* London: Geoffrey Bles. 1955.

-----------. *That Hideous Strength.* London: John Lane The Bodley Head. 1945.

-----------. *The Abolition of Man.* London: Oxford University Press. 1943.

-----------. *The Allegory of Love.* Oxford: Clarendon Press. 1936.

-----------. *The Business of Heaven.* edited by Walter Hooper. London: Collins. 1984.

-----------. *The Dark Tower & Other Stories.* London: Collins. 1977.

-----------. *The Discarded Image.* Cambridge: Cambridge University Press. 1964.

-----------. *The Four Loves.* London: Geoffrey Bles. 1960.

-----------. *The Great Divorce.* London: Geoffrey Bles. 1946.

-----------. *The Horse and His Boy.* London: Geoffrey Bles. 1954.

-----------. *The Joyful Christian.* edited by William Griffin. New York: Macmillan. 1977.

-----------. *The Last Battle.* London: The Bodley Head. 1956.

-----------. *The Lion, The Witch and the Wardrobe.* London: Geoffrey Bles. 1950.

-----------. *The Literary Impact of the Authorized Version.* Philadelphia.: Fortress Press. 1967.

-----------. *The Magician's Nephew.* London: The Bodley Head. 1955.

———. (With E. M. W. Tillyard) *The Personal Heresy.* London: Oxford University Press. 1939.

———. *The Pilgrim's Regress.* London: J. M. Dent. 1933.

———. *The Problem of Pain.* London: The Centenary Press. 1940.

———. *The Screwtape Letters.* London: Geoffrey Bles. 1942.

———. *The Silver Chair.* London: Geoffrey Bles. 1953.

———. *The Voyage of the Dawn Treader.* London: Geoffrey Bles. 1952.

———. *The Weight of Glory.* New York: Macmillan. 1949.

———. *The World's Last Night & Other Essays.* New York: Harcourt, Brace & World. 1960.

———. *They Asked for a Paper.* London: Geoffrey Bles. 1962.

———. *Till We Have Faces.* London: Geoffrey Bles. 1956.

Lewis, W. H. *Letters of C. S. Lewis.* London: Geoffrey Bles. 1966.

Macdonald, Michael H. and Tadie, Andrew A., eds. *The Riddle of Joy.* Grand Rapids, Mich.: Eerdmans. 1989.

Manlove, Colin. *C. S. Lewis: His Literary Achievement.* Hamden, CT: Winged Lion Press, 2010.

Martindale, Wayne & Root, Jerry, eds. *The Quotable Lewis.* Wheaton.: Tyndale House Publishers, Inc. 1989.

Moynihan, Martin, ed. *The Latin Letters of C. S. Lewis.* South Bend, Ind.: St. Augustine's Press. 1998.

Nicholi, Armand. *The Question of God.* New York.: Free Press. 2002.

Payne, Leanne. *Real Presence: The Holy Spirit in the Works of C. S. Lewis.* Westchester, Ill.: Cornerstone Books. 1979.

Peters, John. *C. S. Lewis: The Man and His Achievement.* Exeter,

UK: Paternoster Press. 1985.

Phillips, Justin. *C. S. Lewis at the BBC.* London.: HarperCollins. 2002.

Pow, Harry Lee & Poe, Rebcca Whitten, editors, *C.S. Lewis Remembered.* Grand Rapids: Zondervan, 2006.

Reppert, Victor. *C. S. Lewis' Dangerous Idea: In Defense of the Argument from Reason.* Downers Grove, Il.: InterVarsity Press. 2003.

Sayer, George. *Jack: A Life of C. S. Lewis.* Wheaton, Ill.: Crossway Books. 1994.

Schakel, Peter J. *Reason and Imagination in C. S. Lewis.* Grand Rapids: Eerdmans. 1984.

Vanauken, Sheldon. *A Severe Mercy.* New York: Bantam. 1979.

Vanauken, Sheldon. *Encounter with Light.* Wheaton, Illinois: Marion E. Wade Collection, Wheaton College.

Vaus, Will. *Mere Theology: A Guide to the Thought of C. S. Lewis.* Downers Grove, Illinois: InterVarsity Press. 2004.

Vaus, Will. *The Hidden Story of Narnia: A Book-by-Book Guide to C. S. Lewis' Spiritual Themes.* Cheshire, CT: Winged Lion Press. 2010.

Vaus, Will. *The Professor of Narnia: The C. S. Lewis Story.* Washington D. C.: Believe Books. 2008.

Ward, Michael, *Planet Narnia.* New York: Oxford University Press, 2008.

Wilson, A.N. *C. S. Lewis: A Biography.* New York: Fawcett Columbine. 1990.

Resources for Further Study

Audio & Video Resources

Episcopal Media Center
644 West Peachtree Street, Suite 300
Atlanta, GA 30328-1925
Phone: (404) 815-0640
Toll-Free: 800-229-3788
www.episcopalmedia.org

Books & Other Resources

The C. S. Lewis Foundation
Dr. J. Stanley Mattson, President
P.O. Box 8008
Redlands, CA 92375
Phone: (909) 793-0949
Fax: (909) 335-3501
www.cslewis.org

Cyberspace Resources

Into The Wardrobe: www.cslewis.drzeus.net

Will Vaus Web Site: www.willvaus.com

A C. S. Lewis Discussion Guide

Societies & Publications

The Mythopoeic Society
920 N. Atlantic Blvd. #E
Alhambra, CA 91801
www.mythsoc.org
(Publication: *Mythlore*)

New York C. S. Lewis Society
Clara Sarrocco, corresponding secretary
84-23 77th Avenue
Glendale, NY 11385-7706
(Publication: *CSL: The Bulletin of the New York C. S. Lewis Society*)
www.nycslsociety.com

C. S. Lewis Society of California
100 Swan Way, Suite 200
Oakland, CA 94621
510-635-6892
www.lewissociety.org

Southern California C. S. Lewis Society
http://socalcsl.com/
(Publication: *The Lamppost*)

Arizona C. S. Lewis Society
www.azcslewissociety.org
(Publication: *Sehnsucht: The C. S. Lewis Journal*)

Oxford C. S. Lewis Society
http://sites.google.com/site/lewisinoxford/
(Publication: *The Journal of Inklings Studies*)
http://www.inklings-studies.com/for_author.html

Study Centers

The Marion E. Wade Center
Wheaton College
Wheaton, IL 60187-5593
Phone: (630) 752-5908
Fax: (630) 752-5459
(Publication: *VII: An Anglo-American Literary Review*)
http://www.wheaton.edu/wadecenter/

The Center for the Study of C. S. Lewis and Friends
Taylor University
Upland, Indiana
http://192.195.234.6/academics/supportservices/cslewis/
Biannual colloquium and publication: *Forever Inklings*

Other Titles of Interest

C. S. Lewis

C. S. Lewis: Views From Wake Forest - Essays on C. S. Lewis
Michael Travers, editor

Contains sixteen scholarly presentations from the international C. S. Lewis convention in Wake Forest, NC. Walter Hooper shares his important essay "Editing C. S. Lewis," a chronicle of publishing decisions after Lewis' death in 1963.

"Scholars from a variety of disciplines address a wide range of issues. The happy result is a fresh and expansive view of an author who well deserves this kind of thoughtful attention."
      Diana Pavlac Glyer, author of *The Company They Keep*

The Hidden Story of Narnia:
A Book-By-Book Guide to Lewis' Spiritual Themes
Will Vaus

A book of insightful commentary equally suited for teens or adults – Will Vaus points out connections between the *Narnia* books and spiritual/biblical themes, as well as between ideas in the *Narnia* books and C. S. Lewis' other books. Learn what Lewis himself said about the overarching and unifying thematic structure of the Narnia books. That is what this book explores; what C. S. Lewis called "the hidden story" of Narnia. Each chapter includes questions for individual use or small group discussion.

Why I Believe in Narnia:
33 Reviews and Essays on the Life and Work of C.S. Lewis
James Como

Chapters range from reviews of critical books, documentaries and movies to evaluations of Lewis' books to biographical analysis.
"A valuable, wide-ranging collection of essays by one of the best informed and most accute commentators on Lewis' work and ideas."
Peter Schakel, author of *Imagination & the Arts in C.S. Lewis*

C. S. Lewis: His Literary Achievement
Colin Manlove

"This is a positively brilliant book, written with splendor, elegance, profundity and evidencing an enormous amount of learning. This is probably not a book to give a first-time reader of Lewis. But for those who are more broadly read in the Lewis corpus this book is an absolute gold mine of information. The author gives us a magnificent overview of Lewis' many writings, tracing for us thoughts and ideas which recur throughout, and at the same time telling us how each book differs from the others. I think it is not extravagant to call *C. S. Lewis: His Literary Achievement* a *tour de force.*"
      Robert Merchant, *St. Austin Review*, Book Review Editor

C. S. Lewis & Philosophy as a Way of Life: His Philosophical Thoughts
Adam Barkman

C. S. Lewis is rarely thought of as a "philosopher" per se despite having both studied and taught philosophy for several years at Oxford. Lewis's long journey to Christianity was essentially philosophical – passing through seven different stages. This 624 page book is an invaluable reference for C. S. Lewis scholars and fans alike.

Mythopoeic Narnia: Memory, Metaphore, and Metamorphosis in C. S. Lewis's The Chronicles of Narnia
Salwa Khoddam

Dr. Khoddam, the founder of the C. S. Lewis and Inklings Society (2004), has been teaching university courses using Lewis' books for over 25 years. Her book offers a fresh approach to the *Narnia* books based on an inquiry into Lewis' readings and use of classical and Christian symbols. She explores the literary and intellectual contexts of these stories, the traditional myths and motifs, and places them in the company of the greatest Christian mythopoeic works of Western Literature. In Lewis' imagination, memory and metaphor interact to advance his purpose – a Christian metamorphosis. *Mythopoeic Narnia* helps to open the door for readers into the magical world of the Western imagination.

C. S. Lewis Goes to Heaven: A Reader's Guide to The Great Divorce
David G. Clark

This is the first book devoted solely to this often neglected book and the first to reveal several important secrets Lewis concealed within the story. Lewis felt his imaginary trip to Hell and Heaven was far better than his book *The Screwtape Letters*, which has become a classic. Clark is an ordained minister who has taught courses on Lewis for more than 30 years and is a New Testament and Greek scholar with a Doctor of Philosophy degree in Biblical Studies from the University of Notre Dame. Readers will discover the many literary and biblical influences Lewis utilized in writing his brilliant novel.

George MacDonald

Diary of an Old Soul & The White Page Poems
George MacDonald and Betty Aberlin

The first edition of George MacDonald's book of daily poems included a blank page opposite each page of poems. Readers were invited to write their own reflections on the "white page." MacDonald wrote: "Let your white page be ground, my print be seed, growing to golden ears, that faith and hope may feed." Betty Aberlin responded to MacDonald's invitation with daily poems of her own.

Betty Aberlin's close readings of George MacDonald's verses and her thoughtful responses to them speak clearly of her poetic gifts and spiritual intelligence. Luci Shaw, poet

George MacDonald: Literary Heritage and Heirs
Roderick McGillis, editor

This latest collection of 14 essays sets a new standard that will influence MacDonald studies for many more years. George MacDonald experts are increasingly evaluating his entire corpus within the nineteenth century context.

This comprehensive collection represents the best of contemporary scholarship on George MacDonald. Rolland Hein, author of *George MacDonald: Victorian Mythmaker.*

In the Near Loss of Everything: George MacDonald's Son in America
Dale Wayne Slusser

In the summer of 1887, George MacDonald's son Ronald, newly engaged to artist Louise Blandy, sailed from England to America to teach school. The next summer he returned to England to marry Louise and bring her back to America. On August 27, 1890, Louise died leaving him with an infant daughter. Ronald once described losing a beloved spouse as "the near loss of everything". Dale Wayne Slusser unfolds this poignant story with unpublished letters and photos that give readers a glimpse into the close-knit MacDonald family. Also included is Ronald's essay about his father, *George MacDonald: A Personal Note*, plus a selection from Ronald's 1922 fable, *The Laughing Elf*, about the necessity of both sorrow and joy in life.

A Novel Pulpit: Sermons From George MacDonald's Fiction
David L. Neuhouser

"In MacDonald's novels, the Christian teaching emerges out of the characters and story line, the narrator's comments, and inclusion of sermons given by the fictional preachers. The sermons in the novels are shorter than the ones in collections of MacDonald's sermons and so are perhaps more accessible for some. In any case, they are both stimulating and thought-provoking. This collection of sermons from ten novels serve to bring out the 'freshness and brilliance' of MacDonald's message."

from the author's introduction

Behind the Back of the North Wind:
Critical Essays on George MacDonald's Classic Children's Book
Editors, John Pennington and Roderick McGillis

This collection of 16 essays by various scholars is the first compendium on a particular MacDonald book – *At the Back of the North Wind*. This novel makes a good representative study because it bridges the world of the "realistic" and the fanciful, including a fairy tale and some nonsense poetry. Plus it deals with a central MacDonald theme - death. Essays run the gamut from exploring MacDonald's Christian worldview, to examining the tension between fantasy and reality, to grappling with *North Wind* as children's literature. In every case, the essays illuminate a complex book. This book is also an excellent companion to the critical and scholarly edition of *At The Back of the North Wind* by Pennington and McGillis published by Broadview Press.

Other Titles

To Love Another Person: A Spiritual Journey Through Les Miserables
John Morrison

The powerful story of Jean Valjean's redemption is beloved by readers and theater goers everywhere. In this companion and guide to Victor Hugo's masterpiece, author John Morrison unfolds the spiritual depth and breadth of this classic novel and broadway musical.

Through Common Things: Philosophical Reflections on Popular Culture
Adam Barkman

"Barkman presents us with an amazingly wide-ranging collection of philosophical reflections grounded in the everyday things of popular culture – past and present, eastern and western, factual and fictional. Throughout his encounters with often surprising subject-matter (the value of darkness?), he writes clearly and concisely, moving seamlessly between Aristotle and anime, Lord Buddha and Lord Voldemort.... This is an informative and entertaining book to read!"

    Doug Blomberg, Professor of Philosophy, Institute for Christian Studies

Remembering Roy Campbell: The Memoirs of his Daughters, Anna and Tess
Introduction by Judith Lütge Coullie, Editor
Preface by Joseph Pearce

Anna and Teresa Campbell were the daughters of the handsome young South African poet and writer, Roy Campbell (1901-1957), and his beautiful English wife, Mary Garman. In their frank and moving memoirs, Anna and Tess recall the extraordinary, and often very difficult, lives they shared with their exceptional parents. Over 50 photos, 344 footnotes, timeline of Campbell's life, and complete index.

www.ingramcontent.com/pod-product-compliance
Lightning Source LLC
Chambersburg PA
CBHW020358080526
44584CB00014B/1075